Lecture Notes in Artificial Intelligence   11171

Subseries of Lecture Notes in Computer Science

LNAI Series Editors

Randy Goebel
  University of Alberta, Edmonton, Canada
Yuzuru Tanaka
  Hokkaido University, Sapporo, Japan
Wolfgang Wahlster
  DFKI and Saarland University, Saarbrücken, Germany

LNAI Founding Series Editor

Joerg Siekmann
  DFKI and Saarland University, Saarbrücken, Germany

Thierry Dutoit · Carlos Martín-Vide
Gueorgui Pironkov (Eds.)

Statistical Language and Speech Processing

6th International Conference, SLSP 2018
Mons, Belgium, October 15–16, 2018
Proceedings

 Springer

Editors
Thierry Dutoit
University of Mons
Mons
Belgium

Gueorgui Pironkov 🆔
University of Mons
Mons
Belgium

Carlos Martín-Vide 🆔
Rovira i Virgili University
Tarragona
Spain

ISSN 0302-9743   ISSN 1611-3349 (electronic)
Lecture Notes in Artificial Intelligence
ISBN 978-3-030-00809-3   ISBN 978-3-030-00810-9 (eBook)
https://doi.org/10.1007/978-3-030-00810-9

Library of Congress Control Number: 2018954665

LNCS Sublibrary: SL7 – Artificial Intelligence

This Springer imprint is published by the registered company Springer Nature Switzerland AG
The registered company address is: Gewerbestrasse 11, 6330 Cham, Switzerland

Preface

These proceedings contain the papers that were presented at the 6th International Conference on Statistical Language and Speech Processing (SLSP 2018), held in Mons, Belgium, during October 15–16, 2018.

The scope of SLSP deals with topics of either theoretical or applied interest discussing the employment of statistical models (including machine learning) within language and speech processing, namely:

Anaphora and coreference resolution
Authorship identification, plagiarism and spam filtering
Computer-aided translation
Corpora and language resources
Data mining and semantic web
Information extraction
Information retrieval
Knowledge representation and ontologies
Lexicons and dictionaries
Machine translation
Multimodal technologies
Natural language understanding
Neural representation of speech and language
Opinion mining and sentiment analysis
Parsing
Part-of-speech tagging
Question-answering systems
Semantic role labelling
Speaker identification and verification
Speech and language generation
Speech recognition
Speech synthesis
Speech transcription
Spelling correction
Spoken dialogue systems
Term extraction
Text categorisation
Text summarisation
User modeling

SLSP 2018 received 40 submissions. Every paper was reviewed by 3 Programme Committee members. There were also a few external experts consulted. After a thorough and vivid discussion phase, the committee decided to accept 15 papers (which represents a competitive acceptance rate of about 37%). The conference program included 3 invited talks and some presentations of work in progress as well.

The excellent facilities provided by the EasyChair conference management system allowed us to deal with the submissions successfully and handle the preparation of these proceedings in time.

We would like to thank all invited speakers and authors for their contributions, the Program Committee and the external reviewers for their diligent cooperation, and Springer for its very professional publishing work.

August 2018

Thierry Dutoit
Carlos Martín-Vide
Gueorgui Pironkov

Organization

Program Committee

Steven Abney	University of Michigan, USA
Srinivas Bangalore	Interactions LLC, USA
Jean-François Bonastre	University of Avignon and Pays du Vaucluse, France
Pierrette Bouillon	University of Geneva, Switzerland
Nicoletta Calzolari	Italian National Research Council, Italy
Erik Cambria	Nanyang Technological University, Singapore
Kenneth W. Church	Baidu Research, USA
Walter Daelemans	University of Antwerp, Belgium
Thierry Dutoit	University of Mons, Belgium
Marcello Federico	Bruno Kessler Foundation, Italy
Robert Gaizauskas	University of Sheffield, UK
Ralph Grishman	New York University, USA
Udo Hahn	University of Jena, Germany
Siegfried Handschuh	University of Passau, Germany
Mark Hasegawa-Johnson	University of Illinois, Urbana–Champaign, USA
Keikichi Hirose	University of Tokyo, Japan
Julia Hirschberg	Columbia University, USA
Nancy Ide	Vassar College, USA
Gareth Jones	Dublin City University, Ireland
Philipp Koehn	University of Edinburgh, UK
Haizhou Li	National University of Singapore, Singapore
Carlos Martín-Vide (Chair)	Rovira i Virgili University, Spain
Yuji Matsumoto	Nara Institute of Science and Technology, Japan
Alessandro Moschitti	Qatar Computing Research Institute, Qatar
Hermann Ney	RWTH Aachen University, Germany
Jian-Yun Nie	University of Montréal, Canada
Elmar Nöth	University of Erlangen-Nuremberg, Germany
Cecile Paris	CSIRO Data61, Australia
Jong C. Park	Korea Advanced Institute of Science and Technology, South Korea
Alexandros Potamianos	National Technical University of Athens, Greece
Paul Rayson	University of Lancaster, UK
Mats Rooth	Cornell University, USA
Paolo Rosso	Technical University of Valencia, Spain
Alexander Rudnicky	Carnegie Mellon University, USA
Tanja Schultz	University of Bremen, Germany
Holger Schwenk	Facebook AI Research, France
Vijay K. Shanker	University of Delaware, USA

Richard Sproat	Google Research, USA
Tomoki Toda	Nagoya University, Japan
Gökhan Tür	Google Research, USA
Yorick Wilks	Institute for Human & Machine Cognition, USA
Phil Woodland	University of Cambridge, UK
Dekai Wu	Hong Kong University of Science and Technology, SAR China
Junichi Yamagishi	University of Edinburgh, UK

Additional Reviewers

Banerjee, Somnath	Park, Hancheol
Chung, Jin-Woo	Rosso Mateus, Andrés Enrique
Gaim, Fitsum	Taghizadeh, Nasrin
Joshi, Aditya	Xu, Chang

Contents

Invited Paper

Analysing Speech for Clinical Applications

Isabel Trancoso[1]([⊠])(iD), Joana Correia[1,2](iD), Francisco Teixeira[1](iD),
Bhiksha Raj[2], and Alberto Abad[1](iD)

[1] INESC-ID/Instituto Superior Técnico, University of Lisbon, Lisbon, Portugal
Isabel.Trancoso@inesc-id.pt
[2] Carnegie Mellon University, Pittsburgh, USA

Abstract. The boost in speech technologies that we have witnessed over the last decade has allowed us to go from a state of the art in which correctly recognizing strings of words was a major target, to a state in which we aim much beyond words. We aim at extracting meaning, but we also aim at extracting all possible cues that are conveyed by the speech signal. In fact, we can estimate bio-relevant traits such as height, weight, gender, age, physical and mental health. We can also estimate language, accent, emotional and personality traits, and even environmental cues. This wealth of information, that one can now extract with recent advances in machine learning, has motivated an exponentially growing number of speech-based applications that go much beyond the transcription of what a speaker says. In particular, it has motivated many health related applications, namely aiming at non-invasive diagnosis and monitorization of diseases that affect speech.

Most of the recent work on speech-based diagnosis tools addresses the extraction of features, and/or the development of sophisticated machine learning classifiers [5,7,12–14,17]. The results have shown remarkable progress, boosted by several joint paralinguistic challenges, but most results are obtained from limited training data acquired in controlled conditions.

This talk covers two emerging concerns related to this growing trend. One is the collection of large in-the-wild datasets and the effects of this extended uncontrolled collection in the results [4]. Another concern is how the diagnosis may be done without compromising patient privacy [18].

As a proof-of-concept, we will discuss these two aspects and show our results for two target diseases, Depression and Cold, a selection motivated by the availability of corresponding lab datasets distributed in paralinguistic challenges. The availability of these lab datasets allowed us to build a baseline system for each disease, using a simple neural network trained with common features that have not been optimized for either disease. Given the modular architecture adopted, each component

---

This work was supported by national funds through Fundação para a Ciência e a Tecnologia (FCT) with references UID/CEC/50021/2013, and SFRH/BD/103402/2014.

T. Dutoit et al. (Eds.): SLSP 2018, LNAI 11171, pp. 3–6, 2018.
https://doi.org/10.1007/978-3-030-00810-9_1

of the system can be individually improved at a later stage, although the limited amount of data does not motivate us to exploit deeper networks.

Our mining effort has been focused on video blogs (vlogs), that include a single speaker which, at some point, admits that he/she is currently affected by a given disease. Retrieving vlogs with the target disease involves not only a simple query (i.e. *depression vlog*), but also a post-filtering stage to exclude videos that do not correspond to our target of first person, present experiences (lectures, in particular, are relatively frequent). This filtering stage combines multimodal features automatically extracted from the video and its metadata, using mostly off-the-shelf tools.

We collected a large dataset for each target disease from YouTube, and manually labelled a small subset which we named the in-the-Wild Speech Medical (WSM) corpus. Although our mining efforts made use of relatively simple techniques using mostly existing toolkits, they proved effective. The best performing models achieved a precision of 88% and 93%, and a recall of 97% and 72%, for the datasets of Cold and Depression, respectively, in the task of filtering videos containing these speech affecting diseases.

We compared the performance of our baseline neural network classifiers trained with data collected in controlled conditions in tests with corresponding in-the-wild data. For the Cold datasets, the baseline neural network achieved an Unweighted Average Recall (UAR) of 66.9% for the controlled dataset, and 53.1% for the manually labelled subset of the WSM corpus. For the Depression datasets, the corresponding values were 60.6%, and 54.8%, respectively (at interview level, the UAR increased to 61.9% for the vlog corpus). The performance degradation that we had anticipated for using in-the-wild data may be due to a greater variability in recording conditions (p.e. microphone, noise) and in the effects of speech altering diseases in the subjects' speech. Our current work with vlog datasets attempts to estimate the quality of the predicted labels of a very large set in an unsupervised way, using noisy models.

The second aspect we addressed was patient privacy. Privacy is an emerging concern among users of voice-activated digital assistants, sparkled by the awareness of devices that must be always in the listening mode. Despite this growing concern, the potential misuse of health related speech based cues has not yet been fully realized. This is the motivation for adopting secure computation frameworks, in which cryptographic techniques are combined with state-of-the-art machine learning algorithms. Privacy in speech processing is an interdisciplinary topic, which was first applied to speaker verification, using Secure Multi-Party Computation, and Secure Modular Hashing techniques [1,15], and later to speech emotion recognition, also using hashing techniques [6]. The most recent efforts on privacy preserving speech processing have followed the progress in secure machine learning, combining neural networks and Full Homomorphic Encryption (FHE) [3,8,9].

In this work, we applied an encrypted neural network, following the FHE paradigm, to the problem of secure detection of pathological speech. This was done by developing an encrypted version of a neural network, trained with unencrypted data, in order to produce encrypted predictions of health-related labels. As proof-of-concept, we used the same two above mentioned target diseases, and compared the performance of the simple neural network classifiers with their encrypted counterparts on datasets collected in controlled conditions. For the Cold dataset, the baseline neural network achieved a UAR of 66.9%, whereas the encrypted network achieved 66.7%. For the Depression dataset, the baseline value was 60.6%, whereas the encrypted network achieved 60.2% (67.9% at interview level). The slight difference in results showed the validity of our secure approach.

This approach relies on the computation of features on the client side before encryption, with only the inference stage being computed in an encrypted setting. Ideally, an end-to-end approach would overcome this limitation, but combining convolutional neural networks with FHE imposes severe limitations to their size. Likewise, the use of recurrent layers such as LSTMs (Long Short Term Memory) also requires a number of operations too large for current FHE frameworks, making them computationally unfeasible as well.

FHE schemes, by construction, only work with integers, whilst neural networks work with real numbers. By using encoding methods to convert real weights to integers we are throwing away the capability of using an FHE batching technique that would allow us to compute several predictions, at the same time, using the same encrypted value. Recent advances in machine learning have pushed towards the "quantization" and "discretization" of neural networks, so that models occupy less space and operations consume less power. Some works have already implemented these techniques using homomorphic encryption, such as Binarized Neural Networks [10,11,16] and Discretized Neural Networks [2]. The talk will also cover our recent efforts in applying this type of approach to the detection of health related cues in speech signals, while discretizing the network and maximizing the throughput of its encrypted counterpart.

More than presenting our recent work in these two aspects of speech analysis for medical applications, this talk intends to point to different directions for future work in these two relatively unexplored topics that were by no means exhausted in this summary.

Keywords: Pathological speech · Data mining · Cryptography

References

1. Boufounos, P., Rane, S.: Secure binary embeddings for privacy preserving nearest neighbors. In: International Workshop on Information Forensics and Security (WIFS) (2011)
2. Bourse, F., Minelli, M., Minihold, M., Paillier, P.: Fast homomorphic evaluation of deep discretized neural networks. IACR Cryptology ePrint Archive 2017, 1114 (2017)
3. Chabanne, H., de Wargny, A., Milgram, J., Morel, C., et al.: Privacy-preserving classification on deep neural network. IACR Cryptology ePrint Archive 2017, 35 (2017)

4. Correia, J., Raj, B., Trancoso, I., Teixeira, F.: Mining multimodal repositories for speech affecting diseases. In: INTERSPEECH (2018)
5. Cummins, N., Scherer, S., Krajewski, J., Schnieder, S., Epps, J., Quatieri, T.F.: A review of depression and suicide risk assessment using speech analysis. Speech Commun. **71**, 10–49 (2015)
6. Dias, M., Abad, A., Trancoso, I.: Exploring hashing and cryptonet based approaches for privacy-preserving speech emotion recognition. In: ICASSP. IEEE (2018)
7. Dibazar, A.A., Narayanan, S., Berger, T.W.: Feature analysis for automatic detection of pathological speech. In: 24th Annual Conference and the Annual Fall Meeting of the Biomedical Engineering Society EMBS/BMES Conference, vol. 1, pp. 182–183. IEEE (2002)
8. Gilad-Bachrach, R., Dowlin, N., Laine, K., et al.: CryptoNets: applying neural networks to encrypted data with high throughput and accuracy. In: ICML, JMLR Workshop and Conference Proceedings, vol. 48, pp. 201–210 (2016)
9. Hesamifard, E., Takabi, H., Ghasemi, M.: CryptoDL: deep neural networks over encrypted data. CoRR abs/1711.05189 (2017)
10. Hubara, I., Courbariaux, M., Soudry, D., El-Yaniv, R., Bengio, Y.: Binarized neural networks. In: Lee, D.D., Sugiyama, M., Luxburg, U.V., Guyon, I., Garnett, R. (eds.) Advances in Neural Information Processing Systems 29, pp. 4107–4115. Curran Associates, Inc., New York (2016)
11. Hubara, I., Courbariaux, M., Soudry, D., El-Yaniv, R., Bengio, Y.: Quantized neural networks: training neural networks with low precision weights and activations. J. Mach. Learn. Res. **18**, 187:1–187:30 (2017)
12. Lopez-de Ipiña, K., et al.: On automatic diagnosis of Alzheimers disease based on spontaneous speech analysis and emotional temperature. Cogn. Comput. **7**(1), 44–55 (2015)
13. López-de Ipiña, K., et al.: On the selection of non-invasive methods based on speech analysis oriented to automatic Alzheimer disease diagnosis. Sensors **13**(5), 6730–6745 (2013)
14. Orozco-Arroyave, J.R., et al.: Characterization methods for the detection of multiple voice disorders: neurological, functional, and laryngeal diseases. IEEE J. Biomed. Health Inform. **19**(6), 1820–1828 (2015)
15. Pathak, M.A., Raj, B.: Privacy-preserving speaker verification and identification using gaussian mixture models. IEEE Trans. Audio Speech Lang. Process. **21**(2), 397–406 (2013)
16. Sanyal, A., Kusner, M.J., Gascón, A., Kanade, V.: TAPAS: tricks to accelerate (encrypted) prediction as a service. CoRR abs/1806.03461 (2018)
17. Schuller, B., et al.: The INTERSPEECH 2017 computational paralinguistics challenge: addressee, cold & snoring. In: INTERSPEECH (2017)
18. Teixeira, F., Abad, A., Trancoso, I.: Patient privacy in paralinguistic tasks. In: INTERSPEECH (2018)

Speech Synthesis and Spoken Language Generation

DNN-Based Speech Synthesis for Arabic: Modelling and Evaluation

Amal Houidhek[1,2(✉)], Vincent Colotte[2], Zied Mnasri[1], and Denis Jouvet[2]

[1] Electrical Engineering Department, Ecole Nationale d'Ingénieurs de Tunis,
University Tunis El Manar, Tunis, Tunisia
zied.mnasri@enit.utm.tn
[2] Université de Lorraine, CNRS, Inria, LORIA, 54000 Nancy, France
{amal.houidhek,vincent.colotte,denis.jouvet}@loria.fr

Abstract. This paper investigates the use of deep neural networks (DNN) for Arabic speech synthesis. In parametric speech synthesis, whether HMM-based or DNN-based, each speech segment is described with a set of contextual features. These contextual features correspond to linguistic, phonetic and prosodic information that may affect the pronunciation of the segments. Gemination and vowel quantity (short vowel vs. long vowel) are two particular and important phenomena in Arabic language. Hence, it is worth investigating if those phenomena must be handled by using specific speech units, or if their specification in the contextual features is enough. Consequently four modelling approaches are evaluated by considering geminated consonants (respectively long vowels) either as fully-fledged phoneme units or as the same phoneme as their simple (respectively short) counterparts. Although no significant difference has been observed in previous studies relying on HMM-based modelling, this paper examines these modelling variants in the framework of DNN-based speech synthesis. Listening tests are conducted to evaluate the four modelling approaches, and to assess the performance of DNN-based Arabic speech synthesis with respect to previous HMM-based approach.

Keywords: Parametric speech synthesis · Hidden Markov Models Decision tree · Deep neural network · Arabic language

1 Introduction

Statistical parametric speech synthesis (SPSS) approach has been widely used in the last decade. It presents the advantages of being trainable and making possible changing voice characteristics [4]. SPSS is based on Hidden Markov Models to model speech parameters, as in HTS toolkit (Hidden Markov Models speech synthesis system). HTS has been applied to many languages e.g., English [18], Japanese [24] and Arabic [1] and produces speech of rather good quality. HTS requires the description of each speech segment with a set of contextual features

© Springer Nature Switzerland AG 2018
T. Dutoit et al. (Eds.): SLSP 2018, LNAI 11171, pp. 9–20, 2018.
https://doi.org/10.1007/978-3-030-00810-9_2

that comprises all factors affecting the pronunciation of the corresponding sound (e.g., linguistic, prosodic, phonological information). A standard set of around 50 features was suggested in [18]. Part of the features are language dependent, therefore some modifications of the features set was suggested in [13] and [14] (either ignoring or adding information) to be adapted to the specificities of respectively German and French languages. Actually, the choice of contextual features is primordial as it affects the speech quality.

Arabic speech synthesis using HTS was initiated in [1]; the conventional system was adapted to Arabic with a modification of the excitation model and speech parameters to enhance the speech quality. Later, STRAIGHT vocoder [11] was used in [12] to generate a higher-quality Arabic speech. [7] focused on phonological particularities of Modern Standard Arabic (MSA) [2]. Two phenomena were highlighted, namely gemination [16] (i.e. a geminated consonant is twice as long as its simple counterpart) and vowel quantity (short vowel vs. long vowel) [17] (i.e. a long vowel is twice as long as its short counterpart). In [7] subjective and objective evaluations showed that considering the geminated consonants (resp long vowels) as fully-fledged phonemes or as the same phonemes as their simple (resp short) counterparts leads to similar speech quality as long as the information about gemination and vowel quantity are included in the set of contextual features.

According to [4,23], the naturalness of HTS output speech has never reached the level of unit-selection-generated speech [8]. This is due to three major reasons; vocoding, inaccurate acoustic model and over-smoothing. In SPSS, acoustic models match the contextual features to the corresponding speech parameters. In this approach, the mapping from contextual features to speech parameters is achieved based on decisions trees [10], which are described as shallow architectures, therefore, they are judged inefficient to represent complex dependencies between contextual features and acoustic parameters. Though temporal-domain oversmoothing has almost no effect on quality, frequency-domain oversmoothing is mainly due to the training algorithm accuracy, and may degrade the quality of output speech by causing an envelope effect [25].

To cope with these issues, previous works suggested replacing decision trees by DNN [22] or using external models for duration [21]. Results showed that DNN outperformed HMM in terms of speech quality and naturalness of produced speech for English language [19,23]. This paper aims at introducing DNN in parametric speech synthesis for Arabic and investigating if DNN benefit from the explicit differentiation of different phoneme classes unlike HMM [7]. The paper is organised as follows. Section 2 presents various choices of speech unit modelling for HMM-based speech synthesis in Arabic. Section 3 details DNN-based speech synthesis. Section 4 compares and discusses the various speech unit modelling approaches. Finally, Sect. 5 presents the evaluations of the HMM-based and DNN-based approaches for Arabic speech synthesis.

2   Speech Unit Modelling for Arabic

One of the Arabic speech modelling issues is how should gemination and vowel quantity be regarded: whether is it enough to add gemination and vowel quantity information to the features set, or is it better to consider a geminated consonant (resp. a long vowel) as fully-fledged speech unit in the modelling?

2.1   Speech Unit Modelling

This problem has been dealt with in [7] for HMM-based Arabic speech synthesis, where four modelling approaches are proposed; differentiating geminated consonants (resp long vowels) from simple consonants (resp short vowels) or merging them:

- *C2V2*: This is the most detailed model, where a simple consonant (e.g., /d/) and its geminated counterpart (e.g., /dd/) are modelled by two different units. In the same way, short vowels (e.g., /a/) and their long counterparts (e.g., /aa/) have distinct models.
- *C1V1*: It is the most compact model, where geminated and simple consonants are modelled with the same unit, as well for vowels, long and short vowels are modelled with the same unit.
- *C1V2*: In this approach, a single unit models both a geminated consonant and its simple counterpart, whereas a long vowel and its short counterpart are modelled by two different units.
- *C2V1*: This approach uses a single unit to model both a long vowel and its short counterpart. Whereas for consonants, two units are used, one for the simple consonant and one for its geminated counterpart.

Note that in all cases, gemination and vowel quantities characteristics are included into the set of contextual features.

2.2   Experiments with HMM-Based Modelling

This section summarizes the experiments described in [7], which were conducted to compare the four modelling approaches listed above in the framework of HMM-based synthesizer. The speech data used to train the speaker-dependent models with HTS was extracted from the corpus developed in [6]. The training set consists of 1565 utterances recorded by a male-speaker at 48 KHz sampling rate, whereas the test set comprises 30 utterances. Subjective evaluations showed that the four modelling approaches lead to similar speech quality and present almost the same degree of degradation when compared to the natural speech [7]. Moreover, a one-to-one comparison of the four models showed that listeners had no clear preference for a particular one.

Consequently, differentiating geminated consonants (resp. long vowels) from simple consonants (resp. short vowels) or merging them lead to a similar speech synthesis quality. HMM-based speech synthesis did not benefit from the explicit differentiation between the different classes of phonemes (i.e., simple vs. geminated consonants and short vs. long vowels).

3   DNN-Based Speech Synthesis

3.1   DNN vs. Decision Trees

Decision trees used in HMM-based speech synthesis, present major shortcomings [19,23]. They are inefficient to model complex functions and dependencies between contextual features and acoustic parameters. Since the set of contextual features contains around 50 features, it requires large decision trees to be modelled. Besides, during the training, decision trees split the training data into sub-clusters and use different parameters for each cluster [22]. This process affects the clustering of the context-dependent distributions, thus the estimation of the distributions for speech parameters prediction. According to [3], DNN are able to represent complicated functions, besides, the weights of DNN are trained from all the training data.

3.2   DNN-Based Speech Synthesis System

In DNN-based speech synthesis, the contextual features are mapped to the output vector, which contains spectral and excitation parameters and their dynamic features. Weights of the DNN are trained using pairs of input and output features extracted from training data to minimize the error between the mapped output predicted from the given input and the target output. Finally, a vocoder is used to process the generated speech parameters to produce a speech signal.

3.3   Merlin Toolkit

Merlin speech synthesis toolkit for neural network-based speech synthesis was introduced in [20]. Merlin proposes a variety of architecture e.g., a standard feedforward neural network, recurrent neural network (RNN) and long short-term memory (LSTM). Moreover, Merlin supports WORLD [15] and STRAIGHT [11] vocoder. The input vector of the neural network includes numerical values (e.g., the number of phonemes in the syllable, position of the syllable in the word...) and binary answers to questions about identities of the phonemes context (e.g., is the current phoneme "a"...) and other characteristics.

4   Evaluation of Speech Unit Modelling

4.1   Experiment Conditions

The evaluation of the speech unit modelling approaches (C2V2, C1V1, C1V2 and C2V1) is conducted using the training and test sets described in Sect. 2. The contextual features are the same as in [7]. The input vector consists of 816 features where 771 of them are binary answers to questions about context of the phonemes (e.g., identity of the phoneme, identity of the vowel of the current syllable...), whereas the remaining 45 are numeric values (e.g., position of the phoneme in the syllable, the duration of the phoneme and of the state in frames, frame position within the state and the phoneme, the state position within the phoneme forward and backward etc.). Several tests were conducted to choose the DNN architecture that can generate the best speech quality. In current experiments, the DNN is composed of 4 layers of 1024 units with tanh transfer function plus one BLSTM (bidirectional LSTM) on the upper layer with 512 units to consider the sequential aspect of the speech [5]. During the experiment, WORLD vocoder is used to extract 60-dimensional MCCs (Mel-Cepstral Coefficients), 5-dimensional BAPs (Band APeriodicities) and log (F0) at a frame length of 5 ms.

4.2 Objective Evaluation of Duration

An objective evaluation is conducted with respect to duration of sounds. For speech signals produced with each modelling approach (C2V2, C1V1, C1V2 and C2V1) the average, over the vowels, of the ratios between the mean duration of long vowels (LV) and the mean duration of corresponding short vowels (SV) is calculated as well as the average ratio for geminated consonants (GC) vs. simple consonants (SC). Only phonemes with more than 10 occurrences for each class (simple/geminated consonants and short/long vowels) are considered. The calculated average ratios are compared to those obtained on natural speech.

Table 1. Duration ratios.

Number of occurrence	LV/SV	GC/SC
	262/884	104/1315
C2V2	1.7	2.1
C1V1	1.7	2.1
C1V2	1.7	2.1
C2V1	1.8	2.2
Natural	2.0	2.1

Values in Table 1, show that for the four modelling approaches, the ratios between the predicted durations of long vowels (LV) and short vowels (SV) are lower than those calculated for natural speech. However, the ratios between predicted durations of geminated consonants (GC) and predicted durations of simple consonants (SC) are similar to those calculated on natural speech.

Root mean square error (RMSE) between natural duration and predicted durations was calculated on the different phoneme classes (simple and geminated consonants, and short and long vowels). Values of RMSE are presented in Fig. 1. Results show that for each class, the C2V2 model (the most detailed model) leads to lower RMSE than the other approaches (C1V1, C1V2 and C2V1).

Normalized root mean square error (NRMSE) is calculated by considering the mean duration values of each phoneme class (NRMSE = RMSE/M, where M

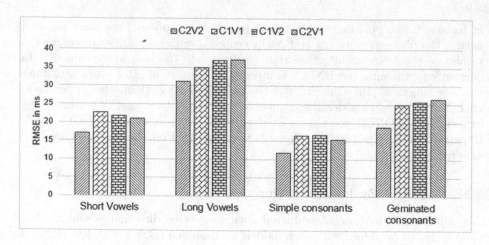

Fig. 1. RMSE between natural and predicted durations

is the mean duration). The obtained results are presented in Fig. 2. NRMSE of
the model C2V2 presents a significant decrease. Meanwhile, for each phoneme
class, the other approaches present similar values of NRMSE.

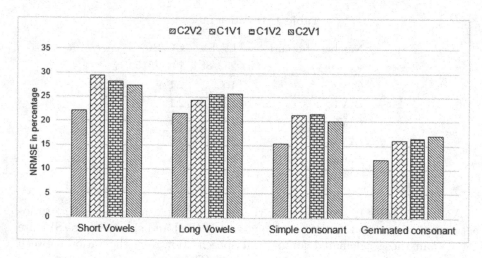

Fig. 2. NRMSE between natural and predicted durations

4.3   Comparison of Modelling Approaches

A preference test [9] was conducted to compare the four proposed approaches. 18
Arabic native speakers participated in this evaluation. Each one evaluated a set
of 20 pairs of speech signals; each pair consists of the same utterance produced
with two different approaches. The order of presentation of the speech signals is

randomly chosen for each trial. During the evaluation, participants were asked to point to the preferred signal based on the global quality of produced speech by answering the following question: *"How do you judge the quality of the second signal compared to the first one?"* and giving a score from 1 to 7 ranging from much worse to much better. Results of comparison are shown in Fig. 3. To analyse the results, scores were grouped to get three possible rates; first preferred (scores 1 and 2 corresponding to much worse and worse), no preference (scores 3, 4 and 5 corresponding to a little worse, about the same and a little better) and second preferred (scores 6 and 7 corresponding to better and much better):

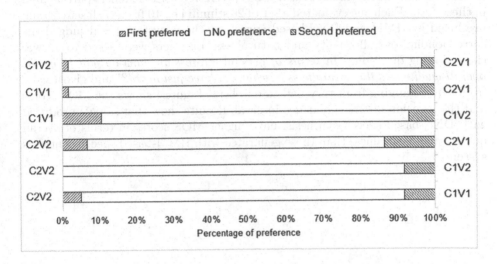

Fig. 3. Results of preference test

The one-to-one comparison shows that listeners had no clear preference for one particular approach. Although, C2V2 leads to a better prediction of duration, the listening tests show that differentiating geminated consonants (resp. long vowels) from simple consonants (resp. short vowels) or merging them leads to similar speech synthesis quality.

5   Evaluation of DNN-Based Speech Synthesis

5.1   Experiments Conditions

DNN-based speech synthesis was evaluated through a comparison to the standard HMM-based speech synthesis (based on decision trees) and to speech processed by the WORLD vocoder. Evaluation data consists of 30 stimuli generated using context-dependent HMM and the model C2V2, 30 stimuli produced using DNN and the model C2V2 and 30 stimuli processed by copy synthesis i.e., natural signals were analysed using the vocoder WORLD, then they were reconstructed based on the extracted speech parameters using the same vocoder WORLD. Note that participants are Arabic native speakers and they are neither specialists in phonetics nor accustomed to speech evaluation.

5.2   Evaluation of Global Quality

MOS (Mean Opinion Score) tests [9] were conducted to assess the global quality and naturalness of produced speech signals. The global quality refers to the overall quality of generated signals. The naturalness is assessed based on the intonation and the rhythm of synthesized speech signals. 15 listeners participated in these tests. Each one evaluated a set of 20 stimuli i.e., 10 from each set (stimuli produced by HMM and DNN-based speech synthesis systems) and judged the corresponding overall quality and naturalness. Listeners were asked to answer the following question: *"In terms of general impression, how do you judge the overall quality and the naturalness of what you have just heard?"* and give a score from 1 to 5 ranging from very bad to excellent. Figure 4 shows the MOS scores and the associated 95% confidence interval. Results show that signals produced with DNN-based speech synthesis, have higher MOS scores in terms of overall quality and naturalness than those generated with HMM-based speech synthesis system.

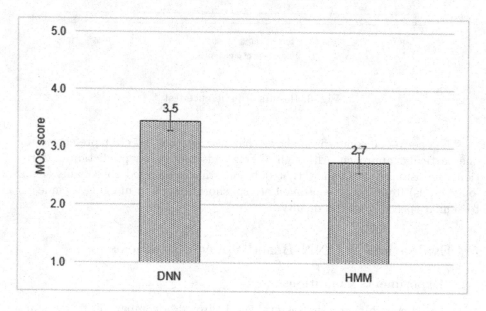

Fig. 4. Results of global quality evaluation.

5.3   Evaluation of Degradation

DMOS (Degradation Mean Opinion Score) tests [9] were conducted to evaluate the degree of degradation caused by the used toolkits HTS (for HMM-based speech synthesis) and Merlin (for DNN-based speech synthesis). Speech signals from each set are compared to the natural speech. Nine listeners participated in these tests, each one evaluated a set of 30 pairs, where each pair consists of the same utterance produced by DNN, HMM-based speech synthesis systems or copy-synthesis and the corresponding natural signal.

Note that the reference (natural signal) is always presented first. Participants evaluated the degradation of signals by answering the following question: *"How do you judge the degradation of the second signal compared to the first one?"*, based on the five-point degradation category scale ranging from very annoying degradation to inaudible degradation. The obtained results are presented in Fig. 5 with the associated 95% confidence interval. The higher the score is, the lower the degradation is.

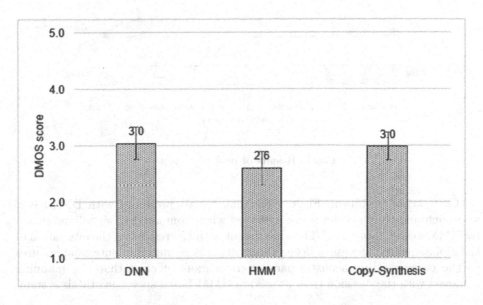

Fig. 5. Results of degradation evaluation.

Results show that the degree of degradation obtained with Merlin is similar to the one obtained by copy-synthesis, and lower than the one obtained with HMM-based speech synthesis system.

5.4   Comparison of DNN and HMM Performance

A preference test [9] was conducted to compare the performance of HMM to DNN-based speech synthesis approaches. Signals generated by Copy-synthesis using the vocoder WORLD were included in this test as well. The comparison was established with respect to the quality of produced speech. Stimuli are compared to each other. 18 listeners participated in this evaluation. Each one evaluated a set of 30 pairs of speech signals; each pair consists of the same utterance produced with two different approaches. The order of presenting the speech signals is randomly chosen for each trial. Participants were asked to point to the preferred signal based on the global quality of produced speech, by answering this question *"How do you judge the quality of the second signal compared to the first one?"* and giving a score from 1 to 7 ranging from much worse to much better. Scores were grouped in the same way like for Fig. 3.

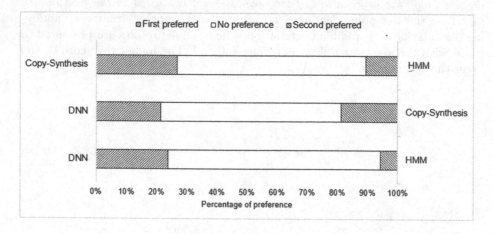

Fig. 6. Results of preference test

Comparison results in Fig. 6 show that signals produced with DNN-based approach and copy-synthesis are preferred when compared to signals produced by HMM-based approach. This is consistent with the results on the evaluation of the global quality: the use of deep neural networks to map the contextual features to the corresponding acoustic parameters is more efficient than the mapping achieved with the decision trees as used in HMM-based speech synthesis system.

6   Conclusions

This paper studied the use of deep neural network in Arabic speech synthesis. Both HMM and DNN-based speech synthesis require the qualification of each text segments with a set of contextual features that comprise all factors (e.g., linguistic, prosodic, phonological...) affecting the pronunciation of the corresponding sound. Part of the set is language dependent, therefore, for Arabic language, two phonological phenomena are highlighted, namely gemination and vowel quantity (short/long). Two extra features are added to the set of contextual features to take into account those specificities.

A variety of possible modelling approaches of speech segments have been investigated such as, the use of different units for modelling long vs. short vowels, and/or the use of different units for modelling simple vs. geminated consonants. These combinations have been compared to another one, where a short vowel and its long counterpart are modelled with the same unit, and a geminated consonant and its simple counterpart are modelled with the same unit. Subjective evaluation of the four speech unit modelling approaches (C2V2, C1V1, C1V2 and C2V1) using Merlin showed that they lead to similar speech quality. However, a better prediction of duration is obtained when using the C2V2 approach (the most detailed). This model attained the lowest RMSE compared to the other models (C1V1, C1V2 and C2V1). Thus, DNN has been more successful to take advantage of specificities of Arabic language.

The second part of this paper focused on assessing the performance of DNN in Arabic speech synthesis. DNN provides an efficient mapping from contextual features to acoustic parameters. This is confirmed by the results of subjective evaluations, which showed that the use of a deep neural architecture in speech synthesis (more specifically in predicting the speech parameters) enhanced the accuracy of acoustic modelling so that the quality of DNN-generated speech is better than the one of HMM-based speech synthesis for Arabic language.

Acknowledgements. This research work was conducted under PHC-Utique Program in the framework of CMCU (Comité Mixte de Coopération Universitaire) grant N 15G1405.

References

1. Abdel-Hamid, O., Abdou, S.M., Rashwan, M.: Improving Arabic HMM based speech synthesis quality. In: 9th International Conference on Spoken Language Processing, INTERSPEECH 2006, Pittsburgh, Pennsylvania (2006)
2. Al-Ani, S.H.: Arabic Phonology: An Acoustical and Physiological Investigation, vol. 61. Walter de Gruyter, Berlin (1970)
3. Bengio, Y.: Learning deep architectures for AI. Found. Trends® Mach. Learn. **2**(1), 1–127 (2009)
4. Black, A.W., Zen, H., Tokuda, K.: Statistical parametric speech synthesis. In: International Conference on Acoustics, Speech and Signal Processing, ICASSP 2007. vol. 4, pp. IV–1229. IEEE (2007)
5. Fan, Y., Qian, Y., Xie, F.L., Soong, F.K.: TTS synthesis with bidirectional LSTM based recurrent neural networks. In: 15th Annual Conference of the International Speech Communication Association, Singapore (2014)
6. Halabi, N.: Modern standard Arabic speech corpus. Ph.D. thesis, University of Southampton (2015)
7. Houidhek, A., Colotte, V., Mnasri, Z., Jouvet, D., Zangar, I.: Statistical modelling of speech units in HMM-based speech synthesis for Arabic. In: 8th Language & Technology Conference, LTC 2017, Poznan, Poland (2017)
8. Hunt, A.J., Black, A.W.: Unit selection in a concatenative speech synthesis system using a large speech database. In: International Conference on Acoustics, Speech, and Signal Processing Conference Proceedings, ICASSP 1996, vol. 1, pp. 373–376. IEEE, Atlanta (1996)

9. ITU: 800, methods for subjective determination of transmission quality. International Telecommunication Union (1996)
10. Jurafsky, D.: Speech and language processing: an introduction to natural language processing. In: Computational Linguistics, and Speech Recognition (2000)
11. Kawahara, H., Masuda-Katsuse, I., De Cheveigne, A.: Restructuring speech representations using a pitch-adaptive time-frequency smoothing and an instantaneous-frequency-based F0 extraction: possible role of a repetitive structure in sounds. Speech Commun. **27**(3), 187–207 (1999)
12. Khalil, K.M., Adnan, C.: Arabic HMM-based speech synthesis. In: International Conference on Electrical Engineering and Software Applications, ICEESA 2013, pp. 1–5. IEEE, Hammamet (2013)
13. Krstulovic, S., Hunecke, A., Schröder, M.: An HMM-based speech synthesis system applied to German and its adaptation to a limited set of expressive football announcements. In: 8th Annual Conference of the International Speech Communication Association, pp. 1897–1900. Citeseer, Antwerp (2007)
14. Maguer, S.L., Barbot, N., Boeffard, O.: Evaluation of contextual descriptors for HMM-based speech synthesis in French. In: 8th Workshop on Speech Synthesis, Barcelona, Spain (2013)
15. Morise, M., Yokomori, F., Ozawa, K.: WORLD: a vocoder-based high-quality speech synthesis system for real-time applications. IEICE Trans. Inf. Syst. **99**(7), 1877–1884 (2016)
16. Newman, D.: The phonetic status of Arabic within the world's languages: the uniqueness of the lughat al-daad. Antwerp Pap. Linguist. **100**, 65–75 (2002)
17. Selouani, S.A., Caelen, J.: Arabic phonetic features recognition using modular connectionist architectures. In: Proceedings of the IEEE 4th Workshop on Interactive Voice Technology for Telecommunications Applications, IVTTA 1998, pp. 155–160. IEEE, Torino (1998)
18. Tokuda, K., Zen, H., Black, A.W.: An HMM-based speech synthesis system applied to English. In: IEEE Speech Synthesis Workshop, Santa Monica, CA, USA, pp. 227–230 (2002)
19. Watts, O., Henter, G.E., Merritt, T., Wu, Z., King, S.: From HMMS to DNNs: where do the improvements come from? In: International Conference on Acoustics, Speech and Signal Processing, ICASSP 2016, pp. 5505–5509. IEEE, Lujiazui (2016)
20. Wu, Z., Watts, O., King, S.: Merlin: an open source neural network speech synthesis system. In: Proceedings of the SSW, Sunnyvale, USA (2016)
21. Zangar, I., Mnasri, Z., Colotte, V., Jouvet, D., Houidhek, A.: Duration modeling using DNN for Arabic speech synthesis. In: 9th International Conference on Speech Prosody, Poznan, Poland, pp. 597–601 (2018)
22. Zen, H.: Deep learning in speech synthesis. In: SSW, Barcelona, Spain, p. 309 (2013)
23. Zen, H., Senior, A., Schuster, M.: Statistical parametric speech synthesis using deep neural networks. In: International Conference on Acoustics, Speech and Signal Processing, ICASSP 2013, pp. 7962–7966. IEEE (2013)
24. Zen, H., Tokuda, K., Masuko, T., Kobayasih, T., Kitamura, T.: A hidden semi-Markov model-based speech synthesis system. IEICE Trans. Inf. Syst. **90**(5), 825–834 (2007)
25. Zhang, M., Tao, J., Jia, H., Wang, X.: Improving HMM based speech synthesis by reducing over-smoothing problems. In: 6th International Symposium on Chinese Spoken Language Processing, ISCSLP 2008, pp. 1–4. IEEE, Kunming (2008)

Phone-Level Embeddings for Unit Selection Speech Synthesis

Antoine Perquin[1]([✉]), Gwénolé Lecorvé[1], Damien Lolive[1],
and Laurent Amsaleg[2]

[1] Univ Rennes, CNRS, IRISA, Lannion, France
{antoine.perquin,gwenole.lecorve,damien.lolive,
laurent.amsaleg}@irisa.fr
[2] Univ Rennes, CNRS, INRIA, IRISA, Rennes, France

Abstract. Deep neural networks have become the state of the art in speech synthesis. They have been used to directly predict signal parameters or provide unsupervised speech segment descriptions through embeddings. In this paper, we present four models with two of them enabling us to extract phone-level embeddings for unit selection speech synthesis. Three of the models rely on a feed-forward DNN, the last one on an LSTM. The resulting embeddings enable replacing usual expert-based target costs by an euclidean distance in the embedding space. This work is conducted on a French corpus of an 11 h audiobook. Perceptual tests show the produced speech is preferred over a unit selection method where the target cost is defined by an expert. They also show that the embeddings are general enough to be used for different speech styles without quality loss. Furthermore, objective measures and a perceptual test on statistical parametric speech synthesis show that our models perform comparably to state-of-the-art models for parametric signal generation, in spite of necessary simplifications, namely late time integration and information compression.

Keywords: Speech synthesis · Unit selection · Embedding

1 Introduction

Unit selection speech synthesis concatenates pre-existing segments of recorded speech, producing high-quality, natural sounding, oral renderings of sentences [2]. This process optimises a *target cost* function selecting the units that best match the linguistic descriptions of the phonemes to synthesize. Quality results from the involvement of linguistic experts who carefully design that function. These methods, however, suffer from concatenation errors and cannot generalize outside the pre-recorded units. Furthermore, they necessitate extremely costly human expertise, which might not exist when targeting or adapting to other domains or languages.

© Springer Nature Switzerland AG 2018
T. Dutoit et al. (Eds.): SLSP 2018, LNAI 11171, pp. 21–31, 2018.
https://doi.org/10.1007/978-3-030-00810-9_3

Instead, this paper proposes an embedding-based method allowing to rely on euclidean distances between units when optimizing their selection. Not only is this cheap compared to human expertise, but embeddings also facilitate domain adaptation. This paper presents four models, with two of them resulting in phone-level embeddings for unit selection. Three of them rely on a feed-forward Deep Neural Network (DNN) whereas the last one uses a Long Short Term Memory layer (LSTM). Experiments using a large French speech corpus show that the use of the embeddings outperforms expert-based unit selection.

A few remarks are in order. One, temporal information can be integrated in different ways. We compare its early or later integration in DNNs, and study the use of temporal dependencies brought by an LSTM layer. Two, in an attempt to understand if mitigating the effects of the curse of dimensionality on the embeddings is beneficial, three models use varying layers sizes at their core. Three, as far as we know, no objective metrics for assessing the quality of such embeddings exist. As a proxy, we evaluate their ability to predict appropriate acoustic features. Four, in contrast to state of the art contributions that work for English, we work with French. This is the opportunity to assess how the embedding-based approach performs on French.

The remainder of this paper is as follows. Section 2 presents related work. Section 3 discusses the handling of time and dimensionality in the embeddings. Finally, Sect. 4 compares our approach to an expert unit selection system.

2   Related Work

The Statistical Parametric Speech Synthesis (SPSS) approach uses vocoders to synthesize speech from acoustic parameters predicted by a so-called *acoustic model* based on linguistic features [1]. Recent models are now based on DNNs [13]. Beside pros and cons of this approach (good flexibility but low quality), the resulting prediction models are interestingly independent of any linguistic expertise.

This approach gave rise to different extensions. On the one hand, the Wavenet model proposes to integrate vocoding in the prediction model, i.e., the raw waveforms are directly predicted [6]. End-to-end approaches such as [9] go further by predicting these waveforms directly from text, that is linguistic features are removed.

On the other hand, prediction models have also been used to transform linguistic features into other representations, based on which a new target cost for unit selection can be defined. In turn, the new representation space can be handled more easily than the symbolic space of the linguistic features. In [12], linguistic features are converted into acoustic ones based on hidden Markov models. The Kullback-Leibler divergence is then used as a target cost. Alternatively, [4,8] have proposed intermediate representations extracted from hidden layers of DNNs, also called *embeddings*.

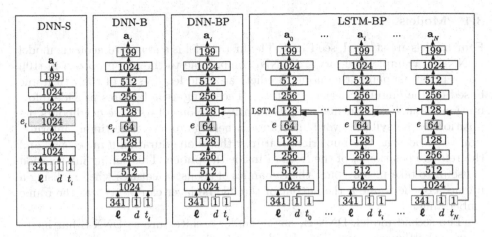

Fig. 1. Architecture of the 4 models. Layer sizes are reported. ℓ denotes the vector of linguistic features, d the phone duration, t_i the time position in the phone for the i-th frame, $\mathbf{a}_i$ the corresponding acoustic features, and N is the total number of frames in the phone.

In [4], each phone is divided into 4 sections for which the mean and variance of the embedding of each frame is computed. The target cost function is the sum of the Kullback-Leibler divergence on the mean and variance of the 4 sections. This showed that there is no loss in the quality of speech when using embeddings instead of acoustic features. The subdivisions, however, still involve some human expertise.

In [8], a phone level embedding is obtained with a multi-modal model composed of an acoustic encoder and a linguistic encoder. The target cost is the euclidean distance in the embedding space. This work is very similar to ours, and was actually conducted at the same time as [7]. Our work focuses on the effect of various time integration and information compression schemes, rather than those of multi-modality.

3   Handling of Time and Dimensionality

A key assumption in our work is that the quality of an embedding is correlated to the quality of the model from which it is derived, in our case acoustic models. In this section, different variants of acoustic models are studied, among which those proposed for unit selection. These models are objectively and perceptually evaluated to assess the behaviour of embeddings with respect to information compression and different strategies for time integration. This section first presents the models under study before describing the experimental dataset, then the objective and perceptual tests.

3.1   Models

Four models are studied, see Fig. 1. The first model is a standard acoustic model (DNN-S), a simple feed-forward DNN, comparable to the one proposed in [10]. For a given phoneme, the model predicts acoustic features $\mathbf{a}_i$ of the i-th frame based on the linguistic feature vector $\boldsymbol{\ell}$. Those linguistic features provide information about the phoneme, e.g., its identity, the one of its close neighbours, its position in the syllable/word/utterance it belongs to, etc. The timing information is encoded as two numerical features: the phone duration d in seconds and the relative position t_i of the frame i inside the phone. This timing information is useful to take into account the dynamics of acoustic features when realising a phone. For the frame i, the output of the middle layer can be seen as the frame embedding e_i.

The second model, DNN-B, has a similar architecture as DNN-S but introduces a bottleneck layer. This bottleneck is obtained by gradually decreasing then increasing the size of the hidden layers. e_i is then a compression of the linguistic features $\boldsymbol{\ell}$. As a side effect, compressing the embedding space avoids the curse of dimensionality and allows for tractable similarity measures.

The limitation of both models is that the resulting embeddings would only represent the frame currently predicted, whereas phone-level embeddings are needed for unit selection. To solve this problem, we propose to postpone making use of the timing information (d and t_i) until after the embedding layer, as in [8]. Applying this principle on DNN-B gives the model DNN-BP, P for Phone-level. For a given linguistic feature vector $\boldsymbol{\ell}$, we obtain a phone-level embedding e.

Finally, to attempt to model the timing dependency across frames, we propose to replace the layer after the embedding layer with an LSTM in DNN-BP to obtain the model LSTM-BP. While the previous models are trained on independent frames, LSTM-BP is trained on the full frame sequence of the considered phone. This method decreases the shuffling possibilities over the training set but could lead to better predictions, and thus better embeddings.

The implementation details of the different models are as follows:

- DNN-S: 5 hidden layers of size 1024. The total number of parameters is 4,75 millions.
- DNN-B: The bottleneck scheme is symmetrically designed: 9 hidden layers of size 1024, 512, 256, 128, 64, 128, 256, 512, 1024. The total number of parameters is 1.95 millions.
- DNN-BP: Same as DNN-B, except timing is postponed. The total number of parameters is 1.95 millions.
- LSTM-BP: Same as DNN-BP, except the second 128 dimensional layer is replaced with an LSTM layer of size 128 too. The total number of parameters is 2.04 millions.

All hidden layers rely on the hyperbolic tangent (*tanh*) activation function. For all models, the output layer is with a linear activation.

3.2 Dataset and Experimental Setup

Our models were trained on a corpus corresponding to the reading of a French audio-book by a professional French speaker resulting in approximately 11 hours of speech for a total of 3300 utterances (approximately 390 000 phonemes). Speech is expressive (narration, acted dialogues), and sentences are complex (long sentences, formal register) due to the style of the audiobook's author (Marcel Proust). 105 utterances were held out for the listening test, while the rest was shuffled at the frame level (or phone level for model LSTM-BP) and then split into three sets: 90% for the training set and 5% each for the validation set and test set.

About 110 linguistic features are considered for each phone. Categorical attributes represent information about quinphones, syllables, articulatory features, and part of speech for the current, previous and following words. They are encoded in one-hot. 34 other features are numerical, such as the position of the phone inside the word or the utterance. After encoding, the overall linguistic vector is of size 341. The linguistic features and the timing information were normalised to the range [0.01, 0.99]. Each linguistic feature was manually extracted, without automatic annotation.

The acoustic features, extracted using the WORLD vocoder [5], consist of a 60 dimension Mel-Generalized Cepstral coefficients (MGC) vector, a 5 dimension band-aperiodicity (BAP) vector and the fundamental frequency F_0. Those features were extracted every 5 ms. The F_0 coefficient was linearly interpolated on unvoiced parts, a boolean attribute keeps track whether the frame was voiced or not and the logarithm was applied to F_0. Finally, the deltas and delta-deltas were computed for MGC, BAP and F_0. In total, the acoustic vector is of size 199. The acoustic features were centered and normalized to unit variance.

The implementation was done using Keras with TensorFlow. Training was done on a GTX 1080 Ti, over 100 epochs using RMSPROP with the mean square error as a loss function. The model weights with the best performance on the validation set were saved. Those models were trained using the true duration values.

3.3 Objective Evaluation

The 4 models were evaluated in an acoustic modelling perspective. Table 1 reports the quality of the predicted acoustic features according to the following measures:

- MCD: Mel-Cepstral Distortion on MGC coefficients.
- BAP: a distortion measure on BAPs.
- V/UV: Voiced/unvoiced error rate.
- RMSE (F0): Root mean squared error on F_0.

Those measures are computed between the acoustic features predicted by the DNNs and the reference acoustic features. The results from a state of the art acoustic model are also directly reported from [11]. They were not trained on the same data, nor even the same language. They are presented for the sake of a sanity check.

Table 1. Objective evaluation of the predictions of our models.

	MCD (dB)	BAP (dB)	V/UV (%)	RMSE (F_0) (Hz)
DNN-S	5.22	0.48	17.2	18.3
DNN-B	5.06	0.35	12.6	17.9
DNN-BP	5.09	0.36	13.7	18.2
LSTM-BP	5.80	0.49	19.7	19.5
DNN (reported from [11])	4.54	0.36	11.38	9.57

First, our measures are higher than those from [11], especially regarding F_0 and voicing error. We believe the high error on those two aspects is due to the high expressiveness of our speech corpus. Taking this into account, these results can be considered as acceptable. Second, by comparing model DNN-B and DNN-BP, we can see that the displacement of the timing information raises the error for all measures by only a small margin. Then, while one would expect DNN-S to lead to the best results, it appears that its performance is a bit worse than for DNN-B and DNN-BP. Possible explanations are the larger number of parameters for model DNN-S (more difficult to reach the global optimum for weights) or the larger number of layers in the DNN-B and DNN-BP. At least, the results show that the bottleneck does not hurt. On the contrary, LSTM-BP leads to the worst results. This is surprising since adding extra information about the previous frames should not degrade the prediction. In our opinion, these results mainly come from the fact that training data are organised as sequences of frames, thus reducing the diversity of observations during training, whereas the other models are trained on shuffled frames. Despite those bad results, we chose to keep LSTM-BP to evaluate the effect of an acoustic model quality on its embeddings and on the resulting synthesized speech.

3.4   Perceptual Evaluation

The previous objective measures are not perfect estimators of the overall speech quality. For example, a significant improvement in MCD does not necessarily translate to a perceptual improvement of the synthesized speech. Thus we want to observe the perceptual impact of embeddings on SPSS.

For each model, synthetic speech has been generated based on the predicted acoustic features using an SPSS approach. In practice, the WORLD vocoder is used. Long utterances were split into breath groups of 4–5 s. The timing information (d and t_i) was derived from a duration model (DNN with 6 hidden layers and *tanh* activation) predicting the number of frames N of a phone based on its linguistic feature vector ℓ. The mean absolute error of this model is 3.7 frames. d is derived by multiplying N by the sampling rate, t_i is simply $\frac{i}{N}$. A listening test was conducted with 21 French native speakers. They were asked to rate between 0 and 10 the overall quality of speech utterances. Synthetic speech coming from the 4 models was presented along with natural speech (NAT) and utterances

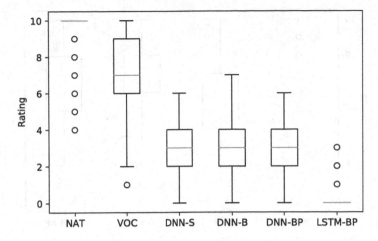

Fig. 2. Results of the listening test for the models in statistic parametric mode for in-domain utterances.

vocoded based on the reference acoustic features (VOC). Each listener was given 10 in-domain utterances and 10 out-of-domain utterances. For in-domain evaluation, we used the 105 sentences left-out from the dataset, while for out of domain evaluation we used 100 phonetically balanced French sentences. Thus, every utterance was rated by at least two different listeners.

In accordance with the objective results, the listening test shows that our models do not perform well in SPSS mode, as can be seen on Fig. 2. While our listeners reacted well to perfect SPSS (analysis-synthesis), giving a 7.2 mean score to the system VOC, they gave a mean score of around 3 to our first 3 models, and agreed that system LSTM-BP's productions were incomprehensible with a mean score of almost 0. This is not surprising since this system had a higher MCD than other systems, which is measured on a log-scale. There is no real statistically significant (p-value greater than 0.05) difference between systems DNN-S, DNN-B and DNN-BP which proves that the displacement of the timing information does not cause any perceptual loss in quality. Surprisingly, the natural speech received a couple of marks below 7. The corresponding utterances were perceived as having unnatural prosody because they were cut to be shortened.

4 Comparison with Expert Unit Selection

In this section, the proposed unit selection method is compared to a system where the target cost is defined based on expert knowledge.

4.1 Unit Selection Engine

Once phone-level embeddings have been extracted, we use them to guide the unit selection process. Before synthesis, for each phone in the database, the

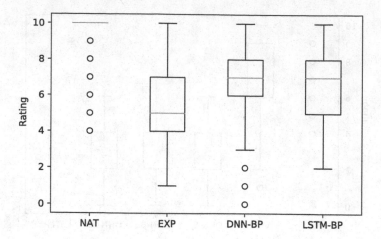

Fig. 3. Results of the listening test for the models working in unit selection mode for in-domain utterances.

corresponding embedding is computed and stored. At synthesis time, a preselection reduces the set of candidate units to those corresponding to the same phoneme as the target, in order to reduce the computation time. The number of candidate units is reduced further by searching the 25 nearest neighbours of the target phone in the embedding space among the pre-selected units. Finally, the lattice of these nearest neighbours for each phone is decoded to find the sequence of units minimizing the sum of the target and concatenation cost.

The target cost is defined as the euclidean distance in the embedding space between the candidate and target phone. For the expert system, the target cost was originally defined as a weighted sum of linguistic features and has since been improved over the years. The join cost for all systems is the same as in [3], defined as a sum of euclidean distances on acoustic features between following candidate units.

4.2   Perceptive Evaluation

Since there is no proposed measure in the literature to evaluate the quality of an embedding in relation to speech synthesis, we directly address the subjective evaluation of the embeddings with listening tests. The results for in-domain and out-of-domain utterances can be found on Figs. 3 and 4 respectively.

For in-domain utterances, the 3 proposed models were all awarded really high grades (multiple times rated with a 10/10 score for each system) but also really low notes (up to 0 for system DNN-BP). However, on average, the expert system received a mean score of 5.4, system DNN-BP received 6.8 and system LSTM-BP received 6.6. While we cannot statistically distinguish the two systems with embeddings (p-value greater than 0.05), both are a statistically significant improvement over the expert system. Interestingly, even if the system LSTM-BP

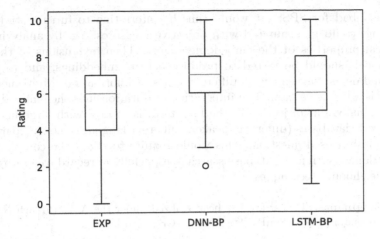

Fig. 4. Results of the listening test for the models working in unit selection mode for out-of domain utterances.

performed really poorly for SPSS, it receives good results for the unit selection paradigm.

For out-of-context utterances, natural speech from the same voice as the one used in the database was unavailable. The expert system received a mean score of 5.9, system DNN-BP received 7.0 and system LSTM-BP received 6.4. This time, the difference between the two systems using embeddings is significant. However, they both perform without significant loss over in-domain synthesis. Surprisingly, the expert system appears to have been better rated on out-of-domain utterances. A probable explanation is the absence of natural speech as a higher baseline during the MUSHRA test. Still, the embedding systems remain significantly better than the expert one proving that the embeddings are general enough to be used in other domains.

5 Conclusion

In this paper, we proposed two models to extract phone-level embeddings in the context of DNN-driven unit selection. The models were compared to other DNNs on the task of acoustic modeling. The experiments highlighted that late integration of time and information compression (bottleneck) do not impact the quality of feature prediction, even though the use of LSTM did not seem conclusive yet. Then, experiments on unit selection showed that quality of synthesized speech based on embeddings resulting from our models is perceptually preferred over an approach with an expertly defined target cost. They also demonstrated that the proposed embeddings are general enough to be used in multiple domains.

Besides these results, our study also highlights the fact that the link between the acoustic feature prediction and the quality of unit embeddings is not clear. For instance, the LSTM-BP model led to good unit selection results whereas it was very bad for SPSS. It would thus be interesting to further study how embeddings could be evaluated with objective measures, e.g. by analyzing the topological properties of the embedding spaces. Then, extensions of the proposed models should be tested to produce better embeddings, and to better understand dependencies across different types of information. Multi-modality, as in [8], is a first direction. The integration of duration into the embeddings is another. Finally, our objective in the long term is to deal with large heterogeneous speech databases (different speakers, different languages, etc.). Apart from the previously raised questions, this would require to study the compliance of the embeddings with fast database searches, especially in regard to approximate nearest neighbours techniques.

Acknowledgments. This study has been realized under the ANR (French National Research Agency) project SynPaFlex ANR-15-CE23-0015.

References

1. Black, A.W., Zen, H., Tokuda, K.: Statistical parametric speech synthesis. In: Proceedings of the IEEE International Conference on Acoustics, Speech and Signal Processing (ICASSP), vol. 4, pp. 1229–1232 (2007)
2. Hunt, A.J., Black, A.W.: Unit selection in a concatenative speech synthesis system using a large speech database. In: Proceedings of the IEEE International Conference on Acoustics, Speech, and Signal Processing (ICASSP), vol. 1, pp. 373–376 (1996)
3. Lolive, D., et al.: The IRISA text-to-speech system for the Blizzard challenge 2017. In: Proceedings of the Blizzard Challenge Workshop (2017)
4. Merritt, T., Clark, R.A., Wu, Z., Yamagishi, J., King, S.: Deep neural network-guided unit selection synthesis. In: Proceedings of the IEEE International Conference on Acoustics, Speech and Signal Processing (ICASSP), pp. 5145–5149 (2016)
5. Morise, M., Yokomori, F., Ozawa, K.: WORLD: a vocoder-based high-quality speech synthesis system for real-time applications. IEICE Trans. Inf. Syst. **99**(7), 1877–1884 (2016)
6. van den Oord, A., et al.: WaveNet: a generative model for raw audio. In: Proceedings of the ISCA Speech Synthesis Workshop (SSW), pp. 125–125 (2016)
7. Perquin, A.: Big deep voice: indexation de données massives de parole grâce à des réseaux de neurones profonds. Master's thesis, University of Rennes 1 (2017)
8. Wan, V., Agiomyrgiannakis, Y., Silen, H., Vit, J.: Googles next-generation real-time unit-selection synthesizer using sequence-to-sequence LSTM-based autoencoders. In: Proceedings of the Annual Conference of the International Speech Communication Association (Interspeech), pp. 1143–1147 (2017)
9. Wang, Y., et al.: Tacotron: towards end-to-end speech synthesis. In: Proceedings of the Annual Conference of the International Speech Communication Association (Interspeech), pp. 4006–4010 (2017)
10. Wu, Z., King, S.: Improving trajectory modelling for DNN-based speech synthesis by using stacked bottleneck features and minimum generation error training. IEEE/ACM Trans. Audio Speech Lang. Process. (TASLP) **24**(7), 1255–1265 (2016)
11. Wu, Z., Watts, O., King, S.: Merlin: an open source neural network speech synthesis system. In: Proceedings of the ISCA Speech Synthesis Workshop (SSW), pp. 218–223 (2016)

12. Yan, Z.J., Qian, Y., Soong, F.K.: Rich-context unit selection (RUS) approach to high quality TTS. In: IEEE International Conference on Acoustics Speech and Signal Processing (ICASSP), pp. 4798–4801 (2010)
13. Ze, H., Senior, A., Schuster, M.: Statistical parametric speech synthesis using deep neural networks. In: Proceedings of the IEEE International Conference on Acoustics, Speech and Signal Processing (ICASSP), pp. 7962–7966 (2013)

Disfluency Insertion for Spontaneous TTS: Formalization and Proof of Concept

Raheel Qader[1], Gwénolé Lecorvé[1(✉)], Damien Lolive[1], and Pascale Sébillot[2]

[1] Univ Rennes, CNRS, IRISA, 22300 Lannion, France
raheel.qader@gmail.com, {gwenole.lecorve,damien.lolive}@irisa.fr
[2] Univ Rennes, Inria, CNRS, IRISA, 35000 Rennes, France
pascale.sebillot@irisa.fr

Abstract. This paper presents an exploratory work to automatically insert disfluencies in text-to-speech (TTS) systems. The objective is to make TTS more spontaneous and expressive. To achieve this, we propose to focus on the linguistic level of speech through the insertion of pauses, repetitions and revisions. We formalize the problem as a theoretical process, where transformations are iteratively composed. This is a novel contribution since most of the previous work either focus on the detection or cleaning of linguistic disfluencies in speech transcripts, or solely concentrate on acoustic phenomena in TTS, especially pauses. We present a first implementation of the proposed process using conditional random fields and language models. The objective and perceptual evalation conducted on an English corpus of spontaneous speech show that our proposition is effective to generate disfluencies, and highlights perspectives for future improvements.

Keywords: Disfluencies · Spontaneous speech
Natural language generation

1 Introduction

Speech disfluencies can be defined as a phenomenon which interrupts the flow of speech and does not add any propositional content [22]. Despite the lack of propositional content, disfluencies have several communicative values. They facilitate synchronization between addressees in conversations [6]. They also improve listening comprehension by creating delays in speech and signaling the upcoming message complexity [14,23] (cited by [3]). Despite this, current Text-To-Speech (TTS) systems only partially integrate disfluencies. They are thus inadequate to express a spontaneous style, and prevent from high user acceptability in some human-machine interactions (e.g. personnal assistants, avatars). To tackle the issue, this paper investigates the automatic insertion of disfluencies.

This study has been realized under the ANR (French National Research Agency) project SynPaFlex ANR-15-CE23-0015.

© Springer Nature Switzerland AG 2018
T. Dutoit et al. (Eds.): SLSP 2018, LNAI 11171, pp. 32–44, 2018.
https://doi.org/10.1007/978-3-030-00810-9_4

This paper proposes a novel formalization of the disfluency generation mechanism. This formalization enables controlling the nature and proportion of the disfluencies to be generated. Our proposal is supported by a proof of concept through a first implementation trained on an English corpus. This implementation relies on conditional random fields (CRFs) and language models (LMs) to experimentally demonstrate the ability of our approach to produce plausible disfluent utterances. As exploratory work, no synthesis experiment is carried out because integrating disfluencies in a TTS system requires adaptations on many aspects (underlying speech corpus, prosody prediction, etc.). Thus, the current work conducts the textual validation of the generated disfluent utterances.

In the remainder, Sect. 2 reviews the domain and presents our motivations. Then, Sect. 3 introduces the formalization of the problem while its implementation is given in Sect. 4. Finally, the validation of our work is provided in Sect. 5 through objective and perceptual evaluations.

2 Review of the Domain and Motivations

According to Shriberg [16], disfluencies are characterized by 3 sections playing a specific role: the *reparandum* region (or RM) which is the sequence of erroneous words; the *repair* region (RR), i.e. the sequence of corrected words for the RM region; and finally the so-called *interregnum* section indicating the interruption in the speech stream. In this schema, the point between the reparandum and the interregnum is the *interruption point* (IP). Below is an example of disfluency:

$$\underbrace{I\ think\ she\ will}_{RM} \quad \underbrace{I\ mean}_{IM}\ \underbrace{he\ will}_{RR}\ not\ come\ today. \qquad \text{(Example 1)}$$
$$\uparrow$$
$$IP$$

Several studies suggest to categorize disfluencies into three main types: pauses, repetitions, and revisions [12,15,24]. Pauses are useful to keep the conversation on while the speaker searches for a phrase. Pauses can be silent, filled (e.g., "uh" or "um") or discourse markers ("you know", "well", etc.). Repetitions can be used to gain time and recover the flow of the speech, intensify the effect of an expression, or signal an upcoming problem in the speech [24]. Finally, revisions occur when the speaker slightly fixes his speech after an error. False starts are an extreme case of revisions in which the speaker completely abandons the interrupted speech and starts a fresh one. Hence, revisions help the speaker monitoring his speech.

Most studies on disfluencies are for automatic speech recognition [8,10,11,17, 18] where the main objective improve language modeling and produce disfluency-free transcripts. On the contrary, disfluency generation is still poorly studied in TTS. According to [2], this is because, most of the time, speech databases for TTS systems do not contain any disfluencies, and linguistic processing pipelines in the front-end still badly integrate disfluent sentences, in spite of NLP progresses in the domain [9]. Among existing work, [19,21] studied the automatic insertion of filled pauses (especially "uh", "um") using finite state acceptors or word lattices. Other studies like [1,4,7] have formalized the problem as searching for an IP using machine learning before selecting, among a set of possibilities, the best words to be inserted according to probabilities given by an LM. This approach is also adopted in our work. Although this approach relies on the reductive hypothesis that disfluencies are predictable based on shallow (non-psychological) cues (raw words, parts of speech, etc.) [7], the resulting disfluencies have shown to feign personality traits [25]. Likewise, recent work has studied the acoustic aspects of lengthenings and filled pauses w.r.t. the perception of uncertainty [20].

Among limitations, most of these studies concentrate on one type of disfluencies (mostly filled pauses). Recently, [5] proposed to model several types of pauses. Following the same objective, we introduce a rich formalization, able to integrate repetitions and revisions in addition to pauses. Then, Shriberg's schema of disfluencies is useful to determine whether an utterance is disfluent or not, but it does not explain how to move from a fluent to a disfluent utterance, especially when disfluencies are interwinted. To solve this problem, we propose to decompose this schema such that it can be used to generate disfluencies in a deterministic way. Finally, it is worth noting that disfluency generation, as usually in natural language generation, is difficult to evaluate since several outputs are generally acceptable in these problems. This makes it particularly difficult to compute objective measures when data, as is the case in our work, contains only one reference to be compared with. This problem is discussed in Sect. 5.

3 Disfluency Generation Process

In this work, we propose a complete process for disfluency generation. The key idea is to compose disfluencies of elementary types. This section presents the whole process, each disfluency type, and the composition mechanism.

3.1 Main Principles

The proposed process considers a disfluency as the result of a transformation function on a fluent utterance. Hence, an utterance with multiple disfluencies results from successively composing transformation functions. In practice, one transformation function is defined for each disfluency type. That is, given a disfluency type T, the transformation function f_T reads a sequence of n words $\mathbf{w} \in V^n$, where V denotes the vocabulary, and returns a sequence of m words, $m > n$. In practice, each function f_T consists of two sub-functions: π_T, which determines the IP position, and ω_T which inserts the actual disfluent words using the result of π_T. Mathematically, these two functions can be defined as below:

$$\pi_T : \quad V^n \quad \rightarrow \quad [\![0, n]\!], \tag{1}$$
$$\text{and } \omega_T : V^n \times [\![0, n]\!] \rightarrow V^m. \tag{2}$$

Thus, f_T is simply calculated as $\omega_T(\mathbf{w}, \pi_T(\mathbf{w}))$. Sub-functions have been chosen to be specific on disfluency types since IPs may not appear in the same context according to the type, and each type has its own structure, expressible through Shriberg's schema and described in the following.

3.2   Disfluency Functions

Pauses can syntactically be seen as a simple interruptions, without any RM nor RR, solely reduced to an IM. This IM can be instantiated by different pause tokens, in our work those present in the corpus used for the experiments: "*<silence>*", "*uh*", "*um*", "*you know*" "*I mean*" and "*well*". This list can obviously be extended in order to make the whole process richer. The following is an example of a pause transformation from a fluent utterance:

$$\mathbf{w} : once\ you\ get\ to\ a\ certain\ degree\ of\ frustration,$$

$$\overset{IM}{\frown}$$
$$f_{\text{pause}}(\mathbf{w}) \quad : once\ you\ get\ to\ a\ certain\ degree\ of \quad \underset{\underset{IP}{\uparrow}}{uh} \quad frustration.$$

(Example 2)

To make the link with the sub-functions presented earlier, the IP here is determined by the π_{pause} function and the choice of the word(s) to be inserted is made by the ω_{pause} function. Repetitions are duplications of one or few words, i.e., their RM and RR regions are identical. Due to the proposed composition mechanism, no IM is considered, as follows: Thus, all repetition are treated as the following example:

$$\mathbf{w} : and\ I\ think\ this\ happens\ to\ a\ lot\ of\ people,$$

$$\qquad\qquad \overset{RM}{\overbrace{\qquad}} \quad \overset{RR}{\overbrace{\qquad}}$$
$$f_{\text{repetition}}(\mathbf{w}) \quad : and\ \overset{}{I \quad think} \underset{\underset{IP}{\uparrow}}{} I\ think\ this\ happens\ to\ a\ lot\ of\ people.$$

(Example 3)

A repetition with a pause in the middle is considered as 2 disfluencies. The scope of the repetition, i.e., length of RM and RR, is determined by the sub-function $\omega_{\text{repetition}}$. In a similar fashion, revisions do not include any IM, and ω_{revision} determines the span of the RR region and generates the RM. As opposed to repetitions, the predicted RM differs from the RR region. An example of revision is given below:

$$\mathbf{w} : that\ is\ so\ that\ if\ whoever\ would\ get\ it,$$

$$\qquad\qquad\qquad \overset{RM}{\overbrace{\qquad}} \quad\quad \overset{RR}{\overbrace{\qquad}}$$
$$f_{\text{revision}}(\mathbf{w}) \quad : that\ is\ so\ that\ \overset{}{if \quad you} \underset{\underset{IP}{\uparrow}}{} if\ whoever\ would\ get\ it.$$

(Example 4)

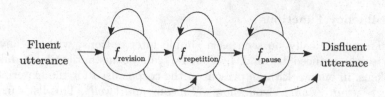

Fig. 1. Whole disfluency generation process.

3.3   Composition of Disfluency Functions

Composition is the only way to generate all disfluency regions and several disfluencies. For instance, an utterance containing a revision and a pause can be seen as the result of $f_{\text{revision}} \circ f_{\text{pause}}$. However, this may be also the result of $f_{\text{pause}} \circ f_{\text{revision}}$. To minimize such ambiguities and make the process deterministic, the following precedence order is defined:

$$\text{revision} \prec \text{repetition} \prec \text{pause}. \tag{3}$$

Thus, for the given example, the composition $f_{\text{pause}} \circ f_{\text{revision}}$ is forbidden. This order is justified by the fact that knowing where revisions and repetitions are can be useful to determine where to insert pauses. Technically, it is also easier to insert a pause in between repeated words than inserting repeated words around one or several pause tokens. Likewise, inserting revisions after repetitions would break repetitions, whereas repetitions applied on top of revisions may help strengthening revisions.

Following this precedence order, the generation process is as given in Fig. 1. Starting from a fluent utterance, and in the respect of, each type of disfluency can be applied zero, one or several times. Below is an example of consecutive transformations:

> I have to go.
>
> f_{rev} $[\textbf{I want to } I \text{ have to}]_{\text{rev}} go.$
>
> $\circ\ f_{\text{rep}}$ $\left[I \text{ want}[\textbf{to } to]_{\text{rep}} I \text{ have to}\right]_{\text{rev}} go.$
>
> $\circ\ f_{\text{pause}}$ $\left[I \text{ want}[to \text{ } to]_{\text{rep}} [\textbf{uh}]_{\text{pause}} I \text{ have to}\right]_{\text{rev}} go.$
>
> $\circ\ f_{\text{pause}}$ $\left[I \text{ want}[to \text{ } to]_{\text{rep}} [uh]_{\text{pause}} [\textbf{I mean}]_{\text{pause}} I \text{ have to}\right]_{\text{rev}} go.$

(Example 5)

These hierarchized iterative compositions can easily be formulated as an actual algorithm and implemented, as described in the next section.

```
   input  : OriginalUtt: a fluent utterance
   output: input utterance with added disfluencies
 1 data:
 2 Types: list of disfluency types
 3 OutputUtt: sequence of words
 4 IP: integer

 5 Types ← [repetition, pause]
 6 OutputUtt ← OriginalUtt
 7 for each T ∈ Types do
 8  │   IP ← πT(OutputUtt)
 9  │   while ¬ StoppingCriterion(T, OutputUtt, IP) do
10  │    │   OutputUtt ← ωT(OutputUtt, IP)
11  │    └   IP ← πT(OutputUtt)
    └
12 return OutputUtt
```

Algorithm 1. Main algorithm for disfluency generation.

4   Implementation

This section presents one way to implement the disfluency generation process. The objective of this implementation is to validate the approach before studying richer and more efficient implementations in the future. For this reason, we limit this study to pauses and repetitions, and set aside the more difficult case of revisions. This configuration is minimal but functional since it enables testing the composition mechanism.

For each disfluency type T, the IP prediction function π_T is treated as a labeling task achieved using a CRF, while the word insertion function ω_T is the selection of the best phrase among a set of automatically built candidates, the selection criterion relying on an LM. In short, the whole process is built on 2 CRFs and 2 LMs. We describe the main algorithm, then these models.

4.1   Main Algorithm

Algorithm 1 presents how to transform an input utterance to a disfluent one. Each type T is examined in a same manner, following the precedence order. The algorithm tries to determine a potential IP (line 8). If this IP is accepted according to a stopping criterion (l. 9), a new disfluency of type T is added to the current version of the utterance being transformed (l. 10). Then, a next IP proposal is computed (l. 11). As soon as an IP is rejected by the stopping criterion, the algorithm moves to the next disfluency type (l. 7) or, if none anymore, returns the transformed utterance (l. 12). The stopping criterion stops insertions as soon as, for the current type T, the proportion of disfluencies of this type in the transformed utterance reaches a maximum threshold fixed by the user. In practice, these thresholds have been set to 1% and 12%, respectively for repetitions and pauses, as observed on average in the training corpus.

4.2   IP Prediction

IP prediction is carried out by a CRF on an input (fluent or disfluent) sequence of words and potentially associated features. This CRF is trained to categorize successive words under two labels: words that are followed by an IP, and the others. At runtime, the CRF produces a list of IPs which are examined in turn until finding out one which has not been exploited yet. This requirement for fresh IPs at each iteration prevents the method from indefinitely adding disfluencies at the sole best place deemed by the CRF. If no new IP is found, the main algorithm moves to the next disfluency type. The examined IPs are those returned for each labelling hypothesis in the N-best list of the CRF. They are sorted by descending posterior probability. Falling back on N-best lists ensures a very large choice of IPs, delegating the termination decision to the stopping criterion.

4.3   Insertion of New Words

Given a chosen IP, the word insertion step seeks to produce a disfluency that best integrates into the utterance. The proposed implementation of ω_T constructs a set of possible word sequences, centered on the IP, and then determines the most probable w.r.t. type T. For repetitions, candidates are RM/RR pairs of various lengths. As for pauses, 6 candidates are proposed, one for each considered pause tokens able to fill the IM. Candidate sequences are discriminated by comparing their probability within their local contexts (± 3 words around the IP). The probability for type T is computed by an n-gram LM trained on T-specific disfluent data. For an IP at position i in a sequence of words $\mathbf{w} = [w_1 \cdots w_N]$, let a disfluent section under examination $\mathbf{d} = [d_1 \cdots d_D]$, and the left/right surrounding words $\mathbf{w}^{(\ell)} = [w_{i-W+1} \cdots w_i]$ and $\mathbf{w}^{(r)} = [w_{i+1} \cdots w_{i+W}]$ respectively. The proper integration of $\mathbf{d}$ within $\mathbf{w}$ can be measured through either the average probability per word or the global probability conditioned on $\mathbf{d}$, respectively defined as:

$$\frac{\Pr(\mathbf{w}^{(\ell)}\mathbf{dw}^{(r)})}{2W + D} \tag{4}$$

$$\text{and } \Pr(\mathbf{w}^{(\ell)}\mathbf{dw}^{(r)}|\mathbf{d}) = \frac{\Pr(\mathbf{w}^{(\ell)}\mathbf{dw}^{(r)})}{\Pr(\mathbf{d})} \tag{5}$$

Since utterances are processed independently, the first measure favors over-insertion of the most frequent tokens from the training corpus. On the contrary, the second disregards the prior probability of the disfluent tokens and solely focuses on how the final word sequence flows well. As a consequence, it leads to over-generating rare tokens. In this paper, a linear interpolation with equal weights associated to each measure is chosen.

5   Experimental Validation

The proposed implementation has been tested on 20 h from the Buckeye corpus [13], an American English conversational speech corpus made of individual interviews with 20 speakers. Manual transcripts (150K words) are annotated with 2,714 repetitions and 20,264 pauses. For each type of disfluencies, a dedicated version of the corpus is derived where utterances with no disfluency of that type were filtered out. To be consistent with precedence order, all pauses were removed from the repetition-specific corpus. An entirely cleaned (fluent) version of the corpus was also built. Data is divided into 3 sets: one to train the models (*train*, 60% of the utterances), another to tune hyper-parameters (*development*, 20%), and a set for evaluation (*test*, 20%). CRFs were trained using Wapiti[1] and LMs are trigrams trained with SRILM[2]. The remainder presents the different evaluations conducted to validate the proposed approach.

5.1   Objective Evaluation

IP predictions are examined through precision, recall and F1-score compared to the reference from our corpus, i.e., a predicted IP is a true positive if it is placed at the exact same position as an IP of the reference utterance. In the absence of multiple references, these measurements are difficult to interpret. Thus, we also propose to introduce the Interruption Rate Ratio (IRR) between the predictions and the reference, i.e., the scale factor between the average number of IPs per sentence in our hypotheses and in the reference. For example, IRR with value 1 indicates an equal proportion of IPs, 0.6 means an under-prediction of 40%, and 2.2 an over-prediction of 120%. Word insertion is evaluated by the LM perplexity given to the generated sequences. Since LMs are also used to select disfluency candidates, this measure is biased but it is primary used to understand the general behavior of the proposition. Disfluent sentences are expected to get lower perplexities than fluent sentences.

Different CRF training settings were studied in preliminary experiments on the development set for IP prediction. Two factors have been studied and adjusted: the optimal set of features and the size of contextual information for each word, i.e., the size of the observed neighborhood window. As a result, it turns out that our best results are obtained with very few attributes, namely raw words and part of speech (POS). As for the neighborhood, a window of a few words (2 in the final experiments) around the word being examined is beneficial.

On the test set, the compared configurations are: the cleaned utterances (*cl.*), their disfluent reference (*ref.*), and utterances produced by our models with the previously exposed features. Regarding pause insertion, an extra feature is introduced to tell the CRF whether a word under study comes from the original fluent sentence or has been added along iterations. This intents to integrate dependencies across transformations, as for instance desired to insert a pause in a repetition. We remind that the reference for repetitions do not contain any pause, whereas the cleaned version for pauses can include repetitions.

Tables 1 and 2 show the results obtained for the repetitions (R) and pauses (P). First, the results are globally low, especially for repetitions. These results

---

[1] http://wapiti.limsi.fr/.
[2] http://www.speech.sri.com/projects/srilm/.

can be explained by the relatively small amount of learning data and the uniqueness of our reference. IRRs show that generated utterances have always fewer
disfluencies than the reference, because of the adopted stopping criterion. To our
knowledge, no comparative work exists for repetitions, and considering a wide
range of pause tokens (not only "uh" and "um") is rather difficult [21]. Hence,
these results are acceptable for a first implementation. In terms of perplexity,
the generated disfluencies are rather close to the reference. Moreover, perplexities and IRRs on pauses highlight, as expected, that a high proportion of pauses
brings a low perplexity. Finally, information about previous iterations of the
algorithm, i.e., knowing which words are inserted (disfluent) words, seems beneficial, as shown in particular by the increase of about 2% points of the F1-score
(P_B $vs.$ P_C).

Table 1. Objective evaluation of repetitions on the test set.

	Features	Window?	Recall	Prec.	F1	IRR	PPL
($R_{cl.}$)	Fluent (cleaned) utterance					0.0	241
($R_{ref.}$)	Disfluent reference utterances					1.0	236
(R_A)	Words	no	0.8%	3.8%	1.3	0.1	236
(R_B)	+ POS	yes	**6.2%**	**17.1%**	**9.2**	0.4	**231**

Table 2. Objective evaluation of pauses on the test set.

	Features	Window?	Recall	Prec.	F1	IRR	PPL
($P_{cl.}$)	Fluent (cleaned) utterances					0.0	242
($P_{ref.}$)	Disfluent reference utterances					1.0	**172**
(P_A)	Words	no	8.2%	29.4%	12.8	0.5	209
(P_B)	+ POS	yes	17.9%	33.6%	23.3	0.7	191
(P_C)	+ prev. disfl.	yes	**19.8%**	**34.5%**	**25.1**	0.7	188

5.2   Perceptual Tests

Two series of perceptual tests were conducted on 24 participants. The first series
separately studies the effects of repetitions and pauses, while the second seeks
to measure their combined effects. Based on a displayed fluent text, testers had
to imagine how it could be uttered during a spontaneous conversation, and gave
their opinion on several proposals, ranging from 0 (impossible utterance) to 10
(perfectly possible). A same set of 40 utterances from the test set is used for all
experiments (4–25 words, all selected so that their disfluent reference contains a
mixture of repetitions and pauses, not necessarily interleaved).

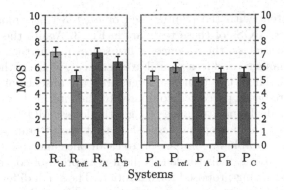

Fig. 2. MOS on repetitions (left) and pauses (right). System labels are as in Table 1.

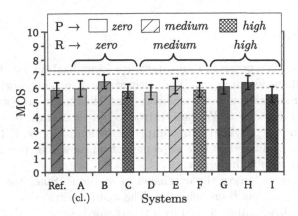

Fig. 3. MOS for mixed repetitions (R) and pauses (P). System labels are as in Table 2.

Mean opinion scores (MOSs, confidence interval $\alpha = 0.05$) are reported in Fig. 2 for the first series of tests. System labels are the same as in Tables 1 and 2. First, these results are close from one configuration to another, and differences are generally insignificant, even between the cleaned and reference utterances. This seems to show that the perception of disfluencies is a difficult task, at least when presented in a textual form. On repetitions, it appears that configurations with no or few repetitions ($R_{cl.}$ and R_A) are preferred to those containing more ($R_{ref.}$ and R_B). This can be explained by the absence of pauses in the middle of the presented repetitions. Then, the results on pauses seem correlated with the proportion of pauses (see IRRs in Table 2), although significance is not proven. On the whole, these two tests show that the automatically generated utterances do not denote w.r.t. the reference.

The incidences of the disfluency proportions, and of combining repetitions and pauses are studied in the second series of experiments. For each type, three insertion levels are considered by modulating the stopping criterion threshold (see Algorithm 1): *zero* means no disfluency of the considered type; *medium*, a proportion consistent with the training set; or *high*, 3 times more disfluencies than in the corpus. MOSs of these tests are in Fig. 3. Again, the results are all very similar. Nevertheless, the absence of low scores means that the disfluency composition mechanism produces plausible utterances, which is the first motivation of these tests. Then, two trends emerge: first, the absence of pause or their strong presence are badly perceived compared to the intermediate setting (B, E, H), then the most disfluent utterances (I) get the lowest MOS.

As a conclusion, the perceptual tests show that the utterances produced by our method are acceptable in comparison to clean ones and to disfluent ones as uttered in real situations. This tends to validate the proof-of-concept implementation and the underlying proposed formalization. The small differences between configurations however encourage one to improve this implementation and to think about more discriminating ways to conduct perceptual tests.

6 Conclusion

In this paper, we have presented an innovative formalization for the automatic insertion of disfluencies in texts. The ultimate goal of this work is to make synthetic speech signals more spontaneous, and thus more acceptable in some human-machine interactions. We have introduced a theoretical process of disfluency composition and provided a first implementation based on CRFs and LMs. The experiments conducted on this implementation show that the proposed process is functional, although perfectible.

A first perspective is now the extension to revisions. Since the validation in this paper, this work has been achieved. The word insertion part, which is the difficult part, has been implemented by altering words from the RR with linguistically similar ones, i.e., words with the same POS and geometrically close in a lexical embedding space. Evaluation will be conducted in the near future. Among other perspectives, more complex models could be tested, for instance to enable including broader, non-lexical, considerations (phonetic confusion, speaker intention, etc.). However, collecting training data is an obstacle here. Finally, evaluation is a challenge. The best improvement track on this point seems to us to provide natural realizations of all the tested utterances. This would avoid bypass the unsuitability of current TTS systems but it requires recording people.

References

1. Adell, J., Bonafonte, A., Escudero, D.: Filled pauses in speech synthesis: towards conversational speech. In: Matoušek, V., Mautner, P. (eds.) TSD 2007. LNCS (LNAI), vol. 4629, pp. 358–365. Springer, Heidelberg (2007). https://doi.org/10.1007/978-3-540-74628-7_47
2. Adell, J., Bonafonte, A., Mancebo, D.E.: On the generation of synthetic disfluent speech: local prosodic modifications caused by the insertion of editing terms. In: Proceedings of the Annual Conference of the International Speech Communication Association (Interspeech) (2008)

3. Adell, J., Escudero, D., Bonafonte, A.: Production of filled pauses in concatenative speech synthesis based on the underlying fluent sentence. Speech Commun. **54**, 459–476 (2012)
4. Andersson, S., Georgila, K., Traum, D., Aylett, M., Clark, R.A.: Prediction and realisation of conversational characteristics by utilising spontaneous speech for unit selection. In: Proceedings of Speech Prosody (2010)
5. Betz, S., Wagner, P., Schlangen, D.: Micro-structure of disfluencies: basics for conversational speech synthesis. In: Proceedings of the Annual Conference of the International Speech Communication Association (Interspeech) (2015)
6. Clark, H.H.: Speaking in time. Speech Commun. **36**, 5–13 (2002)
7. Dall, R., Tomalin, M., Wester, M., Byrne, W.J., King, S.: Investigating automatic & human filled pause insertion for speech synthesis. In: Proceedings of the Annual Conference of the International Speech Communication Association (Interspeech) (2014)
8. Hassan, H., Schwartz, L., Hakkani-Tür, D., Tür, G.: Segmentation and disfluency removal for conversational speech translation. In: Proceedings of the Annual Conference of the International Speech Communication Association (Interspeech) (2014)
9. Honnibal, M., Johnson, M.: Joint incremental disfluency detection and dependency parsing. Trans. Assoc. Comput. Linguist. **2**, 131–142 (2014)
10. Kaushik, M., Trinkle, M., Hashemi-Sakhtsari, A.: Automatic detection and removal of disfluencies from spontaneous speech. In: Proceedings of the Australasian International Conference on Speech Science and Technology (SST) (2010)
11. Liu, Y., Shriberg, E., Stolcke, A., Hillard, D., Ostendorf, M., Harper, M.: Enriching speech recognition with automatic detection of sentence boundaries and disfluencies. IEEE Trans. Audio Speech Lang. Process. **14**, 1526–1540 (2006)
12. de Mareüil, P.B., et al.: A quantitative study of disfluencies in French broadcast interviews. In: Proceedings of Disfluency in Spontaneous Speech Workshop (2005)
13. Pitt, M.A., Johnson, K., Hume, E., Kiesling, S., Raymond, W.: The Buckeye corpus of conversational speech: labeling conventions and a test of transcriber reliability. Speech Commun. **45**, 89–95 (2005)
14. Rose, R.L.: The communicative value of filled pauses in spontaneous speech. Ph.D. thesis, University of Birmingham (1998)
15. Shriberg, E.E.: Phonetic consequences of speech disfluency. Technical report, DTIC Document (1999)
16. Shriberg, E.E.: Preliminaries to a theory of speech disfluencies. Ph.D. thesis, University of California (1994)
17. Stolcke, A., Shriberg, E.: Statistical language modeling for speech disfluencies. In: Proceedings of the IEEE International Conference on Acoustics, Speech and Signal Processing (ICASSP) (1996)
18. Stolcke, A., et al.: Automatic detection of sentence boundaries and disfluencies based on recognized words. In: Proceedings of the International Conference on Spoken Language Processing (ICSLP) (1998)
19. Sundaram, S., Narayanan, S.: An empirical text transformation method for spontaneous speech synthesizers. In: Proceedings of the Annual Conference of the International Speech Communication Association (Interspeech) (2003)
20. Székely, E., Mendelson, J., Gustafson, J.: Synthesising uncertainty: the interplay of vocal effort and hesitation disfluencies. In: Proceedings of the Annual Conference of the International Speech Communication Association (Interspeech) (2017)

21. Tomalin, M., Wester, M., Dall, R., Byrne, W., King, S.: A lattice-based approach to automatic filled pause insertion. In: Proceedinds of the Workshop on Disfluency in Spontaneous Speech (2015)
22. Tree, J.E.F.: The effects of false starts and repetitions on the processing of subsequent words in spontaneous speech. J. Mem. Lang. **34**, 709–738 (1995)
23. Tree, J.E.F.: Listeners' uses ofum and uh in speech comprehension. Mem. Cogn. **29**(2), 320–326 (2001)
24. Tseng, S.C.: Grammar, prosody and speech disfluencies in spoken dialogues. Unpublished doctoral dissertation. University of Bielefeld (1999)
25. Wester, M., Aylett, M.P., Tomalin, M., Dall, R.: Artificial personality and disfluency. In: Proceedings of the Annual Conference of the International Speech Communication Association (Interspeech) (2015)

Speech Recognition and Post-Processing

Forced Alignment of the *Phonologie du Français Contemporain* Corpus

George Christodoulides[(✉)] [iD]

Language Sciences and Metrology Unit, Université de Mons,
Place du Parc 18, 7000 Mons, Belgium
george@mycontent.gr

Abstract. The *Phonologie du Français Contemporain* project is an
international, collaborative research effort to create resources for the
study of contemporary French phonology. It has produced a large,
partially transcribed and annotated corpus of spoken French, consisting of approximately 300 h of recordings, and covering 48 geographical
regions (including Metropolitan France, Belgium, Switzerland, Canada,
and French-speaking countries of Africa). Following a detailed protocol, speakers read aloud a word list and a short text and engage in
guided and spontaneous conversation with an interviewer. The corpus
presents several challenges: significant regional accent variation; variable
recording quality and different types of environment noise; variation in
speaker characteristics (age, sex); and interspersed segments of overlapping speech. In this article, we describe the procedure followed to address
these challenges and produce an automatic forced alignment of the corpus
at the phone, syllable and token level, starting from the initial transcriptions.

Keywords: Forced alignment · Speech recognition · Sociophonetics
Regional variation · French · Corpus linguistics · Language resources

1 Introduction

The *Phonologie du Français Contemporain* project is an international, collaborative research effort to create resources for the study of contemporary French
phonology [7]. It has brought together almost a hundred researchers, who performed recordings of over 600 speakers of French, covering 48 geographical
regions, in Metropolitan France, Belgium, Switzerland, Canada and several countries in Africa. The PFC Project recordings follow a strict protocol, inspired by
Labov's work on sociolinguistics, including two reading tasks and two conversations. The project has produced hundreds of hours of recordings, and approximately 300 h have been transcribed to date. As part of the transcription conventions of the project, expert annotators code two important phonological phenomena of French, namely the realisation of liaisons and the presence or absence

© Springer Nature Switzerland AG 2018
T. Dutoit et al. (Eds.): SLSP 2018, LNAI 11171, pp. 47–55, 2018.
https://doi.org/10.1007/978-3-030-00810-9_5

of schwa, in positions where these phenomena are optional and reflect sociolinguistic factors (regional variation, speaking style variation and sociolinguistic variation).

The corpus has been transcribed in short (5 to 20 s) segments, which contain an orthographic transcription of one or more speakers (i.e. speaker overlaps are only approximately indicated). Two additional coding tiers contain the information on liaison and schwa. The PFC corpus presents several challenges to automatic speech processing: there is significant regional accent variation, since this is one of the objectives of the project; there is significant variation in recording quality, as is often the case with sociolinguistic fieldwork; there is also variation in speaker characteristics, as the project strives to keep a gender balance and cover four age groups from 20 to 80 years old; and finally, the speaking style of free conversation is always challenging to automatic speech recognition (ASR) systems.

In this article, we present our efforts to produce a reliable automatic forced alignment of the entire corpus, at the phoneme, syllable and token level, starting from the source recordings and transcription data. This project is complementary to previous work to provide an automatic part-of-speech and disfluency annotation for the PFC corpus, outlined in [6]. In the following section, we will review relevant work on forced alignment of French speech, and the PFC corpus. In Sect. 3, we present the main characteristics of the PFC corpus which are relevant to our endeavour. In Sect. 4 we present the method used, followed by preliminary evaluation results in Sect. 5, and finally we outline the perspectives of this work, both with respect to improving the forced alignment tools for French and with respect to new uses for an aligned PFC corpus.

2   Related Work

Several automatic forced alignment tools have been developed for French, over the past two decades. Among these, we can cite *EasyAlign* [9], *SPPAS* [2], *Train&Align* [4], the *Montreal Forced Aligner* [13] and *SailAlign* [12].

EasyAlign is based on the HTK toolkit [16] and a monophone model trained on a relatively small corpus; it operates as a plug-in under Praat [3] but only under Windows (due to a dependency on an external DOS-based phonetiser). *Train&Align* is also based on the HTK toolkit, and can be used to produce monophone and triphone models, but is available only for use on the web: due to restrictions in the HTK license, it is not possible to redistribute the files necessary for recognition, training new acoustic models or for performing speaker adaptation as part of an open-source project. For this reason, *SPPAS* uses the Julius open-source toolkit for the aligner, while its models are trained in house using HTK; the triphone model for French is based on a corpus of approximately 10 h. *MFA* is the newest of the tools and is a collection of Python scripts around the Kaldi ASR system [14]. It can generate monophone and triphone models and perform speaker adaptation; an acoustic model is provided for French, albeit without a pronunciation lexicon. Finally, *SailAlign*, which is based on Sphinx [15], focuses on the problem of long sound alignment (finding initial anchor points for a transcription of a long recording).

From the short description of available tools above, it is understood that none of them could cover the needs of our project "out of the box". We have therefore opted to develop a new system in C++ using the Kaldi ASR system; our system is modular and uses the *Praaline* Core Library for corpus and annotation management operations, and a Qt user interface. A phonetisation module is also provided, and has been adapted to the particular needs of this project, as will be explained in Sect. 4.3.

It should also be noted that the C-PROM-PFC corpus [1] comprises of 3-min samples from the PFC corpus. The C-PROM-PFC corpus is approximately 10 h long and its alignment to the phone, syllable and token label has been manually verified by an expert annotator.

3   Corpus Description

3.1   Corpus Composition

The PFC corpus consists of four speaking tasks which are recorded for each participant: reading a list of 94 words, that have been carefully chosen to study phonetic variation; reading a short 300-word text, a fictitious newspaper article that contains multiple points of interest where phonological variation may appear; engage in a guided interview with the researcher; and having a more spontaneous, open-ended conversation with the researcher. Roughly 10 min per conversation are transcribed per speaker.

Table 1 shows the corpus composition, at its current state of transcription. The number of samples per region and task is given, along with their duration in minutes. For the two conversation tasks (guided and free conversation), the percentage of single-speaker utterances in the corpus is indicated: this percentage is calculated as the ratio of the duration of single-speaker transcription segments over the total duration of all transcription segments (after performing the pre-processing steps outlined in Sect. 4.2).

3.2   Available Annotations and Coding Schemes

Information on schwa and liaison realisation is coded based on a common systematic methodology. Schwa coding consists of four fields for each potential schwa realisation in a token: field 1 indicates the presence or absence of the schwa, field 2 the position of the schwa within the word, field 3 its left context and field 4 its right context. Liaison coding consists of four fields: field 1 indicates whether the word is mono-syllabic or poly-syllabic, field 2 indicates the presence or absence (and the type) of liaison, and field 3 indicates the liaison consonant and field 4 gives information about the context. For more information on the coding schemes, refer to [8]. The schwa and liaison coding is valuable for the phonetisation procedure outlined in Sect. 4.3.

Table 1. PFC corpus contents. For each of the four tasks (guided conversation, free conversation, text reading and word reading) the number of speakers is given, along with the duration of the transcribed part of the corpus in minutes. For the two conversational tasks, the percentage of non-overlap utterances (calculated as the ratio of their duration over the total transcription duration) is indicated.

Code	Region	Guided Conv			Free Conv			Text		Words	
		Spk	Dur	Mono	Spk	Dur	Mono	Spk	Dur	Spk	Dur
11a	Douzens	10	255.2	91.2%	5	113.9	83.0%	10	29.3	9	25.0
12a	Rodez	8	236.8	97.2%	8	161.0	87.5%	9	23.0		
13a	Marseille Centre Ville	9	193.0	94.0%	9	175.0	88.5%	9	21.4	9	29.1
13b	Aix-Marseille	7	178.9	97.6%	8	288.7	96.0%	8	21.1	8	34.3
21a	Dijon	7	73.2	84.4%	8	84.8	88.3%	8	19.2	8	25.6
31a	Toulouse	14	296.3	91.6%	9	408.6	94.4%	14	53.4	14	44.5
38a	Grenoble	8	116.9	96.5%	8	109.8	96.1%	7	18.8	9	26.5
42a	Roanne	8	107.9	93.4%	8	148.0	91.9%	8	20.7	8	26.3
44a	Nantes	11	207.1	93.8%	9	289.2	94.7%	10	25.6	11	40.3
50a	Brécey	11	122.6	44.6%	6	61.9	49.6%	9	24.6	11	45.6
54b	Ogéviller	11	269.3	96.2%	11	250.3	96.5%	9	22.1	10	28.0
61a	Domfrontais	12	175.4	74.7%	12	150.3	70.0%	12	34.8	12	40.7
64a	Biarritz	12	204.2	86.7%	4	66.8	67.5%	11	27.4	12	36.4
69a	Lyon	10	232.0	96.8%	11	209.0	96.8%	10	20.6	8	17.6
75c	Paris Centre Ville	12	121.2	49.2%	11	114.9	50.6%	12	27.9		
75x	Aveyronnais à Paris	12	308.3	92.9%	10	286.9	87.8%	8	21.7	12	36.4
80a	Amiens	5	50.0	90.5%	6	60.0	86.7%				
81a	Lacaune	13	172.3	90.9%	11	85.4	68.2%	11	33.9	13	54.8
85a	Vendée	7	71.6	84.1%	8	93.1	86.7%	8	19.0	8	25.2
91a	Brunoy	1	5.2	71.6%	9	23.5	100.0%				
92a	Puteaux-Courbevoie	6	133.9	97.9%	5	155.9	98.0%	5	11.9	4	12.0
974	Ile de la Réunion	7	162.4	97.6%	7	170.4	97.6%	9	28.0	8	32.4
aba	Béjaia	11	250.0	90.4%	10	221.1	90.3%	11	29.6	11	37.5
aca	Chlef	12	213.0	97.3%	12	194.4	96.4%	11	31.7	12	37.9
bfa	Burkina Faso	12	283.7	90.0%	11	282.2	88.6%	9	37.0	11	43.2
bga	Gembloux	12	296.5	92.5%	12	237.3	89.8%	9	27.2	11	27.0
bla	Liège	11	244.0	93.7%	11	281.4	95.7%	12	35.5	11	26.2
bta	Tournai	11	264.0	95.6%	11	253.0	94.7%	12	35.3	12	29.6
caa	Peace River	10	109.0	57.7%	7	22.9	100.0%	9	29.7		
cia	Abidjan	14	267.6	90.6%	12	321.9	92.5%	12	45.0	13	68.1
cqa	Québec ville (université)	9	148.0	93.0%	7	64.2	87.2%	7	18.4	8	28.0
cqb	Saguenay	11	167.3	94.4%	10	321.4	79.9%	11	32.7	10	35.6
cya	Cameroun	6	52.5	91.3%	6	89.9	98.1%	6	29.1	5	20.9
maa	Bamako	10	211.5	66.8%	12	235.5	65.9%	12	61.0	12	52.1
rca	Bangui	11	341.6	99.7%	12	262.7	95.3%	12	51.9	12	43.8
sca	Neuchâtel	12	433.8	89.3%	13	490.6	80.4%	12	33.4	12	47.1
sga	Genève	8	167.8	90.4%	9	206.0	88.5%	9	23.8	9	29.5
sna	Sénégal Dakar	12	235.2	94.5%	11	187.6	88.0%	11	34.0	11	44.9
sva	Nyon	12	147.0	96.9%	9	117.8	76.5%	11	28.5	11	45.2

4   Method

An outline of the method employed in order to align the corpus is shown in
Fig. 1. We used audio processing software to enhance and restore the original
audio recordings, and decrease the variation in the audio properties (e.g. levels).
The original transcriptions were checked for consistency with the annotation
protocol, and were manually corrected where necessary. The transcriptions were
then separated in sequences of segments corresponding to different speakers; overlapping segments were identified at this step. The segments were tokenised and a
phonetic transcription was added: the phonetisation includes pronunciation variants, but these are limited based on the PFC schwa and liaison coding. Forced
alignment of all segments was performed, and acoustic models were trained based
on the data. Special processing was performed on overlapping segments. Finally,
the results of the automatic alignments were combined into the end result.

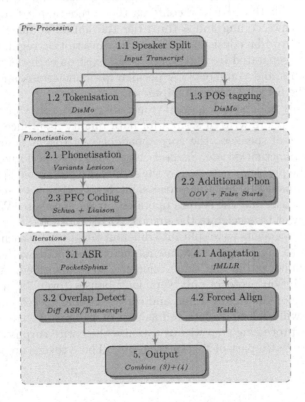

Fig. 1. Methodology used to align the corpus

4.1   Audio Processing and Restoration

We performed an audio enhancing and restoration procedure on all recordings
of the corpus, using the commercial iZotope RX 6 Audio Editor. The following

filters were applied in sequence: De-clip (restore clipped samples at high quality, new maximum level -1 dB), De-click (remove random clicks), De-hum (remove 50 Hz noise and its harmonics), De-reverb (remove reverberation, in light vocal processing mode), Voice De-noise (adaptive noise reduction), De-plosive (light removal of hard microphone puffs), Phase correction (if needed), Equaliser Match (using the "full dialogue" preset) and Leveler (normalisation of audio levels, respecting dialogue dynamics). All subsequent application of ASR models was performed on the processed audio files.

4.2 Pre-processing and Transcription Protocol Validation

According to the PFC transcription protocol, the orthographic transcription shall always indicate the speaker. In cases of overlaps, the overlapping speaker's utterance is transcribed inside angle brackets. Each recording is transcribed on one Praat TextGrid: the first tier contains the orthographic transcription, a second tier the schwa coding and a third tier the liaison coding (the order of tiers was found not to be consistent). For each transcription segment, the same number of words (separated by whitespace) shall exist on each tier. Parentheses are used for events and comments. A peculiar pronunciation can be given in brackets using the SAMPA phonetic alphabet.

As can be easily understood, human transcribers can easily violate this set of rules. We have therefore written scripts for data quality assurance. The scripts verify the number of speakers, the correspondences of tokens across the three tiers, the use of punctuation etc. Several corrections were performed automatically; based on the problems detected by the scripts, we performed approximately 2700 corrections manually. For this process, all TextGrids were imported into a *Praaline* [5] database, and the scripts operated on the database. We developed an interactive editor to accelerate the manual corrections.

Subsequently, segments were split into different timelines for each speaker. As part of this process, single-speaker segments (utterances) and overlaps (multiple speakers transcribed within the same segment) were identified. According to the PFC transcription protocol only very long pauses (over 5 s in length) are transcribed; therefore, normal reading and conversational speech pauses are not transcribed and will have to be detected as part of the forced alignment process.

The final pre-processing step was to tokenise the entire corpus and to annotate it using the *DisMo* part-of-speech tagger [6]. These tokens are the basis for the next step.

4.3 Phonetisation

A dictionary of pronunciation variants for French has been constructed, based on the lexicon distributed with Sphinx ASR (converted to the SAMPA alphabet) and the GLÀFF [10] lexicon. The part-of-speech tags produced by *DisMo* were used to limit the possible pronunciation variants. However, the PFC coding schemes were the most important aid in improving the phonetisation.

For each token, the corresponding tokens from the schwa and liaison tiers were examined, and the pronunciation variants were adjusted accordingly. This reduces the size of the graph of possible pronunciation variants that the forced aligner will have to consider, and it also ensures that the resulting alignment will be coherent with the PFC corpus coding.

4.4   Forced Alignment

The Kaldi automatic speech recogniser [14] was used to perform the main forced alignment of the corpus. In each batch, we first train a monophone model on the data to align, followed by a triphone model, and finally a speaker-adapted triphone model. The acoustic model features consist of Mel-frequency cepstral coefficients (MFCCs) and their deltas. Cepstral mean and variance normalization (CMVN) is applied to all models. The speaker adaptation is performed using Feature space Maximum Likelihood Linear Regression (fMLLR).

First, a separate model is trained for each combination of region and speaking style (reading vs conversation). These models are used to align all data, and perform cross-validation. Aggregate models per speaking style are then trained and used to align the data.

A special procedure is followed for the transcription segments of overlapping speech. A quick constrained speech recognition is performed on the overlapping segment, using PocketSphinx [11], in an effort to detect the overlap in the recording, with a better temporal precision than the one given by the transcription. In cases of success, the utterance boundaries are adjusted (speech correctly recognised as non-overlapping is concatenated with the previous or next utterance as appropriate).

The entire process is automated in a C++ plug-in for *Praaline*, which calls the appropriate external programmes.

5   Evaluation

In the absence of a gold-standard alignment, against which we could compare the outputs of the automatic forced alignment system, we had to devise indirect methods of evaluation. These methods essentially indicate how to improve the process, and can help isolate these utterances in the corpus that may have been incorrectly aligned.

Table 2 shows the preliminary results of cross-validation. The data of each region and speaking style (e.g. 11a-reading) is aligned using the acoustic models trained on each of the other regions, for the same speaking style (e.g. 12a-reading). The alignments are compared by checking the temporal difference between the center of each phoneme; the table indicates the percentage of phonemes where this difference is less than 40 ms.

As expected, read speech is less variable (in phone duration, other prosodic characteristics) than spontaneous speech, and therefore the models achieve better results. However, the results are overall encouraging. This procedure also identifies utterances with important differences between the boundaries of phones,

Table 2. All samples of each region are aligned with each of the acoustic models trained on other regions. The table shows the percentage of phonemes whose center is within 40 ms of the center of the original alignment results.

Region to align	Text			Region to align	Conversation		
	11a	12a	13a		11a	12a	13a
11a		84.8%	84.8%	11a		81.7%	81.8%
12a	87.3%		89.7%	12a	83.5%		84.2%
13a	89.9%	90.1%		13a	82.8%	83.3%	

suggesting a potential problem in the transcription or a particularly difficult to align utterance. We intend to explore whether excluding these "problematic" utterances from the training of the final aggregate models improves the overall performance; however a small dataset of manually checked alignments will be needed for this evaluation.

6 Conclusion and Perspectives

We have presented a procedure for producing an automatic forced alignment of the *Phonologie du Français Contemporain* Corpus at the phone, syllable and token level, starting from the initial transcriptions. As part of this effort, the audio recordings were enhanced and restored, the transcriptions were checked for consistency, the data already coded in the corpus were used to improve the input to the ASR system, and multiple iterations of forced alignment using the Kaldi recogniser were performed.

The PFC corpus has been a valuable resource for studies in French phonology. We hope that this work will allow researchers to use the corpus in new ways and in investigating new research questions. For example, as part of the alignment process, speech pauses were detected with an improved precision: the corpus could be used for studying the dialogue dynamics in socio-linguistic interviews, or in similar studies in prosody. Concordances (text along with the corresponding sound segment) can now be extracted for downstream processing.

We plan to distribute the aligned version of the corpus to the community. To this end we plan to use institutional repositories (such as Ortolang) and also create a custom website using *PraalineWeb* (a tool generating *Django* websites for presenting speech corpora).

Finally, this project resulted in the development of a new tool for speech-to-text alignment of French spoken corpora, that we plan to release in the near future, along with the acoustic models trained on the PFC corpus.

References

1. Avanzi, M.: A corpus-based approach to French regional prosodic variation. Nouveaux Cahiers de Linguistique Française **31**, 309–332 (2014). (Proceedings of the 3rd SWIP)
2. Bigi, B., Hirst, D.: Speech phonetization alignment and syllabification (SPPAS): a tool for the automatic analysis of speech prosody. In: Proceedings of the 6th Speech Prosody Conference, 22–25 May, Shanghai, China (2012)
3. Boersma, P., Weenink, D.: Praat: doing phonetics by computer, ver. 6.0.37 (2018). http://www.praat.org
4. Brognaux, S., Roekhaut, S., Drugman, T., Beaufort, R.: Train & Align: a new online tool for automatic phonetic alignment. In: 2012 IEEE Spoken Language Technology Workshop (SLT), pp. 416–421, December 2012
5. Christodoulides, G.: Praaline: integrating tools for speech corpus research. In: LREC 2014—Proceedings of the 9th International Conference on Language Resources and Evaluation, 26–31 May, Reykjavik, Iceland, pp. 31–34 (2014). http://www.praaline.org
6. Christodoulides, G., Barreca, G.: Expériences sur l'analyse morphosyntaxique des corpus oraux avec l'annotateur multi-niveaux DisMo. Corela: Cognition, Représentation, Langage HS-21 (2017). https://journals.openedition.org/corela/4867
7. Durand, J., Laks, B., Lyche, C.: Phonologie, variation et accents du français. Hermes, Paris (2009)
8. Durand, J., Lyche, C.: French liaison in the light of corpus data. J. Fr. Lang. Stud. **18**(1), 33–66 (2008)
9. Goldman, J.P.: EasyAlign: an automatic phonetic alignment tool under Praat. In: INTERSPEECH 2011—Proceedings of the 12th Annual Conference of the International Speech Communication Association, 27–31 August , Florence, Italy, pp. 3233–3236 (2011)
10. Hathout, N., Sajous, F., Calderone, B.: GLÀFF, a large versatile French lexicon. In: LREC 2014—Proceedings of the 9th International Conference on Language Resources and Evaluation, 26–31 May, Reykjavik, Iceland (2014)
11. Huggins-Daines, D., Kumar, M., Chan, A., Black, A.W., Ravishankar, M., Rudnicky, A.I.: PocketSphinx: a free, real-time continuous speech recognition system for hand-held devices. In: 2006 IEEE International Conference on Acoustics Speech and Signal Processing Proceedings, vol. 1, pp. I-I, May 2006
12. Katsamanis, A., Black, M.P., Georgiou, P.G., Goldstein, L., Narayanan, S.S.: SailAlign: robust long speech-text alignment. In: Proceedings of the Workshop on New Tools and Methods for Very-Large Scale Phonetics Research (2011)
13. McAuliffe, M., Socolof, M., Mihuc, S., Wagner, M., Sonderegger, M.: Montreal forced aligner: trainable text-speech alignment using Kaldi. In: Proceedings of the 18th Conference of the International Speech Communication Association (2017)
14. Povey, D., et al.: The Kaldi speech recognition toolkit. In: IEEE 2011 Workshop on Automatic Speech Recognition and Understanding. IEEE Signal Processing Society, December 2011. IEEE Catalog No. CFP11SRW-USB
15. Walker, W., et al.: Sphinx-4: a flexible open source framework for speech recognition. Technical report, Sun Microsystems Inc., Mountain View, CA, USA (2004)
16. Young, S.J., Kershaw, D., Odell, J., Ollason, D., Valtchev, V., Woodland, P.: The HTK Book Version 3.4. Cambridge University Press, Cambridge (2006)

A Syllable Structure Approach to Spoken Language Recognition

Ruei-Hung Alex Lee[1(✉)] and Jyh-Shing Roger Jang[2]

[1] Taipei European School, Taipei, Taiwan
alex.leeb2019@stu.tes.tp.edu.tw
[2] Department of Computer Science and Information Engineering,
National Taiwan University, Taipei, Taiwan
jang@csie.ntu.edu.tw

Abstract. Spoken language recognition is the task of automatically determining the identity of the language spoken in a speech clip. Prior approaches to spoken language recognition have been able to accurately determine the language within an audio clip. However, they usually require long training time and large datasets since most of the existing approaches heavily rely on phonotactic, acoustic-phonetic and prosodic information. Moreover, the features extracted may not be linguistic features, but speaker features instead. This paper presents a novel approach based on a linguistics perspective, particularly that of syllable structure. Based on human listening experiments, there has been strong evidence that syllable structure is a significant knowledge source in human spoken language recognition. The approach includes a block for labelling common syllable structures (CV, CVC, VC, etc.). Then, a long short-term memory (LSTM) network is used to transform the Mel-frequency cepstral coefficients (MFCC) of an audio clip to its syllable structure, thereby diminishing the influence of speakers on extracted features and reducing the number of dimensions for the final language predictor. The array of syllables is then passed through the second LSTM network to predict the language. The proposed method creates a generalized and scalable framework with acceptable accuracy for spoken language recognition. Our experiments with 10 different languages demonstrate the feasibility of the proposed approach, which achieves a comparable accuracy of 70.40% with a computing time of 37 ms for every second of speech, outperforming most of the existing methods based on acoustic-phonetic and phonotactic features by efficiency.

Keywords: Speech recognition · Spoken language recognition
Syllable structure · Deep convolutional neural network
Long short-term memory (LSTM)

1 Introduction

Spoken language recognition refers to automatically determining the identity of the language spoken in a speech slip. Most approaches to spoken language recognition has relied on phonotactic and acoustic-phonetic features [2,13]. Recent

© Springer Nature Switzerland AG 2018
T. Dutoit et al. (Eds.): SLSP 2018, LNAI 11171, pp. 56–66, 2018.
https://doi.org/10.1007/978-3-030-00810-9_6

efforts, however, has been directed to the extraction of prosodic features and modelling techniques. This emphasis on phonotactic and acoustic-phonetic features has been achieved by transferring written language recognition knowledge to spoken language recognition, as written language can be interpreted as a series of characters, so can spoken language be interpreted as a time sequence of phonemes.

Under this paradigm, previous spoken language recognition approaches has been focusing on identifying phone features and recognizing the resulting phone sequence, such as through N-gram language models that has achieved significant success in the past [18]. However, spoken language encompasses more than mere time sequences of phoneme units. Spoken language involves more characteristics that adds additional information to the speech. These characteristics, referred to as prosody, may often go beyond a phone unit, but instead are feature of an entire syllable and even of a word, sentence or entire speech. These prosodic features include variations of pitch and emphasis on certain words or syllables. Research with foci on prosodic features has yielded successful results [6,11].

Another perspective towards the discovery of new features for spoken language recognition is based upon an investigation into the underlying organization and structure of a language. While previous phonotactic and acoustic-phonetic features relied on phoneme-based structure or word-based structure in certain models that translate phonemes to words through a dictionary, natural languages are typically built upon syllables, rather than words or phonemes. Syllable structure has been investigated in several human listening experiments, yet has received little attention from the community of spoken language recognition. The patterns of different syllable structures, and the presence of different types of syllable structure, can be collectively referred to as syllable structure features.

Syllable structure features have several advantages over traditional features for spoken language recognition, namely phoneme features. As syllable structure features do not require exact phoneme identification, extracting syllable features may be more accurate and time efficient when compared to extracting phoneme units. Moreover, as syllable feature extraction reduces the audio signal directly into non-phoneme-specific syllable structures, it is less likely to be affected by channel noise or other non-language related information, such as variations in speakers or recording devices. Syllable structure also avoids issues of accents or speaker characteristics, as while phonemes may be mispronounced, syllable structures are far less likely to be misread or misspoken. Finally, the reduced number of dimensions in syllable features as opposed to phoneme units, improves training time and reduce the possibility of overfitting.

This paper proposes a two-phase framework for spoken language recognition, based on a LSTM model for syllable feature extraction, and another LSTM model for language recognition based on the extracted syllable features. For the second LSTM model, different architectures are tested to verify the validity of syllable structure as a feature and how the use of the feature can effectively reduce the number of neural network nodes for a comparable accuracy.

2   Syllable Structure as a Feature

Syllable structure had been used within a human listening experiment context before, for the investigation of speech recognition, accent identification, word recognition and infant language acquisition [1,3,9,17]. From these experiments, it has been found that syllable structure can act as useful knowledge sources in human language recognition. It is thus possible to extract these features for spoken language recognition. As we can see in Fig. 1, syllable structures can hold significant correlation to languages.

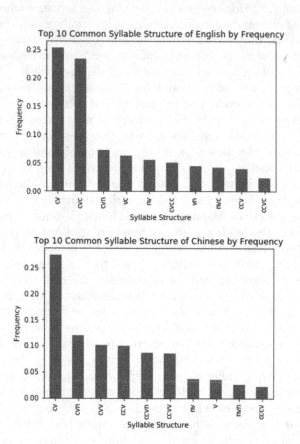

Fig. 1. Bar chart showing the frequencies of the top 10 most common syllable structure in English and Chinese. As can be seen here, different languages have different distributions of syllable structures.

The most basic syllable structure consists of three parts, the onset, the nucleus and the coda. The onset is typically composed of the consonant sound that begins the syllable, the nucleus, the vowel sound in the middle of the syllable, and the coda, the consonant sound that follows the nucleus and ends the syllable. In more complex syllable structures, the onset or coda may be omitted, and additional phonemes may be added to the onset, nucleus or coda. Syllable structures also give rise to another type of speech feature, that is, phonotactic features. However, while syllable structure can be considered to be similar to phonotactics, they hold several distinctions. Phonotactics refers to the exact composition of these syllable structure. Hence, the exact composition of consonant clusters and vowel sequences are a component of phonotactic features. Conversely, include the composition of each syllable (onset and rhyme) and pattern of syllable structure sequences.

2.1 Feature Extraction Based on Syllable Structure

In order to use these syllable structure features for spoken language recognition, we devised a syllable feature extraction model. It was first trained on data from Tatoeba [12], where we have access to the text of each audio clip. These texts are used to create the ground truth part for training the neural network. The text is first translated to International Phonetic Alphabet (IPA) (with epitran [10]) and segmented (with Pyphen [7]) separately. A levenshtein distance algorithm is then used between the IPA transcription and Pyphen segmentation to determine the segmentation of the IPA transcription. In order to avoid investigating phonotactic features instead of syllable structure features, the separated IPA transcriptions are then altered again by converting the distinct consonants and vowels into markers of consonants (C), nasal consonants (N), and vowels (V). After being reduced to C, N and V markers, all possible combinations of C, V and N are identified, such as CV being the representation for the syllable in the word "the (ðə)" or a consonant followed by a vowel. Each of these possible combinations are then assigned an ID number, so as to transform the syllable structure sequence into a numerical sequential representation for training the second LSTM network (Table 1).

Table 1. Common syllable IDs

Syllable structure	ID	Example
CV	0	the (ðə)
V	3	a.pple (æ.pəl)
CVN	6	song (sɒŋ)
VN	16	an (æn)
VC	23	it (ət)
CVC	29	talk (tɔk)

The input to the first LSTM are 13 MFCCs computed from each frame from an audio clip. All signals under 40 dB to the maximum signal at the front and back are first trimmed before the MFCC is extracted. The MFCC is computed from a window of 92.9 ms (2048/22050) separated by a hop size of 23.2 ms (512/22050). For a maximum length of 5 s for the input audio, this results in $(\lceil (5 \times 22050)/512 \rceil \times 13) = 2808$ coefficients as the input for the first LSTM.

2.2 Neural Network Architecture

The configuration for the first syllable feature extraction neural network is a simple 3-layer neural network. 216 element-sequences of 13 dimensional vectors are inputted into the 216 LSTM cells. A hidden LSTM layer with 256 cells is used, as a single syllable may encompass several MFCC cascades of variable total length. The final dense layer output have a softmax activation function and 40 output nodes that each outputs a 225 length array that are the one hot encodings of all possible syllable arrangements. 40 is the maximum number of syllables that can be spoken within 5 s as derived from the data and is thus the dimensions of the vectors.

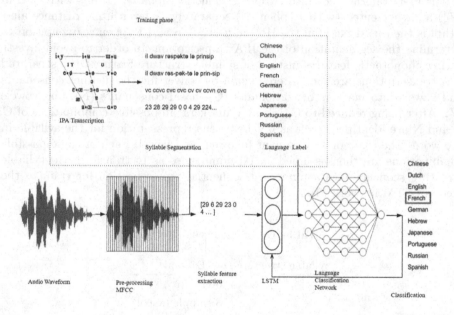

Fig. 2. Diagram of the syllable structure language recognition system

3   Language Recognition Model Architecture

After the extraction of the syllable feature data, another neural network is then used to recognize the language of the syllable feature sequences. The neural network consists of 3 hidden layers and 5 layers in total. The input layer consists of 40 input nodes, each taking a 225 length array (directly following the feature extraction network). The three hidden layers all employ an LSTM structure and have a tanh activation function. The output layer has ten nodes that are a one hot encoding of the 10 languages. The combined model of both syllable extraction and language recognition is shown in Fig. 2.

4 Experiment Set-Up

4.1 LID Training and Evaluation Corpora

We used data from Tatoeba [12], Voxforge [14] and Wide Language Index [8] for evaluation and training. To train our models, we used data sets selected from the databases Tatoeba, Voxforge and the Wide Language Index. Audio files were downloaded, cut into a maximum of 5s and categorized into different languages. Four sets of datasets were defined for training. The first contains 200 utterances for each of the 10 languages (200), the second of 400 utterances for each of the 10 languages (400), the third of 800 utterances (800) and the fourth of 1132 utterances (1132). For evaluation, 100 utterances are selected from each of the 10 languages.

4.2 LID System Description

We based our experiments on LSTM networks [5]. LSTM provides an effective method for processing sequential and temporal information of both MFCC frames and syllables within a neural network system.

Feature Extraction. For syllable structure feature extraction, please refer to Sect. 2 for details. Training corpora was taken from 900 utterances in 7 languages (Chinese, French, German, Spanish, Portuguese, Russian, Dutch) (900-7), which covered all identified syllable structures from parsing textual data. Only 7 languages were selected, because we were unable to conduct IPA transcription of the other 3 languages. The neural network is denoted as SSEM (Syllable Structure Extraction Model) for the rest of the paper. By verifying the syllable structures of the three excluded languages, it can be seen that all possible syllable structure are identified.

Fusion, LSTM Networks and Training. After syllable structure features are extracted as a time series of different syllable structure, the series undergo one hot encoding in order to preserve the categorical characteristic of syllable structure IDs. The encoded output, now of 40 different 225 length arrays are then fed into the language recognition network.

Experiments are done to determine the advantages of discarding all frames labeled as silence (syllable ID 224). Other experiments employed different hidden layers for the language recognition neural network. A layout of (256,256,256) nodes on each of the three layers and one of (60,40,20) nodes are tested. The two layouts are compared to investigate the strength of syllable structure as a lightweight feature.

Training was done on the basis of loss for syllable feature extraction and accuracy for language recognition. RMSprop is used for both networks for optimization.

5 Experimental Results

Experiments are performed on the presence of masking, the layout of different neural network layers for language recognition on syllable structure features, and the use of different datasets. We also evaluated the time and processing efficiency in training and prediction for the models. Here the accuracy refers to the final accuracy of the model on evaluation data at convergence, or the average of the maximum three models at the approximate convergence epoch. The accuracy is calculated by the number of correct predictions divided by the number of all predictions made.

5.1 Masking

We performed a set of experiments to determine the importance of masking, that is, discarding null syllables, to the accuracy of the neural networks. The masking is done to accommodate variable length syllable sequence input within a fixed input array. Experiments on masking were done on dataset (200) and dataset (1132). The same neural network was trained with and without masking on the two datasets. We can see from Table 2 that models with masking outperforms models without masking by a significant margin, the difference increasing as dataset size increases. The smallest difference was 3.94% using dataset (200), model (256,256,256), while the largest difference was 14.34% using dataset (1132), model (60,40,20). The significant average difference of the two test cases implies that a masking layer will be essential for an optimum model, especially with a large dataset.

Table 2. Comparison of neural networks with or without masking

Model	Dataset	Accuracy [%]
(256,256,256)	200	31.51
(256,256,256) Masking	200	35.45
(60,40,20)	1132	55.83
(60,40,20) Masking	1132	70.17
(256,256,256)	1132	61.73
(256,256,256) Masking	1132	70.40

5.2   Neural Network Architecture

We performed experiments to determine the effect on accuracy on two different neural network architectures, in order to determine the suitability of syllable structure features as a lightweight feature. While on average, the (60,40,20) neural network model does have a lower accuracy as compared to the (256,256,256) neural network model, the difference is fairly small. The maximum difference is 4.83% for the two models trained on dataset (200), while the minimum difference is 0.23% for the two models trained on dataset (1132), as shown in Table 3. In light of the difference in training time and evaluation time between (60,40,20) and (256,256,256) models (the (60,40,20) models were faster by 475%), (60,40,20) models should be adopted for most situations, as the accuracy difference is negligible. However, for the purposes for the paper, (256,256,256) models, or models with more nodes in general would be used to discuss overall performance.

Table 3. Comparison of neural networks of different architectures

Model	Dataset	Accuracy [%]
(60,40,20) Masking	200	30.62
(256,256,256) Masking	200	35.45
(60,40,20) Masking	400	41.21
(256,256,256) Masking	400	41.67
(60,40,20) Masking	800	53.47
(256,256,256) Masking	800	55.10
(60,40,20) Masking	1132	70.17
(256,256,256) Masking	1132	70.40

5.3   Prediction Speed

Another characteristic of the model that was investigated was the computing speed in comparison with other approaches to spoken language recognition. Speed is recorded as xRT, or the ratio between the computing time to the total duration of the audio file. As shown in Table 4, the computing speed of finding syllable structure is faster than phoneme extraction or word extraction. It can be seen that the proposed SSEM is faster than all other feature extraction networks with a comparable number of dimensions.

Table 4. Comparison of speeds of the proposed SSEM and other approaches proposed in the literature

Model	Target	Speed [xRT]
SSEM (proposed)	Syllable structure	0.03
CMU Sphinx4 [16]	Word	0.05
OGI [15]	Phoneme	0.40

5.4   Overall Performance and Optimum Model

From Table 3, it is found that the (256,256,256) model with masking was the best performing model, achieving an accuracy of 70.40% and a speed of x0.035 (extraction+processing), a significant decrease from other models. Figure 3 shows the corresponding confusion matrix of this model, where Chinese achieved the highest accuracy of 93%, while Japanese achieved the lowest accuracy of 54%. The accuracy is comparable to the 75.9% accuracy of other LSTM based neural networks on the NIST LRE data set, although comparisons may not be entirely complete due to differences in data [4].

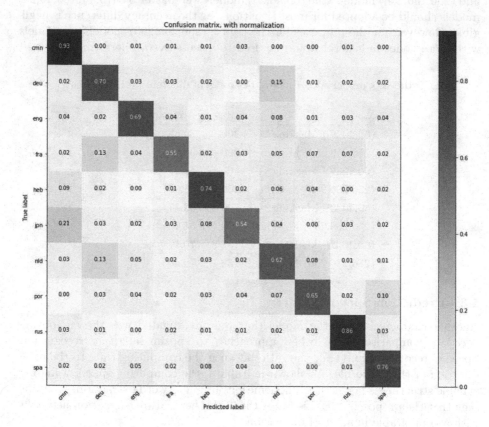

Fig. 3. Confusion matrix of recognized language vs ground truth language

6   Conclusions and Future Work

In this paper, we have proposed a new framework for language feature extraction, with its application to the task of spoken language recognition which has resulted in satisfactory performance. We developed a recurrent neural network that features long short-term memory (LSTM) layers and compared it to the traditional deep convolutional recurrent networks from other papers. An LSTM layer and decoding layer are first used for feature extraction and preprocessing, followed by a more traditional recurrent LSTM network for language identification. In contrast to traditional methods, which take too much time to extract and process features, the proposed network takes syllable sequences as features for better efficiency. Experimental results show that, compared to traditional deep convolutional recurrent networks based on phonotastic or acoustic-phonetic features, our LSTM recurrent network can process the input in slightly over half of the time, while attaining an acceptable accuracy. Specifically, the proposed model with 3 hidden layers of (256,256,256) nodes trained on 1132 utterances for each language can attain an accuracy of 70.40%. Our experiments have shown that syllable features can provide sufficient information to recognize the language of speech, while using less features and dimensions than traditional methods of spoken language recognition. We also showed that for syllable structure features, a large training dataset and masking are essential for optimum performance, but fewer nodes compared to current dominant methods would be needed during training and prediction. Syllable structure features may be used as a complement to existing spoken language recognition models for quicker identification.

While this paper has revealed syllable structures as a promising area for future exploration, improvements and refinements can be made for syllable structure extraction techniques. Better text syllabification techniques, such as silence/pause detection, can be devised to produce more accurate reference data. Moreover, more training data and other neural network architectures or machine learning models may be applied to these syllable structure features for better spoken language recognition. Furthermore, the rudimentary syllable structure classifications can be improved by referring to known syllable structure constraints. These improvements to syllable structure extraction can then be evaluated independently, which would also require IPA transliteration for all relevant languages. Finally, common data sets, such as NIST LRE, can be applied in the future for more complete comparisons against other evaluations.

Acknowledgments. The authors wish to thank Tatoeba and all speakers affiliated for supplying audio speech samples. We also thank members of the NTU MirLab and Ting-Yuan Cheng for their support.

References

1. Anderson-Hsieh, J., Johnson, R., Koehler, K.: The relationship between native speaker judgments of nonnative pronunciation and deviance in segmentais, prosody, and syllable structure. Lang. Learn. **42**(4), 529–555 (1992)
2. Brümmer, N., Strasheim, A., Hubeika, V., Matějka, P., Burget, L., Glembek, O.: Discriminative acoustic language recognition via channel-compensated GMM statistics. In: Tenth Annual Conference of the International Speech Communication Association (2009)
3. Edmondson, W.H., Zhang, L.: The use of syllable structure for speech recognition. Cognitive Science Research Papers-University of Birmingham CSRP (2002)

4. Gelly, G., Gauvain, J.: Spoken language identification using LSTM-based angular proximity. In: Proceedings of Interspeech (2017)
5. Gonzalez-Dominguez, J., Lopez-Moreno, I., Sak, H., Gonzalez-Rodriguez, J., Moreno, P.J.: Automatic language identification using long short-term memory recurrent neural networks. In: Fifteenth Annual Conference of the International Speech Communication Association (2014)
6. Kockmann, M., Ferrer, L., Burget, L., Černocký, J.: iVector fusion of prosodic and cepstral features for speaker verification. In: Twelfth Annual Conference of the International Speech Communication Association (2011)
7. Kozea: Pyphen (2017). https://github.com/Kozea/Pyphen
8. larsyencken: Wide language index. https://github.com/larsyencken/wide-language-index (2017). Accessed 05 June 2018
9. Maïonchi-Pino, N., Magnan, A., Écalle, J.: Syllable frequency effects in visual word recognition: developmental approach in French children. J. Appl. Dev. Psychol. **31**(1), 70–82 (2010)
10. Mortensen, D.R., Dalmia, S., Littell, P.: Epitran: precision G2P for many languages. In: LREC (2018)
11. Ng, R.W., Lee, T., Leung, C.C., Ma, B., Li, H.: Spoken language recognition with prosodic features. IEEE Trans. Audio Speech Lang. Process. **21**(9), 1841–1853 (2013)
12. Tatoeba: Tatoeba. https://tatoeba.org/eng. Accessed 04 Apr 2018
13. Tong, R., Ma, B., Li, H., Chng, E.S.: A target-oriented phonotactic front-end for spoken language recognition. IEEE Trans. Audio Speech Lang. Process. **17**(7), 1335–1347 (2009)
14. Voxforge.org: Free speech... recognition (linux, windows and mac) - voxforge.org. http://www.voxforge.org/. Accessed 05 June 2018
15. Walker, B.D., Lackey, B.C., Muller, J., Schone, P.J.: Language-reconfigurable universal phone recognition. In: Eighth European Conference on Speech Communication and Technology (2003)
16. Walker, W., et al.: Sphinx-4: a flexible open source framework for speech recognition. SML Technical report (2004)
17. Zamuner, T.S., Kharlamov, V.: Phonotactics and syllable structure in infant speech perception. In: Oxford Handbook of Developmental Linguistics, pp. 27–42 (2016)
18. Zissman, M.A.: Comparison of four approaches to automatic language identification of telephone speech. IEEE Trans. Speech Audio Process. **4**(1), 31 (1996)

Investigating a Hybrid Learning Approach for Robust Automatic Speech Recognition

Gueorgui Pironkov[1(✉)], Sean U. N. Wood[2], Stéphane Dupont[1], and Thierry Dutoit[1]

[1] Numediart Institute, University of Mons, Mons, Belgium
{gueorgui.pironkov,stephane.dupont,thierry.dutoit}@umons.ac.be
[2] NECOTIS, University of Sherbrooke, Sherbrooke, Canada
sean.wood@usherbrooke.ca

Abstract. In order to properly train an automatic speech recognition system, speech with its annotated transcriptions is required. The amount of *real* annotated data recorded in noisy and reverberant conditions is extremely limited, especially compared to the amount of data that can be *simulated* by adding noise to clean annotated speech. Thus, using both real and simulated data is important in order to improve robust speech recognition. Another promising method applied to speech recognition in noisy and reverberant conditions is multi-task learning. A successful auxiliary task consists of generating clean speech features using a regression loss (as a denoising auto-encoder). But this auxiliary task uses as targets clean speech which implies that real data cannot be used. In order to tackle this problem a Hybrid-Task Learning system is proposed. This system switches frequently between multi and single-task learning depending on whether the input is real or simulated data respectively. We show that the relative improvement brought by the proposed hybrid-task learning architecture can reach up to 4.4% compared to the traditional single-task learning approach on the CHiME4 database.

Keywords: Speech recognition · Multi-task learning · Robust ASR
Denoising auto-encoder · CHiME4

1 Introduction

In a scenario of clean and non-reverberant acoustic environment, the amount of available annotated data is very substantial for ASR. This eases speech recognition considerably, with some researchers even suggesting that we may have reached human-like performance [24]. However, these ideal acoustic conditions are not very realistic since in many real-life situations, we are faced with degradations of the speech signal. Degradations may come from the surrounding noise (e.g. cars, babble, industrial noises, etc.) [11] or from the acoustic properties of the room (when the microphone used for recording is not a close-talking

© Springer Nature Switzerland AG 2018
T. Dutoit et al. (Eds.): SLSP 2018, LNAI 11171, pp. 67–78, 2018.
https://doi.org/10.1007/978-3-030-00810-9_7

microphone) leading to reverberations of the speech [8]. Another problem in this noisy and reverberant scenario is the limited amount of annotated *real* data. A method frequently used to tackle this problem is to artificially create *simulated* data by adding noise and reverberation on top of clean speech, this way the massive amounts of clean annotated speech can be reused in order to improve ASR in this degrading conditions. Nevertheless, there is a considerable difference between the simulated and real data. The mismatch between these two types of noisy and reverberant data leads to poor results in real-life situations when the acoustic model is trained using simulated data only [23]. Among the different explanations for this mismatch includes the Lombard effect [6], when a speaker talking in a noisy environment naturally tends to raise his/her voice, changing the properties of the speech compared to speech recorded in clean environment.

In this paper, we propose a Hybrid-Task Learning (HTL) architecture that benefits from both real and simulated data. We use the word *hybrid* as the HTL system is a mix of Single-Task Learning (STL) and Multi-Task Learning (MTL) [1]. STL refers to the traditional ASR training where the acoustic model tries to solve only one task, i.e. the phone-state posterior probability estimation for ASR, whereas during an MTL training, the acoustic model is trained to jointly solve one main task (the same one as for STL) plus at least one auxiliary task (for instance, gender recognition or speaker classification). The main motivation for this HTL setup is that simulated data has an advantage compared to real data: we have access to the original clean speech. Thus, the MTL system can be used to train the acoustic model where simulated data is applied as input, and the auxiliary task consists of regenerating the original clean speech, similarly to a Denoising Auto-Encoder (DAE) for instance. However, training an MTL setup exclusively would mean that only simulated data could be used, as we do not have access to the clean speech when real data is applied. Hence, we investigate this mixed STL/MTL architecture that behaves as an MTL system when the input is simulated data and as an STL system when the input data is real. An important point is that the system changes between MTL to STL depending of the random variation of real and simulated data fed to the network. The main goal of the HTL system is to take advantage of the large amount of annotated simulated data easily available while simultaneously integrating real data to the acoustic model, thus improving ASR performance for real-life acoustic conditions. To evaluate this HTL setup, we use the CHiME4 database [23], which is mainly composed of simulated data, but also contains a smaller quantity of real data.

2   Related Work

Several studies have previously focused on applying MTL for ASR. The main task for the acoustic model in ASR consists of predicting the phone-state posterior probabilities, that are subsequently used as input of a Hidden-Markov Model (HMM) that deals with the temporality of speech (or more recently and alternatively, a network with recurrent connections is used instead). Some of the earliest studies use gender classification as an auxiliary task [12,20], where the goal is to increase the awareness of the acoustic model concerning the correlation between gender and speech. Recent studies have also focused on increasing the speaker-awareness of the network in order to increase the generalization ability, by using speaker classification or i-vectors [3] estimation as auxiliary tasks (rather than concatenating the i-vector to the input features) [14,21,22]. More details about these auxiliary tasks and their application for ASR can be found in [13].

Using a variety of different tasks in order to improve speech recognition in noisy and reverberant acoustic environment is also a field of interest. For instance, some studies have focused on improving ASR in solely reverberant condition, by using reverberant data for training and applying a de-*reverberant* auto-encoder as an auxiliary task [5,17]. Instead of using a regression auxiliary task (the DAE here), other researches try classification auxiliary tasks for robust ASR. In this case, the auxiliary task recognizes and classifies the type of noise present in the corrupted sentence [7,19]. The improvement brought by this approach is very limited though. A far more promising method previously cited consists of using a denoising auto-encoder as auxiliary task [2,10,12,18], where the DAE targets for training are the clean features (which implies having access to clean features and making training with real data almost impossible). Very similarly, another work used the same DAE MTL system for robust ASR, but in their case an additional bottle-neck layer was added. As a result, this bottle-neck layer was further used as the input of a classic STL ASR system [9]. Finally, in a previous work, we obtained promising results by generating the noise only as auxiliary task (instead of the clean speech only) [15].

The novelty of this work focuses on the Hybrid-Task Learning architecture for ASR, leveraging both simulated and real data. To our best knowledge, it is the first time that such a hybrid architecture is tested for speech recognition.

3   Hybrid-task Learning

In this work, we present and review the capacity and improvement brought by the hybrid-task learning approach compared to single and multi-task learning, where the auxiliary task investigated in order to improve the ASR robustness is a denoising auto-encoder. The HTL architecture is directly derived from multi-task learning, and can actually be seen as a special case of MTL, where the MTL architecture is data dependent.

3.1   Multi-task Learning

Multi-Task Learning was initially introduced at the end of the twentieth century [1]. The basic concept of MTL consists of training one system (e.g. a neural network) to solve multiple different, but still related tasks. More specifically, in an MTL setup, there should be one *main task* plus at least one *auxiliary task*. The purpose of the auxiliary task is to improve the convergence of the system to the benefit of the main task. An MTL system with one main task and N auxiliary tasks is presented in Fig. 1 as an example.

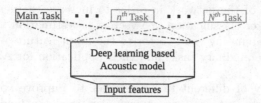

Fig. 1. A multi-task learning network with one main task and N auxiliary tasks.

The update of the parameters of the network is done by backpropagating a mixture of the error of all tasks, with a term:

$$\epsilon_{MTL} = \epsilon_{Main} + \sum_{n=1}^{N} \lambda_n * \epsilon_{Auxiliary_n}, \tag{1}$$

where ϵ_{MTL} is the mixture error to be minimized, ϵ_{Main} and $\epsilon_{Auxiliary_n}$ are the errors computed from the *main* and *auxiliary* tasks respectively, λ_n is a nonnegative weight associated to each auxiliary task, and N is the total number of auxiliary tasks added to the main task of this system.

The influence of the auxiliary task with respect to the main task is controlled by the value of λ_n. If the nth auxiliary task has its λ_n close to 1, then its contribution to the error estimation will be as important as the main task's contribution. On the contrary, for λ_n close to 0, the auxiliary task's influence will be very small (or nonexistent), leading to a single-task system. Most frequently, only the main task is kept during testing, the auxiliary tasks being withdrawn.

3.2 Hybrid-task Learning Mechanism

The novelty of HTL comes from its flexibility compared to MTL. The core idea is to have a system that adapts the number of output tasks, and more specifically the presence or absence of auxiliary tasks, depending on the input features. The setup is applicable to the specific situation where the same training set contains to two types of data, some of which that may be used to train the auxiliary task(s), whereas the rest of the data could not be applied for the auxiliary task(s). In this case, a setup that is able to adapt its auxiliary task(s) dynamically is required in order to train the whole system using all the available data. An illustration of the proposed hybrid architecture is shown in Fig. 2.

Computing the error to be backpropagated in this setup will be very similar to the MTL Eq. (1), with the difference being an additional term which value will depend of the feature type currently processed, leading to:

$$\epsilon_{HTL} = \epsilon_{Main} + \gamma_{feature} * \left(\sum_{n=1}^{N} \lambda_n * \epsilon_{Auxiliary_n} \right), \tag{2}$$

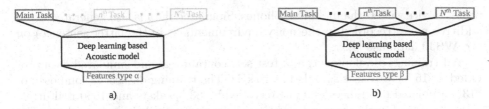

Fig. 2. A hybrid-task learning (HTL) system which adapts its architecture depending of the input features. The same system is represented, where α and β are two different kind of input features randomly fed to the system (for instance real and simulated data). (a) As the input features are α type, the HTL system behaves as a single-task learning system. (b) The β type features force the system to behave as multi-task learning system wit N auxiliary tasks.

with $\gamma_{feature}$ a binary variable equal to 1 if the error ϵ_{HTL} is computed from features supporting MTL, or equal to 0 if the input features can be used only for the main task.

In this paper, the hybrid setup is investigated for robust ASR. This setting is a particularly suitable candidate for HTL. As discussed previously, on the one hand, the amount of annotated clean speech if far more significant than the amount of annotated noisy and reverberant speech, more specifically the amount of *real* noisy and reverberant data. On the other hand, it is possible to generate *simulated* noisy and reverberant data by adding noise to the original (annotated) clean speech and convolving it with the impulse response of a reverberant room. The limitation of the simulated data is the mismatch between the real data and the artificially generated data. Thus, a solution is to create databases containing real and simulated data, where the ratio of real-to-simulated data will be biased towards the simulated data (as the annotations are required for ASR). In this case though, the MTL setup could not be applied if the auxiliary task is a denoising auto-encoder (one of the rare truly effective auxiliary task for robust ASR), as there would be no ground-truth for the real data due to the lack of clean features in real-life conditions. Applying an HTL setup to this database will allow us to benefit from the DAE task with simulated data while the acoustic model still learns valuable information from the real data.

4 Experimental Setup

This section presents the tools and techniques specifically used to evaluate the HTL setup for ASR in noisy and reverberant conditions.

4.1 Database

To evaluate the proposed HTL setup for robust ASR, we use the CHiME4 database [23]. This database contains 1-channel, 2-channel, and 6-channel microphone array data. Real acoustic mixing were recorded in four different noisy environments (café, street junction, public transport and pedestrian area) through a tablet device with 6-channel microphones. Simulated data is also generated using additive noise (recorded in the noisy environments as in the latter sentence) on the WSJ0 database [4].

All training, development, and test sets contain real and simulated data provided as 16 bit wav files sampled at 16 kHz. The training dataset is composed of 7138 simulated utterances ($\approx$15 h) recorded by 83 speakers and 1600 real utterances ($\approx$4 h) of real noisy and reverberant speech recorded by 4 speakers. The development contains the same division of real and simulated data, that is a total of 3280 utterances ($\approx$5.6 h) from 4 other speakers respectively. Similarly, the test set consists of a total of 2640 sentences leading to approximately 4.5 h recorded by 4 speakers for real and 4 others for simulated data.

In this work, an DAE is used as auxiliary task, as a result we use only one channel (channel n°5) during training, while the development and test sets are created from randomly selected channels.

4.2   Features

The features used as input of our system as well as targets for the DAE task are obtained following this traditional ASR pipeline: (1) 13-dimensional Mel-Frequency Cepstral Coefficients (MFCC) features are extracted from the row audio wav files, and normalized via Cepstral Mean-Variance Normalization (CMVN). (2) The adjacent ±3 frames are spliced for each frame. (3) The concatenate features dimension is reduced by a projection into a 40-dimension feature space using Linear Discriminative Analysis (LDA) transformation. (4) The final features are obtained through feature-space Maximum Likelihood Linear Regression (fMLLR), that is a feature-space speaker adaptation method.

Furthermore, these 40-dimensional features are spliced one more time with the surrounding ±5 frames for the input features of the acoustic model, whereas there is no splicing concerning the DAE task targets.

4.3   Acoustic Model Training

Training and testing the HTL setup was done using the *nnet3* version of the Kaldi toolbox [16].

The acoustic model used to evaluate the HTL performance is single-task learning feed-forward Deep Neural Network (DNN). The DNN has 4 hidden layers, each composed of 1024 neurons using rectified linear unit (ReLU) activations. The 1972 phone-state posterior probabilities of the STL main task are computed after a softmax output layer. The DNN training is achieved through 14 epochs with an initial learning rate of 0.0015 which is progressively reduced to 0.00015. The error of the main ASR task is computed using the *cross-entropy* loss function. Whereas for the DAE auxiliary task, the *quadratic* loss function is applied (as this is a regression issue and not a classification task). The parameters (weights and biases) of the network are updated by backpropagating the error derivatives using stochastic gradient descent (SGD) and no momentum nor regularization. The input features are processed through mini-batches of a size

$N = 512$. Since the HTL DAE task requires knowing the type of features, e.g. features extracted from real or simulated data, each mini-batch contains features coming from only one of these two datasets (whereas usually all features would be voluntarily mixed up in the mini-batch). The value of the coefficient $\gamma_{feature}$ of the Eq. (2) is automatically updated during training, by keeping track of the origin (real or simulated) of the mini-batches.

During decoding, the most likely transcriptions are obtained using the output state probabilities computed by the network, and applying them to an HMM system and a language model, the language model being the 3-gram KN language model trained on the WSJ 5K standard corpus.

4.4 Baseline

Using the settings presented in the previous section, we train and test a feed-forward single-task learning deep neural network as the baseline acoustic model. The Word Error Rate (WER) is computed on both development and test sets, for each type of data (real and simulated), and for all four noisy environments. The results are shown in Table 1.

The effects of a significant mismatch between the development and test datasets can be noticed for both real and simulated data. For the *pedestrian* noisy environment for instance, the dev set WER on real data is 11.36% whereas for the real data of the test set the WER more than doubles to 25.37%. Beside the *street* environment, all other environments suffer from the mismatch between the dev and test set, especially for real data. This tendency is also confirmed on simulated data with the overall WER going from 18.12% to 26.00% for the development set and test set respectively. This mismatch is even more noticeable on real data with the overall WER dropping from 16.46% to 29.30%. The mismatch is partially due to the variability of the recording conditions. Another explanation can be the impact of the Lombard effect described in Sect. 1.

Table 1. Word error rate (WER) in % on the development and test sets of CHiME4 dataset used as baseline. *Overall* is the mean WER of all 4 environmental noises and *Avg.* is the mean WER over real and simulated data.

	Avg.	Dev set			Test set		
		Mean	Simu	Real	Mean	Simu	Real
Overall	22.47	17.29	18.12	16.46	27.65	26.00	29.30
Bus	24.93	18.51	16.02	20.99	31.35	20.58	42.12
Café	24.98	19.12	21.81	16.43	30.84	30.01	31.66
Pedestrian	19.33	12.95	14.53	11.36	25.71	26.04	25.37
Street	20.66	18.60	20.12	17.08	22.71	27.36	18.06

Finally, it can also be noted that both the development and test sets contain speech uttered by 8 different speakers (whereas 83 speakers are used for training).

This lack of diversity can also explain the difference of WER between the two datasets, as the impact of one or two speakers harder to recognize compared to the others would be much more severe compared to having more speakers in those datasets. As a general remark, our goal here is to provide a proof-of-concept of the benefits of HTL and not directly challenge the state-of-the-art results on CHiME4.

5   HTL Performance

In this section, we compare the HTL setup to an STL setup. The improvement brought by the hybrid flexibility is also compared to MTL. For each experimental situation, the results for the development set and test set are computed, as well as the results on real and simulated data, and the average over all four datasets.

5.1   Denoising Auto-Encoder Auxiliary Task Impact

In order to evaluate the hybrid task setup, we vary the value of λ present in Eq. (2). If $\lambda = 0$, the setup is behaving as single-task learning system, which is our baseline. The higher the value of λ, the more influential the DAE task will be compared to the ASR main task. Both the STL and HTL setups are trained using real and simulated data, with the data fed to the networks being randomly selected between real and simulated. Results are presented in Table 2.

Table 2. Performance of the hybrid-task learning architecture when the auxiliary task is a denoising auto-encoder, with λ the weight attributed to the DAE auxiliary task during training. The baseline, which is the single-task learning architecture, is obtained for $\lambda = 0$. The *Avg.* value is computed over all four datasets.

Value of λ	Avg.	Dev set			Test set		
		Mean	Simu	Real	Mean	Simu	Real
0 (STL)	*22.47*	*17.29*	*18.12*	*16.46*	*27.65*	*26.00*	*29.30*
0.05	22.07	16.82	17.44	16.20	27.31	25.57	29.05
0.1	21.96	16.77	17.42	16.11	27.16	25.36	28.95
0.15	**21.88**	**16.72**	**17.32**	16.11	**27.04**	**25.23**	28.84
0.2	21.93	16.82	17.60	**16.04**	**27.04**	25.39	**28.69**
0.3	22.10	17.02	17.71	16.32	27.18	25.43	28.92
0.5	22.75	17.60	18.43	16.77	27.89	26.32	29.46
0.7	23.08	17.92	19.05	16.79	28.27	26.96	29.57

There is a persistent improvement brought by the hybrid-task learning architecture, overall all four possible datasets, especially for a value of λ less than 0.4. The relative improvement of HTL compared to STL reaches up to 4.4% for the development dataset applied on simulated noisy and reverberant speech for $\lambda = 0.15$. More generally, an overall relative improvement of 2.6% is obtained over all four datasets for $\lambda = 0.15$, showing the positive impact of the hybrid auxiliary task in all cases. In light of the above best WER obtained while varying the impact of the DAE auxiliary task, we set $\lambda = 0.15$ for the next sections.

5.2 Evaluating the "Hybrid" Impact

Despite the improvement brought by the HTL setup compared to single-task learning, it is questionable if this improvement comes from the hybrid architecture that frequently switches from single to multiple tasks depending of the input features, or only from the usage of multiple tasks. In order to evaluate the HTL impact we train an HTL and STL system using both real and simulated data and compare the results to STL and MTL systems trained using only simulated data, we also train an STL system on real data only. The results are presented in Table 3.

Before discussing the HTL impact it can be noticed that the idea that "more data is always better" applies here when comparing all three STL systems. Using only real data (the smallest dataset) for training gives the worst results with a WER of 54.57% over all four datasets. And when looking at the test results, surprisingly, the WER on the simulated data is lower (62.92%) than for real data (65.57%), despite the mismatch between real and simulated data (simulated data that is unseen here), highlighting a even larger mismatch between the real data used for training and the real data used for testing. Using simulated and real data (largest dataset) for training gives an WER of 22.47% over all four datasets, whereas using only simulated data reaches a word error rate of 23.73%.

Table 3. Comparing the word error rate (%) of different task learning (TL) systems depending of training datasets, where the hybrid-TL and multi-TL auxiliary tasks are DAE with $\lambda = 0.15$. *Avg.* is the average WER over all four datasets.

Training dataset(s)	System architecture	Avg.	Dev set			Test set		
			Mean	Simu	Real	Mean	Simu	Real
Real + Simu	Single-TL	22.47	17.29	18.12	16.46	27.65	26.00	29.30
Real + Simu	Hybrid-TL	**21.88**	**16.72**	**17.32**	**16.11**	**27.04**	**25.23**	**28.84**
Simu only	Single-TL	23.73	18.27	18.45	18.09	29.18	26.55	31.81
Simu only	Multi-TL	23.28	17.91	17.99	17.82	28.63	26.06	31.20
Real only	Single-TL	54.57	44.89	49.83	39.95	64.25	62.92	65.57

Again having more data (and more diversified data) helps. Training with added real data to the simulated data significantly improves the real data results (going from 18.09% to 16.46% for the dev set for instance), whereas, as expected this improvement is much smaller for simulated data (from 18.45% to 18.12% on the same dataset) but still present.

Both the MTL and HTL architectures appear to improve results compared to their respective STL setups, with an averaged WER of 23.28% over all four datasets for MTL and 21.88% for HTL. But as discussed earlier comparing directly the WER of HTL and MTL directly would be incorrect as both systems train on a different amount (and type) of features, making it hard to estimate if the improvement comes from the hybrid architecture or from the greater amount of data used during the HTL training.

Thus, we compute the relative improvement brought by HTL compared to STL when real and simulated is used for training and compare it to the relative improvement brought by MTL compared to STL when only simulated is used. The results are shown in Fig. 3.

It can be observed that on average, and more specifically for three out of the four datasets, using HTL gives better relative improvement than MTL. The highest gap between the HTL and MTL relative improvements can be noticed on the simulated datasets. Interestingly, for the test set using real data, MTL gives a slightly higher relative improvement (0.3% better than for HTL), where for MTL no real data was used during training. This result can be explained by the fact that the WER on the real data testset are worst on STL when training on simulated data only, thus in this situation MTL provides a better generalization than HTL to the unseen data as a higher gap exists between the STL and MTL WER.

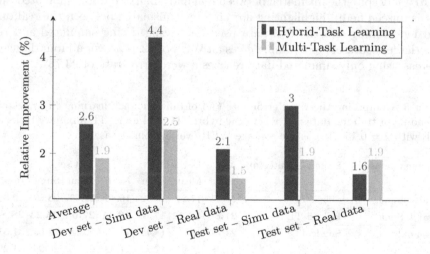

Fig. 3. Evaluation of the relative improvement brought by hybrid-task learning compared to single-task learning versus the relative improvement brought by multi-task learning compared to single-task learning.

6   Conclusion

In this work, a novel task learning mechanism is proposed which is refereed to as Hybrid-Task Learning. This mechanism is based on mixing the Multi-Task Learning architecture with the tradition Single-Task Learning architecture, leading to a dynamic hybrid system that switches between single and multi-task learning depending of the input feature's type. A relative improvement of 4.4% can be achieved by HTL compared to STL. Additionally, it can be noted that, as for MTL, implementing and training the proposed HTL setup is not time consuming and does not require additional information, as the clean data used for training the auxiliary task is already available when the simulated data is generated. In future work, we would like to investigate other auxiliary tasks for the proposed HTL setup, for instance generating only the noise as auxiliary task (as opposed to the DAE), as well as evaluating HTL performance on other databases and feature combinations other than real and simulated data.

Acknowledgments. This work has been partly funded by the Walloon Region of Belgium through the SPW-DGO6 Wallinov Program n°1610152.

References

1. Caruana, R.: Multitask learning. In: Thrun, S., Pratt, L. (eds.) Learning to Learn. Springer, Boston (1997). https://doi.org/10.1007/978-1-4615-5529-2_5
2. Chen, Z., Watanabe, S., Erdogan, H., Hershey, J.R.: Speech enhancement and recognition using multi-task learning of long short-term memory recurrent neural networks. In: INTERSPEECH, pp. 3274–3278. ISCA (2015)
3. Dehak, N., Kenny, P., Dehak, R., Dumouchel, P., Ouellet, P.: Front-end factor analysis for speaker verification. IEEE Trans. Audio Speech Lang. Process. (ICASSP) **19**(4), 788–798 (2011)
4. Garofolo, J., Graff, D., Paul, D., Pallett, D.: CSR-I (WSJ0) Complete LDC93S6A. Web Download. Linguistic Data Consortium, Philadelphia (1993)
5. Giri, R., Seltzer, M.L., Droppo, J., Yu, D.: Improving speech recognition in reverberation using a room-aware deep neural network and multi-task learning. In: IEEE International Conference on Acoustics, Speech and Signal Processing (ICASSP), pp. 5014–5018. IEEE (2015)
6. Hansen, J.H.: Morphological constrained feature enhancement with adaptive cepstral compensation (MCE-ACC) for speech recognition in noise and lombard effect. IEEE Trans. Speech Audio Process. **2**(4), 598–614 (1994)
7. Kim, S., Raj, B., Lane, I.: Environmental noise embeddings for robust speech recognition. arXiv preprint arXiv:1601.02553 (2016)
8. Kinoshita, K., et al.: A summary of the reverb challenge: state-of-the-art and remaining challenges in reverberant speech processing research. EURASIP J. Adv. Sig. Process. **2016**(1), 1–19 (2016)
9. Kundu, S., Mantena, G., Qian, Y., Tan, T., Delcroix, M., Sim, K.C.: Joint acoustic factor learning for robust deep neural network based automatic speech recognition. In: IEEE International Conference on Acoustics, Speech and Signal Processing (ICASSP), pp. 5025–5029. IEEE (2016)

10. Li, B., Sainath, T.N., Weiss, R.J., Wilson, K.W., Bacchiani, M.: Neural network adaptive beamforming for robust multichannel speech recognition. In: Proceedings of INTERSPEECH (2016)
11. Li, J., Deng, L., Gong, Y., Haeb-Umbach, R.: An overview of noise-robust automatic speech recognition. IEEE/ACM Trans. Audio Speech Lang. Process. **22**(4), 745–777 (2014)
12. Lu, Y., et al.: Multitask learning in connectionist speech recognition. In: Proceedings of the Tenth Australian International Conference on Speech Science and Technology, Sydney, 8–10 December 2004, pp. 312–315 (2004)
13. Pironkov, G., Dupont, S., Dutoit, T.: Multi-task learning for speech recognition: an overview. In: Proceedings of the 24th European Symposium on Artificial Neural Networks (ESANN) (2016)
14. Pironkov, G., Dupont, S., Dutoit, T.: Speaker-aware multi-task learning for automatic speech recognition. In: 23rd International Conference on Pattern Recognition (ICPR) (2016)
15. Pironkov, G., Dupont, S., Wood, S.U.N., Dutoit, T.: Noise and speech estimation as auxiliary tasks for robust speech recognition. In: Camelin, N., Estève, Y., Martín-Vide, C. (eds.) SLSP 2017. LNCS (LNAI), vol. 10583, pp. 181–192. Springer, Cham (2017). https://doi.org/10.1007/978-3-319-68456-7_15
16. Povey, D., et al.: The kaldi speech recognition toolkit. In: IEEE 2011 Workshop on Automatic Speech Recognition and Understanding. IEEE Signal Processing Society (2011)
17. Qian, Y., Tan, T., Yu, D.: An investigation into using parallel data for far-field speech recognition. In: IEEE International Conference on Acoustics, Speech and Signal Processing (ICASSP), pp. 5725–5729. IEEE (2016)
18. Qian, Y., Yin, M., You, Y., Yu, K.: Multi-task joint-learning of deep neural networks for robust speech recognition. In: IEEE Workshop on Automatic Speech Recognition and Understanding (ASRU), pp. 310–316. IEEE (2015)
19. Sakti, S., Kawanishi, S., Neubig, G., Yoshino, K., Nakamura, S.: Deep bottleneck features and sound-dependent i-vectors for simultaneous recognition of speech and environmental sounds. In: 2016 IEEE Spoken Language Technology Workshop (SLT), pp. 35–42. IEEE (2016)
20. Stadermann, J., Koska, W., Rigoll, G.: Multi-task learning strategies for a recurrent neural net in a hybrid tied-posteriors acoustic model. In: INTERSPEECH, pp. 2993–2996 (2005)
21. Tan, T., et al.: Speaker-aware training of LSTM-RNNS for acoustic modelling. In: IEEE International Conference on Acoustics, Speech and Signal Processing (ICASSP), pp. 5280–5284. IEEE (2016)
22. Tang, Z., Li, L., Wang, D.: Multi-task recurrent model for speech and speaker recognition. arXiv preprint arXiv:1603.09643 (2016)
23. Vincent, E., Watanabe, S., Nugraha, A.A., Barker, J., Marxer, R.: An analysis of environment, microphone and data simulation mismatches in robust speech recognition. Comput. Speech Lang. **46**, 535–557 (2016)
24. Xiong, W., et al.: Achieving human parity in conversational speech recognition. arXiv preprint arXiv:1610.05256 (2016)

A Comparison of Adaptation Techniques and Recurrent Neural Network Architectures

Jan Vaněk$^{(\boxtimes)}$ (iD), Josef Michálek (iD), Jan Zelinka (iD), and Josef Psutka (iD)

University of West Bohemia, Univerzitní 8, 301 00 Pilsen, Czech Republic
{vanekyj,orcus,zelinka,psutka}@kky.zcu.cz

Abstract. Recently, recurrent neural networks have become state-of-the-art in acoustic modeling for automatic speech recognition. The long short-term memory (LSTM) units are the most popular ones. However, alternative units like gated recurrent unit (GRU) and its modifications outperformed LSTM in some publications. In this paper, we compared five neural network (NN) architectures with various adaptation and feature normalization techniques. We have evaluated feature-space maximum likelihood linear regression, five variants of i-vector adaptation and two variants of cepstral mean normalization. The most adaptation and normalization techniques were developed for feed-forward NNs and, according to results in this paper, not all of them worked also with RNNs. For experiments, we have chosen a well known and available TIMIT phone recognition task. The phone recognition is much more sensitive to the quality of AM than large vocabulary task with a complex language model. Also, we published the open-source scripts to easily replicate the results and to help continue the development.

Keywords: Neural networks · Acoustic model · TIMIT · LSTM
GRU · Phone recognition · Adaptation · i-vectors

1 Introduction

Neural Networks (NNs) and deep NNs (DNNs) became dominant in the field of the acoustic modeling several years ago. Simple feed-forward (FF) DNNs were faded away in recent years. The current progress is based on the modeling of a longer temporal context of individual feature frames. Main two ways are actually popular: First, a larger context is modeled by a time-delayed NN (TDNN) [9,16]. TDNNs model long term temporal dependencies with training times comparable to standard feed-forward DNNs. In the TDNN architecture, the initial transforms learn narrow contexts and the deeper layers process the hidden activations from a wider temporal context. Hence the higher layers have the ability to learn wider temporal relationships. The second way to learn the

© Springer Nature Switzerland AG 2018
T. Dutoit et al. (Eds.): SLSP 2018, LNAI 11171, pp. 79–90, 2018.
https://doi.org/10.1007/978-3-030-00810-9_8

longer temporal context is to use recurrent NNs (RNNs). The most popular RNN architecture is a long short-term memory (LSTM) that has been designed to address the vanishing and exploding gradient problems of conventional RNNs. Unlike feed-forward neural networks, RNNs have cyclic connections making them powerful for modeling sequences [12]. The main drawback is much slower training due to the sequential nature of the learning algorithm. An unfolding of the recurrent network during training was proposed in [13] to speed-up the training, however it is still significantly slower than FF NNs or TDNNs. More recently, another type of recurrent unit, a gated recurrent unit (GRU), was proposed in [2,3]. Similarly to the LSTM unit, the GRU has gating units that modulate the flow of information inside the unit, however, without having a separate memory cells. Further revising GRUs leaded to a simplified architecture potentially more suitable for speech recognition in [11]. First, removing the reset gate in the GRU design resulted in a simpler single-gate architecture called modified GRU (M-GRU). Second, replacing *tanh* with *ReLU* activations in the state update equations was proposed and called M-reluGRU. A more detailed overview of the RNN architectures follows in Sect. 3.

Even if large datasets are used for the DNN training, an adaptation of an acoustic model (AM) to a test speaker and environment is beneficial. A lot of techniques have been reported on the adaptation, such as the classical maximum a posterior (MAP) and maximum likelihood linear regression (MLLR) for traditional GMM-HMM acoustic models. Although this technique can be modified for an NN-based acoustic model, a much simpler application has so-called feature space MLLR (fMLLR) [4] because fMLLR changes only features and it does not adapt NN parameters. This speaker adaptation technique can be easily applied in an NN-based acoustic model [8,10,15]. Therefore, fMLLR can be used to any DNN architecture. i-vectors originally developed for speaker recognition can be used to the speaker and environment adaptation also [7,14]. Alternative approach is using of discriminative speaker codes [6,17]. More detailed description of the adaptation techniques used in this paper follows.

2   Adaptation of DNNs

The simplest way of the adaptation is a feature level adaptation. When adapting input features, NN can have any structure. The most popular and well known technique is fMLLR based on an underlying HMM-GMM that is used during initial stage of the NN training.

2.1   fMLLR

The fMLLR transforms feature frames with a speaker-specific square matrix A and a bias b. For HMM-GMMs, A and b are estimated to maximize the likelihood of the adaptation data given the model [4,15]. In the training phase, the speaker-specific transform may be updated several-times alternating HMM-GMM update. These approach is usually called a speaker adaptive training (SAT). The result of the training phase is a canonical model that requires using adaptation during testing phase. However, two-pass processing is required during test phase. The first pass produces unsupervised alignment that is used to estimate the transform parameters via maximum likelihood. The model used for alignment does not need to be the identical model to the final canonical one. Because all the steps are using the underline HMM-GMM any NN architecture may be used to train the final NN acoustic model.

2.2   i-vectors

The i-vector extraction is a well known technique, so we focused here to more practical points. An detailed description of i-vectors can be found in [7, 14] and further papers referenced in there.

The i-vector extraction is comprised from following steps:

1. An universal background model (UBM) needs to be trained. Usually a GMM with 512 to 2048 diagonal components is used. The quality of GMM is not critical, so some speed-up methods can be utilized. Features for UBM do not need to match witch features for NN nor i-vector accumulators. Usually, features with cepstral mean normalization (CMN) or cepstral mean and variance normalization (CMVN) are used for UBM. The normalization techniques reduce speaker and environment variability. Features without any normalization are used for the i-vector accumulators to carry more speaker- and environment-related information.
2. Zero-order and centered first-order statistics are accumulated for every speaker according to the UBM posteriors.
3. The i-vector extraction transforms are estimated iteratively by expectation/maximization (EM) algorithm.
4. The i-vector for individual speakers is evaluated. For training speakers, zero-order and centered first-order statistics have been already accumulated. For other speakers, statistics must be accumulated. Then, the i-vector is evaluated by the i-vector extraction transforms computed in the third step.

The four step process seems simple but there are some details that need to be mentioned:

– CMN or CMVN may be computed online or offline. The offline variant may be per-utterance or per-speaker. The online variant starts from global cepstral mean and it is subsequently updated. An exponential forgetting is usable for very long utterances. The training setup should match with the testing one.
– The accumulated statistic should be saturated or scaled-down for long utterances due to an i-vector overfitting.

– The offline scenario is not proper for training. The number of speakers and thus variants of i-vectors is very limited and leads to NN overfitting. The online scenario is recommended for training, in the Kaldi Switchboard example recipe the number of speakers is also boosted by pseudo-speakers. Two training utterances represent one pseudo-speaker. The offline scenario may be used in the test phase.

3   Recurrent Neural Network Architectures

3.1   Long Short-Term Memory

Long short-term memory (LSTM) is a widely used type of recurrent neural network (RNN). Standard RNNs suffer from both exploding and vanishing gradient problems. Both of these problems are caused by the fact, that information flowing through the RNN passes through many stages of multiplication. The gradient is essentially equal to the weight matrix raised to a high power. This results in the gradient growing or shrinking at an exponential rate to the number of timesteps.

The exploding gradient problem can be solved simply by truncating the gradient. On the other hand, the vanishing gradient problem is harder to overcome. It does not simply cause the gradient to be small; the gradient components corresponding to long-term dependencies are small while the components corresponding to short-term dependencies are large. Resulting RNN can then learn short-term dependencies but not long-term dependencies.

The LSTM was proposed in 1997 by Hochreiter and Scmidhuber [5] as a solution to the vanishing gradient problem. Let c_t denote a hidden state of a LSTM. The main idea is that instead of computing c_t directly from c_{t-1} with matrix-vector product followed by an activation function, the LSTM computes Δc_t and adds it to c_{t-1} to get c_t. The addition operation is what eliminates the vanishing gradient problem.

Each LSTM cell is composed of smaller units called gates, which control the flow of information through the cell. The forget gate f_t controls what information will be discarded from the cell state, input gate i_t controls what new information will be stored in the cell state and output gate o_t controls what information from the cell state will be used in the output.

The LSTM has two hidden states, c_t and h_t. The state c_t fights the gradient vanishing problem while h_t allows the network to make complex decisions over short periods of time. There are several slightly different LSTM variants. The architecture used in this paper is specified by the following equations:

$$i_t = \sigma(W_{xi}x_t + W_{hi}h_{t-1} + b_i)$$
$$f_t = \sigma(W_{xf}x_t + W_{hf}h_{t-1} + b_f)$$
$$o_t = \sigma(W_{xo}x_t + W_{ho}h_{t-1} + b_o)$$
$$c_t = f_t * c_{t-1} + i_t * \tanh(W_{xc}x_t + W_{hc}h_{t-1} + b_c)$$
$$h_t = o_t * \tanh(c_t)$$

The Fig. 1 shows the internal structure of LSTM.

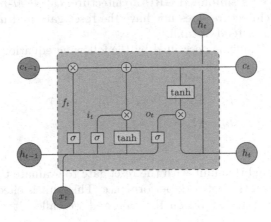

Fig. 1. Structure of a LSTM unit

3.2 Gated Recurrent Unit

A gated recurrent unit (GRU) was proposed in 2014 by Cho et al. [3] Similarly to
the LSTM unit, the GRU has gating units that modulate the flow of information
inside the unit, however, without having a separate memory cells.

The update gate z_t decides how much the unit updates its activation and
reset gate r_t determines which information will be kept from the old state. GRU
does not have any mechanism to control what information to output, therefore
it exposes the whole state.

The main differences between LSTM unit and GRU are:

- GRU has 2 gates, LSTM has 3 gates
- GRUs do not have an internal memory different from the unit output, LSTMs
  have an internal memory c_t and the output is controlled by an output gate
- Second nonlinearity is not applied when computing the output of GRUs.

The GRU unit used in this work is described by the following equations:

$$r_t = \sigma(W_r x_t + U_r h_{t-1} + b_r)$$
$$z_t = \sigma(W_z x_t + U_z h_{t-1} + b_z)$$
$$\tilde{h}_t = \tanh(W x_t + U(r_t * h_{t-1}) + b_h)$$
$$h_t = (1 - z_t) * h_{t-1} + z_t * \tilde{h}_t$$

3.3   Modified Gated Recurrent Unit with ReLU

Ravanelli introduced a simplified GRU architecture, called *M-reluGRU*, in [11]. This simplified architecture does not have the reset gate and uses ReLU as an activation function instead of tanh.

The *M-reluGRU* unit is described by the following equations:

$$z_t = \sigma(W_z x_t + U_z h_{t-1} + b_z)$$
$$\tilde{h}_t = \mathrm{ReLU}(W x_t + U h_{t-1} + b_h)$$
$$h_t = (1 - z_t) * h_{t-1} + z_t * \tilde{h}_t$$

We have also used this unit with the reset gate to evaluate the impact of the missing reset gate on the network performance. This unit is effectively a normal GRU with ReLU as an activation function and we called it *reluGRU* in this paper.

The Fig. 2 shows the internal structure and difference of GRU and M-reluGRU units.

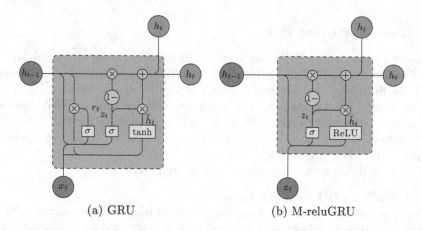

(a) GRU   (b) M-reluGRU

Fig. 2. Structure of GRU and M-reluGRU units

4   Experiments

We have chosen TIMIT, a small phone recognition task, as a benchmark of the NN architectures and adaptation techniques. The TIMIT corpus is well known and available. The small size allows a rapid testing and simulates a low-resource scenario that is still an issue for many minor languages. The phone recognition is much more sensitive to quality of AM than large vocabulary task with a complex language model.

The TIMIT corpus contains recordings of phonetically-balanced prompted English speech. It was recorded using a Sennheiser close-talking microphone at 16 kHz rate with 16 bit sample resolution. TIMIT contains a total of 6300 sentences (5.4 h), consisting of 10 sentences spoken by each of 630 speakers from 8 major dialect regions of the United States. All sentences were manually segmented at the phone level.

The prompts for the 6300 utterances consist of 2 dialect sentences (SA), 450 phonetically compact sentences (SX) and 1890 phonetically-diverse sentences (SI).

The training set contains 3696 utterances from 462 speakers. The core test set consists of 192 utterances, 8 from each of 24 speakers (2 males and 1 female from each dialect region). The training and test sets do not overlap.

4.1 Speech Data, Processing, and Test Description

As mentioned above, we used TIMIT data available from LDC as a corpus LDC93S1. Then, we ran the Kaldi TIMIT example script s5, which trained various NN-based phone recognition systems with a common HMM-GMM tied-triphone model and alignments. The common baseline system consisted of the following methods: It started from MFCC features which were augmented by Δ and $\Delta\Delta$ coefficients and then processed by LDA. Final feature vector dimension was 40. We obtained final alignments by HMM-GMM tied-triphone model with 1909 tied-states (may vary slightly if rerun the script). We trained the model with MLLT and SAT methods, and we used fMLLR for the SAT training and a test phase adaptation. We dumped all training, development and test fMLLR processed data, and alignments to disk. Therefore, it was easy to do compatible experiments from the same common starting point. We also dumped MFCC processed by LDA with no normalization and CMN calculated both per speaker and per utterance.

We employed a bigram language/phone model for the final phone recognition. A bigram model is a very weak model for phone recognition; however, it forced focus to the acoustic part of the system, and it boosted benchmark sensitivity. The training, as well as the recognition, was done for 48 phones. We mapped the final results on TIMIT core test set to 39 phones (as is usual for TIMIT corpus processing), and phone error rate (PER) was evaluated by the provided NIST script to be compatible with previously published works. In contrast to the Kaldi recipe, we used a different phone decoder. It is a standard Viterbi-based triphone decoder. It gives better results than the Kaldi standard WFST decoder on the TIMIT phone recognition task.

We have used an open-source Chainer 3.2 DNNs Python tranining tool that supports NVidia GPUs [1]. It is multiplatform and easy to use.

4.2 DNN Training

First, as a reference to RNNs, we trained feed-forward (FF) DNN with ReLU activation function without any pre-training. We used dropout $p = 0.2$. We stacked 11 input feature frames to 440 NN input dimension, like in Kaldi example s5. We have used a network with 8 hidden layers and 2048 ReLU neurons, because it gave the best performance according to our preliminary experiments. The final softmax layer had 1909 neurons. We used SGD with momentum 0.9. The networks were trained in 3 stages with learning rate 1e–2, 4e–3 and 1e–4. The batch size was gradually increased from initial 256 to 1024, and finally to 2048. The training in each stage was stopped when the development data criterion increased in comparison to the last epoch.

Then we have trained LSTM, GRU, reluGRU and M-reluGRU networks. For all of these recurrent networks, we have used identical training setup. We used 4 layers with 1024 units in each. The dropout used was $p = 0.2$. We have used output time delay equal to 5 time steps. RNNs were trained in 4 stages. The first stage used Adam optimization algorithm with batch size 512. The other stages used SGD with momentum 0.9, batch size 128 and learning rate equal to 1e–3, 1e–4, and 1e–5 respectively. The training in each stage was stopped when the development data criterion increased in comparison to the last epoch, as in FF network case.

We have trained each network on several input data and i-vector combinations. We used fMLLR data described in the previous section, MFCC and MFCC with CMN. The normalization was calculated either per speaker or per utterance. For training and testing, we used no i-vectors, online i-vectors and offline i-vectors calculated also either per speaker or per utterance. We also evaluated online i-vectors for training and offline i-vectors for testing. The i-vectors were computed according to Kaldi Switchboard example script. However, because of small TIMIT size, we did not use any reduction of data. Entire training dataset was used to estimate i-vector extractor in all steps. The i-vector extractor has been trained only once and online, per-speaker, and per-utterance i-vectors sets were extracted by the same extractor transforms.

Because of stochastic nature of results due to random initialization and stochastic gradient descent, we have performed each experiment 10 times in total. Then, we have calculated the average phone error rate (PER) and its standard deviation.

4.3 Results

We have evaluated average PER, its standard deviation for all combinations of three features variants, six i-vector variants, and five NNs architectures. We had to split the results into two tables because of the page size. Table 1 shows the average PER for each experiment for FF, LSTM, and GRU NNs architectures. Table 2 compares three variants of GRU-based NNs: GRU, reluGRU, M-reluGRU. A subset of the most valuable results is also depicted in Fig. 3. It is clear that fMLLR adaptation technique worked quite well. All the NN architectures gave the best result with fMLLR. The i-vector adaptation had a stable gain only for FF NN. Two variants of the i-vector adaptation were the best: online i-vectors for training and online or offline per-speaker for testing. Results of RNNs with the i-vector adaptation were interesting, because there was no significant gain. The results with adaptation were rather worse. Between RNN architectures, LSTM was the winner (PER 15.43% with fMLLR). The GRU and reluGRU gave comparable PERs, 15.7% with fMLLR, that was slightly worse than LSTM. M-reluGRU did not performed well and the results were often worse than FF.

Table 1. Phone error rate [%] for FF, LSTM and GRU networks

Data	i-vectors		Phone error rate [%]		
	Training	Testing	FF	LSTM	GRU
fMLLR	–	–	17.00 ± 0.13	$\mathbf{15.43 \pm 0.28}$	15.69 ± 0.19
	Off. spk.	Off. spk.	17.17 ± 0.16	16.08 ± 0.19	$\mathbf{16.04 \pm 0.29}$
	Off. utt.	Off. utt.	17.32 ± 0.15	$\mathbf{16.34 \pm 0.32}$	16.43 ± 0.25
	Online	Off. spk.	17.17 ± 0.16	$\mathbf{16.14 \pm 0.22}$	16.15 ± 0.28
	Online	Off. utt.	17.10 ± 0.21	16.27 ± 0.34	$\mathbf{16.14 \pm 0.24}$
	Online	Online	17.18 ± 0.14	$\mathbf{16.23 \pm 0.26}$	16.23 ± 0.19
MFCC	–	–	19.42 ± 0.18	$\mathbf{16.98 \pm 0.27}$	17.48 ± 0.19
	Off. spk.	Off. spk.	19.02 ± 0.15	$\mathbf{17.50 \pm 0.19}$	17.63 ± 0.22
	Off. utt.	Off. utt.	19.29 ± 0.19	18.12 ± 0.27	$\mathbf{18.09 \pm 0.29}$
	Online	Off. spk.	18.22 ± 0.19	17.19 ± 0.26	$\mathbf{17.00 \pm 0.28}$
	Online	Off. utt.	18.48 ± 0.16	17.27 ± 0.26	$\mathbf{17.21 \pm 0.20}$
	Online	Online	18.19 ± 0.19	$\mathbf{17.21 \pm 0.15}$	17.33 ± 0.37
MFCC with CMN per speaker	–	–	18.49 ± 0.19	$\mathbf{16.53 \pm 0.20}$	17.00 ± 0.25
	Off. spk.	Off. spk.	18.47 ± 0.20	$\mathbf{17.20 \pm 0.23}$	17.33 ± 0.21
	Off. utt.	Off. utt.	18.59 ± 0.10	17.45 ± 0.19	$\mathbf{17.36 \pm 0.21}$
	Online	Off. spk.	18.11 ± 0.24	$\mathbf{16.90 \pm 0.24}$	17.04 ± 0.16
	Online	Off. utt.	18.17 ± 0.22	17.34 ± 0.31	$\mathbf{17.06 \pm 0.20}$
	Online	Online	18.21 ± 0.19	17.25 ± 0.26	$\mathbf{17.24 \pm 0.31}$
MFCC with CMN per utterance	–	–	19.44 ± 0.27	$\mathbf{16.98 \pm 0.20}$	17.54 ± 0.20
	Off. spk.	Off. spk.	19.10 ± 0.17	$\mathbf{17.60 \pm 0.31}$	17.64 ± 0.33
	Off. utt.	Off. utt.	19.32 ± 0.14	18.28 ± 0.35	$\mathbf{18.15 \pm 0.35}$
	Online	Off. spk.	18.70 ± 0.18	17.53 ± 0.23	$\mathbf{17.33 \pm 0.18}$
	Online	Off. utt.	18.63 ± 0.16	17.60 ± 0.23	$\mathbf{17.46 \pm 0.19}$
	Online	Online	18.73 ± 0.18	17.66 ± 0.23	$\mathbf{17.43 \pm 0.19}$

Table 2. Phone error rate [%] for GRU and its modifications

Data	i-vectors		Phone error rate [%]		
	Training	Testing	GRU	reluGRU	M-reluGRU
fMLLR	–	–	**15.69 ± 0.19**	15.70 ± 0.56	17.06 ± 0.77
	Off. spk.	Off. spk.	**16.04 ± 0.29**	16.28 ± 0.38	17.50 ± 0.72
	Off. utt.	Off. utt.	16.43 ± 0.25	**16.33 ± 0.13**	18.25 ± 0.85
	Online	Off. spk.	**16.15 ± 0.28**	16.19 ± 0.22	17.76 ± 0.94
	Online	Off. utt.	**16.14 ± 0.24**	16.23 ± 0.18	17.85 ± 0.76
	Online	Online	**16.23 ± 0.19**	16.39 ± 0.33	17.60 ± 0.67
MFCC	–	–	17.48 ± 0.19	**17.30 ± 0.50**	19.64 ± 1.05
	Off. spk.	Off. spk.	**17.63 ± 0.22**	18.32 ± 0.39	20.13 ± 0.93
	Off. utt.	Off. utt.	**18.09 ± 0.29**	18.35 ± 0.37	20.70 ± 0.65
	Online	Off. spk.	**17.00 ± 0.28**	17.30 ± 0.38	19.38 ± 0.96
	Online	Off. utt.	**17.21 ± 0.20**	17.52 ± 0.47	19.44 ± 0.89
	Online	Online	**17.33 ± 0.37**	17.41 ± 0.44	19.29 ± 0.89
MFCC with CMN per speaker	–	–	17.00 ± 0.25	**16.91 ± 0.22**	18.23 ± 0.53
	Off. spk.	Off. spk.	**17.33 ± 0.21**	17.70 ± 0.39	19.44 ± 0.66
	Off. utt.	Off. utt.	**17.36 ± 0.21**	17.91 ± 0.35	19.43 ± 1.17
	Online	Off. spk.	**17.04 ± 0.16**	17.39 ± 0.27	19.03 ± 1.07
	Online	Off. utt.	**17.06 ± 0.20**	17.48 ± 0.29	18.93 ± 0.74
	Online	Online	**17.24 ± 0.31**	17.45 ± 0.27	18.89 ± 0.78
MFCC with CMN per utterance	–	–	17.54 ± 0.20	**17.50 ± 0.29**	19.26 ± 0.85
	Off. spk.	Off. spk.	**17.64 ± 0.33**	18.05 ± 0.27	19.08 ± 0.77
	Off. utt.	Off. utt.	**18.15 ± 0.35**	18.52 ± 0.33	21.04 ± 0.97
	Online	Off. spk.	**17.33 ± 0.18**	17.79 ± 0.31	20.10 ± 0.95
	Online	Off. utt.	**17.46 ± 0.19**	18.05 ± 0.24	19.63 ± 0.99
	Online	Online	**17.43 ± 0.19**	17.85 ± 0.18	20.01 ± 0.69

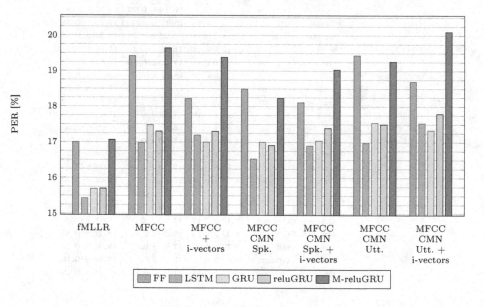

Fig. 3. Phone error rate [%] on features with best performing i-vector variants

5 Conclusion

In this paper, we have compared feed-forward and several recurrent network architectures on input data with fMLLR or i-vector adaptation techniques. The used recurrent networks were based on LSTM and GRU units. We have also evaluated two GRU modifications: reluGRU, with ReLU activation function, and M-reluGRU, with ReLU activation function and without the reset gate. As features, we have used MFCC processed by LDA without normalization or with CMN calculated either per speaker or per utterance, and also fMLLR adaptation. We have also augmented the features with several variants of i-vectors: online or offline calculated either per speaker or per utterance. Due to the stochastic nature of the used optimizers, we have performed all experiments 10 times in total and calculated the average phone error rate and its standard deviation.

For all networks, we have obtained the best results with fMLLR adaptation. The i-vector adaptation consistently improved the results only for FF networks. In the case of RNN, i-vectors did not lead to any significant improvement; it even gave worse results in all LSTM experiments and in some experiments with GRU variants. We have achieved the best results with LSTM network (PER 15.43% with fMLLR). GRU and reluGRU were slightly worse (both having PER 15.7% with fMLLR). M-reluGRU was in some cases even worse than FF network.

For all our experiments, we have used Chainer 3.2 DNN training framework with Python programming language and we have published our open-source scripts at https://github.com/OrcusCZ/NNAcousticModeling to easily replicate the results and to help continue the development.

Acknowledgement. This work was supported by the project no. P103/12/G084 of the Grant Agency of the Czech Republic and by the grant of the University of West Bohemia, project No. SGS-2016-039. Access to computing and storage facilities owned by parties and projects contributing to the National Grid Infrastructure MetaCentrum provided under the programme "Projects of Large Research, Development, and Innovations Infrastructures" (CESNET LM2015042), is greatly appreciated.

References

1. A flexible framework of neural networks for deep learning. https://chainer.org
2. Cho, K., Van Merriënboer, B., Bahdanau, D., Bengio, Y.: On the properties of neural machine translation: encoder-decoder approaches. arXiv preprint arXiv:1409.1259 (2014)
3. Chung, J., Gulcehre, C., Cho, K., Bengio, Y.: Empirical evaluation of gated recurrent neural networks on sequence modeling. arXiv preprint arXiv:1412.3555 (2014)
4. Gales, M.: Maximum likelihood linear transformations for HMM-based speech recognition. Comput. Speech Lang. **12**(2), 75–98 (1998)
5. Hochreiter, S., Schmidhuber, J.: Long short-term memory. Neural Comput. **9**(8), 1735–1780 (1997)
6. Huang, Z., Tang, J., Xue, S., Dai, L.: Speaker adaptation of RNN-BLSTM for speech recognition based on speaker code. In: ICASSP, vol. 1, pp. 5305–5309 (2016). https://doi.org/10.1109/ICASSP.2016.7472690

7. Karafiát, M., Burget, L., Matějka, P., Glembek, O., Černocký, J.: iVector-based discriminative adaptation for automatic speech recognition. In: Proceedings of 2011 IEEE Workshop on Automatic Speech Recognition and Understanding, ASRU 2011, pp. 152–157 (2011). https://doi.org/10.1109/ASRU.2011.6163922

8. Parthasarathi, S.H.K., Hoffmeister, B., Matsoukas, S., Mandal, A., Strom, N., Garimella, S.: fMLLR based feature-space speaker adaptation of DNN acoustic models. In: INTERSPEECH, pp. 3630–3634. ISCA (2015)

9. Peddinti, V., Povey, D., Khudanpur, S.: A time delay neural network architecture for efficient modeling of long temporal contexts. In: Proceedings of the Annual Conference of the International Speech Communication Association, INTERSPEECH January 2015, pp. 3214–3218 (2015)

10. Rath, S.P., Povey, D., Veselý, K., Černocký, J.: Improved feature processing for deep neural networks. In: INTERSPEECH, pp. 109–113. ISCA (2013)

11. Ravanelli, M., Brakel, P., Omologo, M., Bengio, Y., Kessler, F.B.: Improving speech recognition by revising gated recurrent units. In: INTERSPEECH 2017, pp. 1308–1312 (2017). https://doi.org/10.21437/Interspeech.2017-775

12. Sak, H., Senior, A., Beaufays, F.: Long short-term memory based recurrent neural network architectures for large vocabulary speech recognition. In: INTERSPEECH, vol. 1, pp. 338–342 (2014). arXiv:1402.1128

13. Saon, G., Soltau, H.: Unfolded Recurrent Neural Networks for Speech Recognition. In: INTERSPEECH, vol. 1, pp. 343–347 (2014). http://mazsola.iit.uni-miskolc.hu/~czap/letoltes/IS14/IS2014/PDF/AUTHOR/IS141054.PDF

14. Saon, G., Soltau, H., Nahamoo, D., Picheny, M.: Speaker adaptation of neural network acoustic models using i-vectors. In: 2013 IEEE Workshop on Automatic Speech Recognition and Understanding, pp. 55–59 (2013)

15. Seide, F., Chen, X., Yu, D.: Feature engineering in context-dependent deep neural networks for conversational speech transcription. In: ASRU (2011)

16. Waibel, A., Hanazawa, T., Hinton, G., Shikano, K., Lang, K.J.: Phoneme recognition using time-delay neural networks. IEEE Trans. Acoust. Speech Sig. Process. 37(3), 328–339 (1989). https://doi.org/10.1109/29.21701

17. Xue, S., Abdel-Hamid, O., Jiang, H., Dai, L., Liu, Q.: Fast adaptation of deep neural network based on discriminant codes for speech recognition. IEEE/ACM Trans. Speech Lang. Process. 22(12), 1713–1725 (2014). https://doi.org/10.1109/TASLP.2014.2346313

Restoring Punctuation and Capitalization Using Transformer Models

Andris Vāravs[✉] and Askars Salimbajevs

Tilde, Vienibas gatve 75A, Riga, Latvia
{andris.varavs,askars.salimbajevs}@tilde.lv

Abstract. Restoring punctuation and capitalization in the output of automatic speech recognition (ASR) system greatly improves readability and extends the number of downstream applications. We present a Transformer-based method for restoring punctuation and capitalization for Latvian and English, following the established approach of using neural machine translation (NMT) models. NMT methods here pose a challenge as the length of the predicted sequence does not always match the length of the input sequence. We offer two solutions to this problem: a simple target sequence cutting or padding by force and a more sophisticated attention alignment-based method. Our approach reaches new state of the art results for Latvian and competitive results on English.

Keywords: Speech recognition · Punctuation restoration
Capitalization restoration · Transformer

1 Introduction

The raw output of a generic automatic speech recognition (ASR) system typically consists of single-case word sequences, without any punctuation symbols. Adding punctuation and capitalization greatly improves the readability of automatic speech transcripts and can also help many of the natural language processing (NLP) and understanding (NLU) tools that can be applied downstream.

There have been many previous studies on automatic punctuation restoration in speech transcripts using data-driven methods. Language models (LM) and prosody based systems have been commonly used as baseline methods [13,22, 24], which are outperformed by using conditional random fields (CRFs) [21] and recurrent neural networks (RNN) [27]. Machine translation based models, which translate non-punctuated text into punctuated text [14,23], showed their effectiveness in spoken language translation evaluation campaigns [8–10]. While phrase-based machine translation (PBMT) can be used for this task, the best results [15] are achieved using neural machine translation (NMT) methods like those based on encoder-decoder architectures [3].

Capitalization recovery has also been explored with various methods for statistical machine translation [11,30], but it has received less attention for enriching transcribed speech [7,16]. Commonly used methods are similar to punctuation

© Springer Nature Switzerland AG 2018
T. Dutoit et al. (Eds.): SLSP 2018, LNAI 11171, pp. 91–102, 2018.
https://doi.org/10.1007/978-3-030-00810-9_9

restoration: n-gram language models [2,20] and maximum entropy models for sequence labeling [5,11]. While there have been attempts to integrate capitalization directly into the ASR language model [6], both punctuation and capitalization recovery is usually performed as post-processing.

In NMT, a new architecture called Transformer [29] has provided a strong alternative to RNNs and convolutional neural networks (CNNs) with a number of considerable advantages. Transformer models can process sequences in parallel during training, use fewer parameters for the same or better translation quality versus RNNs and CNNs, and also converge considerably faster [29], thus reducing the required time and hardware for obtaining a high quality model.

In this work, we propose to tackle the problems concerning both punctuation restoration for Latvian and English and capitalization restoration for Latvian by using the NMT approach, and basing our models on Transformer architecture. We first describe our modeling method for these problems in Sect. 2 and then outline experiment details in Sect. 3. Results and discussion follow in Sects. 4 and 5.

2   Method

In this section, we outline the modeling architecture we used and any adaptations we made for the task of punctuation or capitalization restoration.

2.1   Transformer Model

Our method closely follows the Transformer models in NMT [29], adapted for the purposes of punctuation restoration, capitalization, or both.

Transformer models eliminate the requirement for sequential processing during training that RNNs have without having the size of the network scale up with the length of the sequence to be processed (either in width or depth), a property that CNNs exhibit for sequence processing tasks [4].

Instead, Transformer uses a novel combination of position-wise fully connected feedforward networks (FFNs) and self-attention layers that allow the Transformer to process each position in the sequence differently, while sharing the same parameters across all positions. This allows Transformer to process sequences of arbitrary length using a constant number of parameters. Furthermore, typically the number of parameters required for Transformer to achieve the same or better quality is lower than RNN or CNN-based solutions for machine translation [12,29].

The overall architecture of the model follows that of the encoder-decoder architecture [3], where the encoder and decoder both consist of several Transformer specific self-attention and position wise feed-forward layers; however, the input and output word piece embeddings and a softmax function for predicting the next word piece remain unchanged from conventional NMT architectures.

2.2 Input and Output Vocabularies

The previous best model for punctuation restoration in Latvian [25] used word stems for creating a vocabulary 100,000 units large, which is more efficient than creating the vocabulary using full words. However, using word stems loses a considerable amount of morphological information, which might be important for a morphologically rich language like Latvian, while still retaining a rather large vocabulary for an NMT model. Instead, we choose to follow the by now standard practice in NMT of using word piece vocabularies [26] with a desired vocabulary size of 32,000 units for both Latvian and English.

We use a method similar to [15] for target vocabulary size reduction. Unlike NMT, the target sequence in both the punctuation and capitalization problems does not change word wise, it only alters the capitalization or inserts punctuation respectively. This information can be captured in the output sequence by treating this as a sequence labeling problem. The model must learn to output a target class for each word in the input sequence, where target class describes what should be done with the input at this position in the sequence to restore punctuation or capitalization. We call a position for a target label corresponding to a full word in the input a "word slot".

The number of classes differ from experiment to experiment. When the source dataset contains more punctuation symbols than we want the model to learn in a particular experiment, we use simple rule-based substitutions to reduce the number of punctuation classes, e.g., "!" and "?" might be mapped to a ".".

Another difference from the previous best model for Latvian is the interpretation of the word slot classes. Where [25] used classes to indicate punctuation that should be following after a word, we make the classes describe the punctuation symbols that should come before the given word. This was validated experimentally using the BLSTM model, see Table 1. Datasets in this table are described in Sect. 3.1.

Table 1. Predicting punctuation after and before a word slot for Latvian using BLSTM [25].

Test set	Word slot interpretation	Classes	Prec., %	Recall, %	F1, %
Webnews	After	Comma	82.7	67.5	74.3
		Period	74.6	64.2	69.0
		Average	78.7	65.8	71.7
	Before	Comma	82.9	67.8	74.6
		Period	77.8	66.2	71.6
		Average	80.3	67.0	73.0

While all the relevant classification metrics do go up for this new interpretation, it also presents two additional complications: (1) sentence boundaries are now tied to the beginning of the next sentence, as it is the first word of the next sentence that will have the closing symbol of the last sentence attached to it; (2) the closing symbol of the last sentence has nothing to be attached to, forcing us to add an end-of-segment marker during training.

To make sure the model does not learn to cheat by relying on end-of-segment markers for predicting sentence boundaries, we randomly concatenate sentences from training data into longer segments, forcing the model to learn that sentences can end at any point inside a segment. However, the end-of-segment marker still has to be appended at the end of a batch during inference, and given that we can not assume exact sentence boundaries, this end-of-segment most likely does not match an actual sentence boundary. But practically speaking, this does not matter because it is possible to batch the text to be evaluated by using predicted sentence boundaries between second-to-last and last potential sentence in a batch and then moving this last sentence, which might have been a partial sentence, to the next batch. This approach is basically the same as [27].

2.3 Mapping Word Pieces to Word Slots

A significant problem with using word pieces for our input vocabulary is that the target sequence no longer matches the input sequence in terms of length. There are two possible solutions here: (1) have the output sequence classify individual word pieces, thus making the sequence lengths match, or (2) rely on the seq2seq ability to generate sequences of different lengths for a given input sequence and have the model learn the mapping from input word pieces to target word slots.

The former solution is problematic because the model could assign different classes to different pieces of the same word, as outlined by [15]. The latter solution, however, can result in mismatch of sequence lengths, where a model mispredicts the number of word slots and breaks the alignment. But, given that doing predictions on a word piece level does not actually guarantee that the alignment will never be broken, we need some sort of a strategy for dealing with the cases with broken alignment anyway. This motivated us to choose the second option, and perform predictions on the whole word level.

There seem to be several potential solutions for dealing with broken alignment between input word pieces and target word slots.

The simplest option (1) is correcting sequence length by cutting or filling the sequence with likely, but hard-coded tokens until the sequence matches the target length. If the word slot alignment breaks somewhere in the middle of the sequence, this solution does nothing to repair such a case. It is, however, very simple to implement and fast to perform. We call this the "brute force" approach to sequence mismatch correction.

A more promising option (2) is to use wider beam search for decoding and to only consider those hypotheses that match the desired word slot number like [15]. However, there is no guarantee of such a hypothesis being produced even with a very large beam, which would also make decoding very slow. When none of the beam entries contain a hypothesis with the correct length, we still need some other method to correct the alignment mismatch.

Another solution (3) is to try to repair the alignment by analyzing the attention alignment matrices for a given sequence. Several post-processing techniques in NMT rely on the alignment between input and output sequences typically produced by the attention layer between encoder and decoder in conventional NMT systems following [3]. But this is more complicated in Transformer models due to the presence of multiple attention distributions for each Transformer layer, each of which learns to attend to something else.

Practically speaking, however, there is usually at least one attention head that still produces a seemingly reliable alignment between input and output, particularly in the final layers of the model. We checked manually for such a head and found it present in all our punctuation models. The attention alignment information can then be used to map any predicted word slots that have punctuation to the exact input word pieces, padding or cutting the word slots in between that have no punctuation attached to them. This approach has only the extra cost of producing the attention matrices after the best hypothesis has been obtained, but it should otherwise be faster than (2) and perhaps more robust, if the alignment turns out to be reliable.

We implemented (1) as a fast and simple baseline, and also implemented a version of (3) to test whether the alignments produced by any of the heads in Transformer models can be used to reliably repair alignment for seq2seq tasks like this.

3   Experiments

3.1   Datasets

We used three internal text corpora for experiments in Latvian and English monolingual data from Europarl corpus [18] for a point of comparison with [27].

All three Latvian corpora are created automatically by crawling Latvian internet resources. First corpus with the name "webnews" consists of 50 million sentences that were collected automatically from Latvian web news portals. The corpus consists of about 905 million tokens, i.e., words and punctuation symbols. Due to the automatic nature of web crawling, this corpus is noisy, with lots of spelling mistakes, incorrect grammar, and otherwise unusable text for our purposes, so we apply extensive filtering to this corpus. This dataset is the same as the one used in [25]. We also refer to that paper for detailed filtering steps, with the only notable differences being that we do not employ stemming for vocabulary size reduction and we do not replace punctuation symbols with their word forms, e.g., we do not replace "," with "comma".

Additionally, we use a 1.3 million sentence "SaeimaHalf" and a 2.1 million sentence "SaeimaFull" corpora, where SaeimaHalf is a subset of SaeimaFull. Both were created from the public transcripts of Latvian Parliament (Saeima) sessions. The total number of words in both corpora is 34M. Even though these corpora are also collected automatically, their quality is much higher than webnews, so filtering leaves proportionally more data for experiments.

The total size of English data is approximately 2.2M sentences and 54M words. We adapted the data preparation script for Europarl from [27] so that we have a point of comparison for English.

After processing, development and evaluation held-out sets are created. The sizes of the respective training, development and test sets as well as the impact of filtering for each corpora can be found in Table 2.

Table 2. Datasets used

Language	Name	Raw/filtered, sentences	Train/dev/test, sentences
Latvian	Webnews	50M/40.5M	40.4M/50K/50K
	SaeimaHalf	1.3M/1M	1M/5K/10K
	SaeimaFull	2.1M/2.1M	2M/25K/25K
English	Europarl_en [18]	2.2M/2M	1.6M/200K/200K

3.2 Experiment Details

All Transformer models are implemented in Tensorflow [1], based on reference implementations in Tensor2Tensor [28]. All of the models are trained on a single nVidia GTX 1080 Ti GPU, using a batch size of 8192, and the "transformer_small" hyerparameter set from Tensor2Tensor. This corresponds to only 2 layers in encoder and 2 layers in decoder, 4 attention heads per layer, a hidden and vocabulary embedding size of 256, and an FFN size of 1024. Dropout and label smoothing is applied for regularization, following the Transformer defaults in Tensor2tensor. All models use an input vocabulary of roughly 32,000 word pieces. Adam [17] optimizer was used for all experiments.

For punctuation, we have trained a total of 3 Transformer models for Latvian datasets, and a single model for the English Europarl dataset. To identify the Latvian models, we use their training dataset name and the number of punctuation classes modeled for their naming. The models are: "T_webnews_3", "T_saeima_3", and "T_saeima_5" for Latvian and "T_europarl_en_8" for English. All of the Latvian models have been trained for 1M iterations, while the English one was trained for 0.5M steps. Since these models are concerned only with predicting with punctuation, we preprocess the data by removing all capitalization, and then we create a separate file with filtered inputs without any punctuation and a file with target labels describing the now lost punctuation.

We train a single dedicated model for capitalization using the same hyperparameter set as for punctuation, just with a different list of classes for output, indicating that word slot contains a word to be left alone or capitalized. The model is called "T_saeima_capitalization", as it is trained on the SaeimaFull dataset. The main reason for training a separate capitalization model on the more narrow domain SaeimaFull dataset, and not the larger webnews, is the specifics of the domain: the model needs to learn to non-trivial patterns for commission names, ministries, and laws. Extra preprocessing is used for this model: all punctuation is removed from the training data, while capitalization is left intact. To have a point of comparison for this scenario, we also train the recaser tool from Moses toolkit [19].

We also train a single combined model for Latvian that performs restoration of both punctuation and capitalization at the same time. This model follows the same hyperparameters as the rest, and is trained for 1M steps, like other Latvian models. We use combined labels for predictions, where each word slot predicts both the punctuation mark to be used and whether or not the word at this word slot should be capitalized. This model is called "T_webnews_comb_3", and is evaluated on punctuation and capitalization tasks separately.

All the models we have trained and points of comparison from literature are summarized in Table 3.

Table 3. Models used in experiments

Name	Train set	Punctuation classes	Capitalization	Train steps
BLSTM [25]	Webnews	word, comma, period	No	-
T_webnews_3			No	1M
T_webnews_comb_3			Yes	1M
T_saeima_3	SaeimaHalf	word, comma, period	No	1M
T_saeima_5	SaeimaHalf	word, comma, period, question mark, dash	No	1M
Punctuator2 [27]	Europarl_en	word, comma, period, quest. m., dash, excl. m., colon, semicolon	No	1.5M
T_europarl_8				1M
Moses recaser	SaeimaFull	-	Yes	-
T_saeima_cap				1M

4   Results and Discussion

We have summarized all of the punctuation results in Table 4, grouped together by the respective test set. We have also added BLSTM results from [25] as baseline, where available for Latvian. We use [27] as baseline for English Europarl results[1]. For capitalization we use the recaser tool from Moses toolkit [19] as a strong baseline. All the numbers presented here have been computed after applying the sequence length fix hack outlined in Sect. 2.3. We also try out sequence alignment repair from attention alignments on webnews test data for comparison.

---

[1] Europarl results were not in print version of the paper, but they can be found at https://github.com/ottokart/punctuator2

We can see the basic improvement Transformer models obtain over our BLSTM baseline model for Latvian on webnews test set. Of particular note is the considerable increase in recall performance of these models, while precision is boosted to a lesser degree. Models have also learned well how word pieces in the input map to word slots in the output. T_webnews_3 exhibits sequence length mismatch in only 1.8% cases, while T_saeima_3 in only 3.7%. However, the amount of sequence length mismatch increases significantly if we try to apply a model trained on a more narrow domain to a test set from a wider domain, as evidenced by the behavior of T_saeima_3 on the webnews dataset.

Interestingly enough, the combined punctuation and capitalization model T_webnews_comb_3 shows both better precision and recall for all punctuation classes and a very low mismatch amount. This demonstrates that the ability of the model to perform well on punctuation restoration task does not suffer, when paired together with another task. We evaluate the capitalization ability separately in Table 5.

We carry out our attempts to repair the sentences with broken alignments between inputs and predictions using the T_webnews_3 model. This procedure produces some improvements for long sequences, however, as reflected in the results for webnews dataset, the macro average F1 is actually the exact same as for the brute force approach. In particular, the precision and recall seems to be better for commas, but worse for periods.

Looking at individual examples, we can find both examples where the repair from attention has salvaged a broken alignment and examples, where the alignment was correct, but trying to re-align the outputs with inputs using the attention breaks it by shifting the predictions a token to the left or right side of the truth. We also tried out using attention values from other heads, but all of them produced substantially worse results. For our purposes repairing alignment from attention is, thus, not reliable enough to be used over the brute force approach, which is simpler and faster.

On the SaeimaHalf dataset, we perform experiments with more than 3 punctuation classes, training both a 3 (word, period, comma) and a 5 class (word, comma, period, question mark, and dash) model on it. Furthermore, we tried applying a more general domain model to the Saeima test set, which presents a more narrow domain, and observe good, but worse results than a domain-specific model.

In the case of English and the Punctuator2 model from [27], the advantage of Transformer models becomes less pronounced. We still observe a noticeable increase in recall performance across all punctuation classes; however, for the less common punctuation classes, precision is worse than Punctuator2. Overall, the macro average F1 score is slightly better for Transformer, but the improvement is marginal. It is possible the model could do better with more training time, as this model was only trained for 500,000 steps instead of the 1,000,000 for other models.

In Table 5, our Transformer capitalization model demonstrates a small but considerable improvement over the Moses recaser tool for the Latvian Saeima

Table 4. Results on the punctuation restoration task.

Test set	Model	Mismatch, %	Classes	Prec., %	Recall, %	F1, %
Webnews	BLSTM [25]	-	Comma	82.8	70.0	75.9
			Period	77.8	69.5	73.4
			Average	80.3	69.8	74.7
	T_webnews_3	1.8	Comma	84.5	83.3	83.9
			Period	83.3	86.3	84.7
			Average	84.0	84.8	84.4
	T_webnews_3 with alignment repair	0.0	Comma	84.7	83.5	84.1
			Period	83.2	86.1	84.6
			Average	84.0	84.8	84.4
	T_saeima_3	12.4	Comma	60.4	63.9	62.1
			Period	62.3	63.6	63.0
			Average	61.4	63.8	62.6
	T_webnews_comb_3	0.3	Comma	85.7	83.8	84.7
			Period	84.1	87.6	85.8
			Average	84.9	85.7	85.3
SaeimaHalf	T_saeima_5	1.0	Comma	91.3	92.1	91.7
			Period	88.8	88.2	88.5
			Quest.m.	77.5	73.6	75.5
			Dash	77.7	66.7	71.8
			Average	83.8	80.2	82.0
	T_saeima_3	0.8	Comma	91.8	90.9	91.4
			Period	89.4	89.4	89.4
			Average	90.6	90.2	90.4
	T_webnews_3	4.7	Comma	84.6	80.5	82.5
			Period	84.2	74.0	78.7
			Average	84.4	77.3	80.7
Europarl_en	Punctuator2 [27]	-	Comma	68.9	72.0	70.4
			Period	84.7	84.1	84.4
			Quest.m.	77.7	73.2	75.4
			Dash	55.9	8.8	15.2
			Excl.m.	50.0	0.1	0.1
			Colon	60.9	23.8	34.2
			Semicolon	44.7	1.1	2.2
			Average	63.3	37.6	47.2
	T_europarl_en_8	1.3	Comma	67.1	73.6	70.2
			Period	89.3	90.0	89.7
			Quest.m.	77.9	81.8	79.8
			Dash	38.8	11.7	18.0
			Excl.m.	25.8	1.6	3.0
			Colon	47.0	34.1	39.5
			Semicolon	25.9	11.0	15.4
			Average	53.1	43.4	47.8

dataset. This model still suffers from mismatch between input and output sequence lengths, but to a much lesser degree than punctuation models: the actual mismatch amount is just 0.27%.

We also try out our combined model for both punctuation and capitalization T_webnews_comb_3 on both webnews and Saeima datasets. It shows good results on webnews test set, as expected, but the performance does noticeably degrade on the more narrow and specialized domain Saeima test set. Domain sensitivity is even more pronounced, when we try to truecase webnews test set using the model trained on Saeima: performance degrades massively, as the model is unable to cope with a more general domain, showing an F1 score of only 35.5 versus an F1 score of 74.1, displayed by a model that was trained on webnews, but evaluated on Saeima test set.

Table 5. Capitalization results on Latvian Saeima and webnews datasets.

Model	Test set	Prec., %	Recall, %	F1, %
T_saeima_capitalization	SaeimaFull	99.1	98.7	98.9
Moses recaser	SaeimaFull	97.2	97.5	97.3
T_webnews_comb_3	SaeimaFull	89.9	63.1	74.1
T_webnews_comb_3	webnews	94.9	91.2	93.0
T_saeima_capitalization	webnews	37.5	33.7	35.5

5   Conclusions

In this paper, we have presented a method for punctuation restoration and capitalization restoration tasks using the novel Transformer models. These models are fast and show strong results on both tasks, but they do exhibit considerable domain sensitivity both in terms of classification metrics and in terms of decoded sequence length mismatch.

The problem of sequence length mismatch remains without a complete solution. In our experiments we found the brute force sequence cutting or padding approach to provide good results most of the time, when the test domain is close to train domain. Our attempts to improve the alignment in mismatched cases using Transformer attention heads did not yield the expected improvements, as there was no overall improvement, compared to the brute force approach.

We achieve new state of the art results on our internal datasets for Latvian, improving the average F1 score from 74.7 to 85.3 on webnews corpus, and establish strong baselines for SaeimaHalf dataset, where our 3 class model achieves an average F1 score of 90.4, but a more complex 5 class model reaches an average F1 of 82.0. Our combined capitalization and punctuation model also displays good results for capitalization on the test set from its domain, showing an F1 score of 93.0 on webnews, but a more modest 74.1 on the more narrow domain SaeimaHalf test set.

Acknowledgements. The research has been supported by the European Regional Development Fund within the project "Neural Network Modelling for Inflected Natural Languages" No. 1.1.1.1/16/A/215.

References

1. Abadi, M., et al.: Tensorflow: a system for large-scale machine learning. In: OSDI, vol. 16, pp. 265–283 (2016)
2. Agbago, A., Foster, G.: Truecasing for the portage system. In. Recent Advances in Natural Language Processing (2005)
3. Bahdanau, D., Cho, K., Bengio, Y.: Neural machine translation by jointly learning to align and translate. arXiv preprint arXiv:1409.0473 (2014)
4. Bai, S., Kolter, J.Z., Koltun, V.: An empirical evaluation of generic convolutional and recurrent networks for sequence modeling. arXiv preprint arXiv:1803.01271 (2018)
5. Batista, F., Moniz, H., Trancoso, I., Mamede, N.: Bilingual experiments on automatic recovery of capitalization and punctuation of automatic speech transcripts. IEEE Trans. Audio Speech Lang. Process. **20**(2), 474–485 (2012)
6. Beaufays, F., Strope, B.: Language model capitalization. In: 2013 IEEE International Conference on Acoustics, Speech and Signal Processing (ICASSP), pp. 6749–6752. IEEE (2013)
7. Brown, E.W., Coden, A.R.: Capitalization recovery for text. In: Coden, A.R., Brown, E.W., Srinivasan, S. (eds.) IRTSA 2001. LNCS, vol. 2273, pp. 11–22. Springer, Heidelberg (2002). https://doi.org/10.1007/3-540-45637-6_2
8. Cettolo, M., Niehues, J., Stüker, S., Bentivogli, L., Federico, M.: Report on the 10th IWSLT evaluation campaign. In: Proceedings of the International Workshop on Spoken Language Translation, Heidelberg, Germany (2013)
9. Cettolo, M., Niehues, J., Stüker, S., Bentivogli, L., Federico, M.: Report on the 11th IWSLT evaluation campaign, IWSLT 2014. In: Proceedings of the International Workshop on Spoken Language Translation, Hanoi, Vietnam (2014)
10. Cettolo, M., Niehues, J., Stüker, S., Bentivogli, L., Federico, M.: Report on the 12th IWSLT evaluation campaign, IWSLT 2015. In: Proceedings of the International Workshop on Spoken Language Translation, Da Nang, Vietnam (2015)
11. Chelba, C., Acero, A.: Adaptation of maximum entropy capitalizer: little data can help a lot. Comput. Speech Lang. **20**(4), 382–399 (2006)
12. Chen, M.X., et al.: The best of both worlds: combining recent advances in neural machine translation. arXiv preprint arXiv:1804.09849 (2018)
13. Cho, E., et al.: A real-world system for simultaneous translation of German lectures. In: INTERSPEECH, pp. 3473–3477 (2013)
14. Cho, E., Niehues, J., Waibel, A.: Segmentation and punctuation prediction in speech language translation using a monolingual translation system. In: International Workshop on Spoken Language Translation (IWSLT) 2012 (2012)
15. Cho, E., Niehues, J., Waibel, A.: NMT-based segmentation and punctuation insertion for real-time spoken language translation. In: Proc. Interspeech 2017. pp. 2645–2649 (2017), https://doi.org/10.21437/Interspeech.2017-1320
16. Gravano, A., Jansche, M., Bacchiani, M.: Restoring punctuation and capitalization in transcribed speech. In: IEEE International Conference on Acoustics, Speech and Signal Processing, ICASSP 2009, pp. 4741–4744. IEEE (2009)
17. Kingma, D.P., Ba, J.: Adam: a method for stochastic optimization. arXiv preprint arXiv:1412.6980 (2014)
18. Koehn, P.: Europarl: a parallel corpus for statistical machine translation. In: MT Summit, vol. 5, pp. 79–86 (2005)

19. Koehn, P., et al.: Moses: open source toolkit for statistical machine translation. In: Proceedings of the 45th Annual Meeting of the ACL on Interactive Poster and Demonstration Sessions, pp. 177–180. Association for Computational Linguistics (2007)

20. Lita, L.V., Ittycheriah, A., Roukos, S., Kambhatla, N.: tRuEcasing. In: Proceedings of the 41st Annual Meeting on Association for Computational Linguistics, ACL 2003, vol. 1. pp. 152–159. Association for Computational Linguistics, Stroudsburg (2003). https://doi.org/10.3115/1075096.1075116

21. Lu, W., Ng, H.T.: Better punctuation prediction with dynamic conditional random fields. In: Proceedings of the 2010 Conference on Empirical Methods in Natural Language Processing, pp. 177–186. Association for Computational Linguistics (2010)

22. Ostendorf, M., et al.: Speech segmentation and spoken document processing. IEEE Sig. Process. Mag. **25**(3), 59–69 (2008)

23. Peitz, S., Freitag, M., Mauser, A., Ney, H.: Modeling punctuation prediction as machine translation. In: International Workshop on Spoken Language Translation (IWSLT) 2011 (2011)

24. Rao, S., Lane, I., Schultz, T.: Optimizing sentence segmentation for spoken language translation. In: Eighth Annual Conference of the International Speech Communication Association (2007)

25. Salimbajevs, A.: Bidirectional LSTM for automatic punctuation restoration. In: Human Language Technologies-The Baltic Perspective: Proceedings of the Seventh International Conference Baltic HLT 2016, vol. 289, p. 59. IOS Press (2016)

26. Sennrich, R., Haddow, B., Birch, A.: Neural machine translation of rare words with subword units. arXiv preprint arXiv:1508.07909 (2015)

27. Tilk, O., Alumäe, T.: Bidirectional recurrent neural network with attention mechanism for punctuation restoration. In: Interspeech, pp. 3047–3051 (2016)

28. Vaswani, A., et al.: Tensor2tensor for neural machine translation. CoRR abs/1803.07416 (2018), http://arxiv.org/abs/1803.07416

29. Vaswani, A., et al.: Attention is all you need. In: Advances in Neural Information Processing Systems, pp. 6000–6010 (2017)

30. Wang, W., Knight, K., Marcu, D.: Capitalizing machine translation. In: Proceedings of the Main Conference on Human Language Technology Conference of the North American Chapter of the Association of Computational Linguistics, pp. 1–8. Association for Computational Linguistics (2006)

Natural Language Processing and Understanding

Arabic Name Entity Recognition Using Deep Learning

David Awad[(✉)], Caroline Sabty[(✉)], Mohamed Elmahdy[(✉)],
and Slim Abdennadher[(✉)]

Computer Science and Engineering Department, German University in Cairo,
New Cairo, Egypt
david.awad@student.guc.edu.eg,
{caroline.samy,mohamed.elmahdy,slim.abdennadher}@guc.edu.eg

Abstract. Many applications that we use on a daily basis incorporate
Natural Language Processing (NLP), from simple tasks such as automatic text correction to speech recognition. A lot of research has been
done on NLP for the English language but not much attention was given
to the NLP of the Arabic language. The purpose of this work is to implement a tagging model for Arabic Name Entity Recognition which is an
important information extraction task in NLP. It serves as a building
block for more advanced tasks. We developed a deep learning model
that consists of Bidirectional Long Short Term Memory and Conditional
Random Field with the addition of different network layers such as Word
Embedding, Convolutional Neural Network, and Character Embedding.
Hyperparameters have been tuned to maximize the F1-score.

Keywords: Natural Language Processing · Name Entity Recognition
Deep Learning · Arabic · Bidirectional Long Short Term Memory
Word Embedding · Convolutional Neural Network

1 Introduction

Nowadays, Natural Language Processing (NLP) is extensively discussed and
researched. It has been used in large fields like machine translation, speech recognition, and text processing. NLP has brought a serious development in the field
of computation and Artificial Intelligence [10]. It focuses on transforming human
language into an acceptable presentation for computers to understand. Recently,
applications involve information extraction, machine translation, summarization,
search, and human-computer interface. To reach the goal of fully semantic understanding, researchers used divide and conquer approach and established a few
subtasks functional for application development and analysis [6]. These vary
from the syntactic, such as part-of-speech tagging, chunking, and parsing, to
the semantic, such as word sense disambiguation, semantic-role labeling, named
entity extraction and anaphora resolution.

© Springer Nature Switzerland AG 2018
T. Dutoit et al. (Eds.): SLSP 2018, LNAI 11171, pp. 105–116, 2018.
https://doi.org/10.1007/978-3-030-00810-9_10

Name Entity Recognition (NER) systems were found to be extremely significant for various tasks in NLP as Information Retrieval and Question Answering tasks. NER manages to identifying proper name entities such as person, location, organization, and miscellaneous. Several methods have been implemented for NER that depends on manual features and pays attention to improve feature selection and engineering [19].

Arabic is a language spoken by around 420 million people, making it one of the most spoken languages in the world. Arabic is the official language in 24 countries dominantly lying in the middle east and north Africa [18]. The rapid increase in globalization, languages are becoming a key part in technology due to the wide variety of applications and tools for translation, speech recognition, question answering and information retrieval. Research in Arabic language processing should be of an importance to keep up with recent technology because of the increase in Arabic language presence in the technology and social media scene.

What makes English NER easier than Arabic NER is that most of the names begin with capital letters which is not an option in Arabic. In addition, Arabic nature as is a morphologically complex language due to its extremely inflectional, it has a general form of a word: Prefix (es) + Stem + Suffix (es) and the number of prefixes and suffixes could be 0 or more. Another problem is that a letter in the Arabic language could have up to three various forms according to its position in the word [1, 2].

One of the major problems that faces NER, in general, is the lack of labeled data. To perform a task like NER, a large corpus specifically labeled data is needed. Another problem is the building of complex hand-designed features which come from various linguistic analysis [17]. The use of the deep neural network like the Recurrent Neural Network (RNN) approach is well known for its efficiency for sequential inputs like speech and languages. Moreover, RNN enables the model to process variable length input.

The main aim of this work is to implement a tagger for Arabic Name Entity Recognition using a Recurrent Neural Network (RNN) model. Since it is a new promising approach and there is only one tagger for the Arabic language in Neural Networks (NN).

In this work, several RNN layers have been investigated, to reach the final model with the best performance. The final model uses the combination of character- and word-level representations as input to Bidirectional Long Short Term Memory (BLSTM) in order to model contextual information. The word embedding are passed into a CNN layer before being fed into the BLSTM. After the BLSTM layer, a sequential CRF was used to cooperatively decode labels for the whole sentence. This model requires no feature engineering, task-specific resources or data pre-processing beyond character embedding and pre-trained word embedding.

Our model has been evaluated on combining two datasets ANERCorp which is a Corpus of more than 150,000 words annotated for the NER task [2] and AQMAR Arabic Wikipedia Named Entity Corpus and Tagger that is a 74,000-

token corpus of 28 Arabic Wikipedia articles hand-annotated for named entities [15]. Finally, our model has obtained 76.65% F1 score for ANER.

2   Related Work

Deep Learning has shown good performance in Name Entity Recognition (NER) field for English language but there is not much research done for Arabic Name Entity recognition (ANER).

A Name Entity Recognition System for English based on Recurrent Neural Network was proposed in [9]. It proposed several models for sequence tagging and the model that produced accurate tagging performance without resorting to word embedding was BLSTM-CRF. The advantage of using BLSTM is the efficiency in using the previous and the future input features. CRF added to the model the use of sentence-level tag information. They scored 90.10% F1 using Senna embedding and Gazetteer features.

In [11] they tackle the problem of developing resources and features for new languages and domains. They obtain an NER performance using LSTM-CRF model for different languages other than English without gazetteers or hand-engineered features. Their Model does not need any language-specific resources or features. They also used character-based word representation model to capture orthographic sensitivity. The model got 90.94% F1 score for LSTM-CRF added to it pre-trained word embedding, dropout rate and character-based modeling of words.

Another NER model developed in [4] is hybrid bidirectional LSTM and CNN architecture. Its advantages are to detect word and character features and no need to use most feature engineering. For modeling character-level information they used CNN. A special bidirectional recursive neural network connected to a convolutional network was explored in [12]. This approach is to divide each sentence into chunks of meaningful sentences holed by nodes then BRNN-CNN model categorizes each node by these hidden features and evaluates hidden state features of every node. They got 90.91% F1 for BLSTM-CNN added to it Word Embedding only and 91.55% F1 score with lexicon features and capitalization feature, which is a feature not applicable for the Arabic language because there are no capital words in Arabic to define name entities. They also Scored 91.62% F1 BLSTM-CNN + lex and added to it word embedding.

[14] introduced an updated model BI-LSTM-CRF, they added to it a CNN to benefit from its capability to convert character-level data of a word into its character-level presentation. After that, they combined word and character level representation to be the input to BI-directional LSTM and like in [9] a CRF layer was connected on top of BI-LSTM to decode labels for the entire sentence. They also obtained 91.21% F1 Score for NER. One of the advantages of their model is applying data from several domains to the model easily because it doesn't require data from a specific domain or task-specific knowledge.

All the previous stated work mainly tackle the English language. One of the most effective learner for Arabic Name Entity Recognition task is implemented using CRF. This was proposed in [1]. Due to the small size corpora and selected features for the Arabic language, a model may lose identification of some name entities. Their solution was using CRF which is one of the machine learning techniques. Their CRF Model results of this are 72.16%, 79.20% and 67.18% for Person, Location and Organization classes.

[8] used deep learning for Arabic NER. It takes advantage of both character- and word-level representations by applying them to an integration between BLSTM and CRF, as well as not requiring most feature engineering. Not only did this paper uses unannotated corpora dataset but its model also depends on unsupervised word representations learned from this corpora. They obtained 85.71% F1 Score for Arabic NER in social media. One of the differences between this paper and our work is the datasets. NER is usually easier especially in social media like Twitter as most of the Named Entities are preceded with hashtags. The dataset used in this paper is an unsupervised dataset and it was collected from Twitter. In addition, this paper did not add the CNN layer, which was observed in our work to boost performance.

3   Dataset Pre-processing

The dataset used for training and testing is the ANERCorp and AQMAR. ANERCorp is a Corpus of more than 150,000 words annotated for the NER task [2] and AQMAR Arabic Wikipedia Named Entity Corpus and Tagger is a 74,000-token corpus of 28 Arabic Wikipedia articles hand-annotated for named entities [15]. Both datasets were added together to get more than 200K words. Since tags across the two corpora do not follow the same labeling guideline, they have been normalized. The different tags in the data are PER, LOC, ORG and MISC. For each type of tag there are two different forms one for indicating the beginning of a name entity and the other for indicating the inside of a named entity. The whole dataset was divided into chunks of 150 words. The vocabulary was created using all distinct words. For tags, we used One Hot Encoder because every tag needs to have a different vector from each other. Otherwise, the model might get confused when predicting the tag of a word.

A word2Vec Arabic model, which contains 600k vocabulary and 100 dimensions has been used for word embedding. Out-of-Vocabulary words have been assigned embedding vector of zeros. The main usage of character embedding is to give another representation for words. This should help our model to learn the word embedding OOV rather than ignoring them. So the words are represented by an array of characters and these characters represented by one hot encoder. The model also takes a second input sequence of words in the form of character embedding. Finally, after granting a format for words, characters and tags, we need to use these forms to represent three different sequences to be trained and tested.

4   Model Architecture

Our model had several layers that we could modify to understand their impact on the overall performance. The first layers that come after the input layer are the Word Embedding and Character Embedding. After computing their outputs, these outputs are concatenated together to get the best result. Then two Convolutional Neural Network layers were added on top of the word embedding before concatenation of word embedding with character embedding. Now the main layers of our models come, they are the BLSTM then the CRF layers. They are mainly responsible for training the model on the input sequence and connecting the tags of a sequence together as shown in Fig. 1.

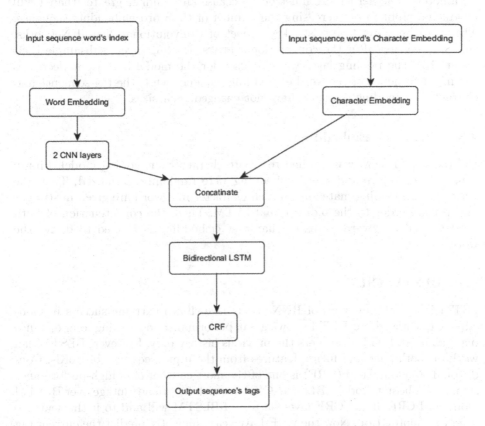

Fig. 1. Proposed Arabic NER Deep Learning Model

4.1   Word Embedding

In the first stage of BLSTM-CRF model was using index encoding for word sequences but the performance of the model was not high compared to most models that used Word2Vec. Thus, Word2Vec was fed to BLSTM-CRF. The advantage to our model from using Word2Vec is capturing the characteristics of the neighbors of a word and similarities between words.

4.2   Convolutional Neural Network

A multiple of convolutional layers with nonlinear activation function form a Convolutional Neural Network (CNN). It is used to directly manipulate the output layer. It could apply different filters and then add their results. In our model we used 2 layers of CNN after pre-trained word embedding to improve accuracy. Each with filter equal to 800 which is the best filter count after tuning the hyperparameters. The kernel size must be 1 because any number greater than 1 will produce a problem of decreasing the number of the word embedding sequence. The use of pooling layers is a key aspect of Convolutional Neural Networks, typically defined after the convolutional layers. Pooling layers subsample their input [13]. The pooling layer was not used for the model because it decreases the input sequence of the word embedding sequence while the tag sequence and character embedding sequence have not changed their sizes.

4.3   Character Embedding

Bidirectional LSTM was applied to create character embedding model. Firstly a list of characters and their embedding were randomly initialized. Then the character embedding matching to each character in a word are given in straight and reverse order to the bidirectional LSTM. Then, the concatenation of both forward and backward forms of character embedding is formed to derive the word.

4.4   BLSTM-CRF

LSTM is one of the types of RNNs that have shown extreme success in modeling sequential data. LSTM shows great performance in learning long-distance dependencies. LSTM considers the previous history only. However, BLSTM can work on both past and future features from the input sequence of words. Conditional Random Field (CRF) is one of the most conventional high-performance sequence labeling models. BLSTM-CRF network has an advantage over BLSTM alone and CRF alone. CRF layer on top of BLSTM will add to it the sentence level tag information. Now the CRF Layer can efficiently predict the current tag from past and future tag which is equal to the BLSTM past and future input features. These extra features can boost tagging accuracy [9].

4.5   Model Hyper-parameters

One of the most important properties that affect the learning of Artificial Neural Network (ANN) is the activation function which calculates the output from the summation of the weighted input signals of the neural network. It also maps the result between 0 to 1 or −1 to 1 depending on the function. The main reason for using it is transforming the input signal of a node in an ANN to an output signal. It is applied to the summation of the product of input nodes and their weights. A Neural Network unaccompanied by Activation function would directly be a Linear regression Model, which will not fulfill learning complicated functional mappings from data [3]. The activation function that was used by our model was softplus. Softplus showed the best performance after tuning the activation function for BLSTM layer and Tanh for the 2 CNN layers.

Another function that affects the training of deep learning models is Optimization function. Optimization function used to minimize the output of error function. It depends on the internal learn-able parameters of a model that are applied to the input to compute the predicted output. The internal parameters of a model have a tremendously important job in effectively and efficiently training the model and process accurate outcomes. Thus, several optimization functions were tried to improve the output [3]. Nadam is the optimization function that was used in our model and it outperformed other optimization functions.

Deep neural networks have various non-linear hidden layers, which make the model exceedingly expressive model to be able to learn very complicated relationships between the outputs and the inputs. Some of the complicated relationships will be the outcome of sampling noise due to the limited training data. The dropout rate is used to tackle the problem of overfitting, which is due to the noise found in the training dataset but not in the test dataset [16]. The dropout used in the model 0.2 it reduced over fitting slightly and improved the F1 score.

5   Evaluation and Results

The dataset has been divided into training, validation, and testing of 72%, 8%, and 10%. In this section, the different evaluations and results will be discussed. The sections start by introducing the different stages or layers of the model. Afterward, it presents the process of tuning the Hyper-parameters.

5.1   Model Results

We will discuss the output results of each stage until it reaches the final stage as shown in Table 1. The first model consisted of BLSTM and CRF. The input of the model was sequences of words with word represented by an index. The result of the precision is 86.07% and recall equal to 34.5%. Due to the very low recall percentage, the F1 score was the lowest, which is equal to 50.17%. The accuracy of the model is 91.93% which is the lowest accuracy we got too.

After we added the Word2Vec, as it boosts deep learning models. Our model experienced remarkable improvement after adding the word2vec layer. We used the word2vec on LSTM layer first then we tried on BLSTM to show the difference between LSTM and Bidirectional LSTM. Word2vec on LSTM and CRF has precision equal to 76.2% and recall equal to 65.1%, then F1 score equal to 70.2%

and accuracy equal to 96.26%. The precision of the model using BLSTM is 86.78%, recall is 62.47% and an F1 score is equal to 72.65%. The model accuracy has increased by 0.32%. Thus, BLSTM is better than regular LSTM. Two CNN layers with 800 Filters joined our model. The new precision is equal to 80.5%, recall is 68% and the F1 score is 73.7%.

Our final model had a character embedding concatenated to its word embedding to solve the problem of OOV and enable our model to enhance prediction. The final results of the precision reached 84.15%, recall reached 68.74% and the F1 score is 75.68%. The accuracy is the highest accuracy compared to our previous models, its accuracy is equal to 95.71%.

Table 1. Results of different models

Models	Precision	Recall	F1 score	Validation accuracy	Testing accuracy
BLSTM-CRF	86.07	34.50	50.17	91.93	94.33
LSTM-CRF-WE	76.20	65.10	70.20	95.26	97.28
BLSTM-CRF-WE	86.78	62.47	72.65	95.58	98.85
BLSTM-CRF-WE-CNN	80.50	68.00	73.70	95.54	98.17
BLSTM-CRF-WE-CNN-CE	84.15	68.74	75.68	95.71	98.06

5.2   Tuning Hyper-parameters

The tuned parameters are the optimizer, activation function, epoch number and batch size. These Parameters affect the performance of the model as explained below.

Epoch. Epoch is a random cutoff, usually defined as "one pass over the whole dataset", used to separate training into different phases, which is useful for logging and periodic assessment [5]. The epoch of our model was tuned between 5, 10 and 50. The best results came from 10 epochs as shown in Table 2.

Batch Size. Batch size is the number of sentences that will be propagated through the networks. The training dataset, which is 1252 sequences, will be divided by the number of batch size. Small batch sizes are attractive since they are able to make convergence in fewer epochs. However, large batch sizes provide more data-parallelism which successively enhance computational efficiency and scalability [7]. Table 3 show the best batch sizes according to our experiment which are 10 and 32.

Table 2. F1-score versus number of epochs

Number of epochs	F1 score
5	72.15
10	75.86
15	73.84
20	74.84
25	74.21
30	73.97
35	74.97
40	74.13
45	74.17
50	74.24

Table 3. F1-score versus batch sizes

Batch size	F1 score
10	76.05
20	73.64
32	75.15
40	74.81
60	74.39
80	74.62
100	73.25

Activation Function. Activation functions are used to establish nonlinearity to models, which allows deep learning models to learn nonlinear prediction. There are multiple activation functions that have been experimented with in our model to find the best match for the model. These activation functions are Softmax, Softplus, Softsign, Relu, Tanh, Sigmoid, Hard-Sigmoid and Linear. The model has 2 different layers CNN and BLSTM, each one of them needs an activation function. For CNN the activation function that could improve the F1-score is Tanh and for BLSTM are Linear, Softplus, Tanh and Sigmoid as shown in Table 4.

Optimization Function. To minimize the output of the error function, the optimization function has been tuned, to get the best optimization function for our model. The different optimization functions that were tried out are RMSprop, Adagrad, Adadelta, Adam, Adamax, and Nadam. As shown in Table 5 Nadam was the best optimizer found in Keras and it has improved the F1-score of the model.

Table 4. F1-score for different activation functions applied on CNN and BLSTM

Activation functions	CNN F1	BLSTM F1
Softmax	43.4	19.6
Softplus	72.2	75.3
Softsign	74.7	74.7
Relu	72.8	71.8
Tanh	76.7	75.3
Sigmoid	68.2	75.2
Hard-Sigmoid	74.6	66.4
Linear	69.8	75.6

Table 5. F1-score for different activation functions applied on CNN and BLSTM

Optimization function	F1 score
RMSProp	71.41
Adagrad	72.63
Adadelta	63.4
Adam	72.28
Adamax	73.84
Nadam	75.43

Dropout Rate. The model was using a dropout equal to 0.1 which has a high over fitting between the accuracy and the validation accuracy. After tuning the drop out 0.2 was chosen by us to be the best performing dropout rate. The F1 score of the 0.1 is 75.11% and of the 0.2 is equal to 76.65%.

Final Model. The final model that consists of all layers after tuning their hyper-parameters to get the highest F1-score and accuracy. It consists of BLSTM-CRF, Word Embedding, 2 CNN layers and Character Embedding. Its activation functions are Tanh for CNN layers and Softplus for the BLSTM layer. In addition, Nadam was used as the optimization function and dropout rate equal to 0.2. The accuracy is equal to 95.94%, recall is equal to 69.66% and the final F1-score is 76.65%.

6   Conclusion and Future Work

We have introduced a tagger for Arabic Name Entity Recognition using deep learning techniques. The dataset used in this work is a combination of ANER-Corp and AQMAR. Various deep learning models have been investigated such as LSTM-CRF, BLSTM-CRF, Word Embedding, CNN and Character Embedding to reach the model with the highest F1-score. In addition, various hyper-parameters have been tuned such as the optimizer, activation function, epoch number and batch size. We concluded that the final model with the highest F1-score and accuracy consists of BLSTM-CRF with Word Embedding, CNN, and Character Embedding after tuning their hyper-parameters. The F1-Score of the final model is equal to 76.65% and the accuracy is equal to 95.94%. For future work, we are intending to add different layers to test their performance. In addition, the learning rate hyper-parameter could be tuned.

References

1. AbdelRahman, S., Elarnaoty, M., Magdy, M., Fahmy, A.: Integrated machine learning techniques for Arabic named entity recognition. IJCSI **7**, 27–36 (2010)
2. Benajiba, Y., Rosso, P., BenedíRuiz, J.M.: ANERsys: an Arabic named entity recognition system based on maximum entropy. In: Gelbukh, A. (ed.) CICLing 2007. LNCS, vol. 4394, pp. 143–153. Springer, Heidelberg (2007). https://doi.org/10.1007/978-3-540-70939-8_13
3. Buduma, N., Locascio, N.: Fundamentals of Deep Learning: Designing Next-Generation Machine Intelligence Algorithms. O'Reilly Media Inc., Sebastopol (2017)
4. Chiu, J.P.C., Nichols, E.: Named entity recognition with bidirectional LSTM-CNNs. arXiv preprint arXiv:1511.08308 (2015)
5. Chollet, F., et al.: Keras (2015). https://keras.io
6. Collobert, R., Weston, J.: A unified architecture for natural language processing: deep neural networks with multitask learning. In: Proceedings of the 25th International Conference on Machine Learning, pp. 160–167. ACM (2008)
7. Devarakonda, A., Naumov, M., Garland, M.: AdaBatch: adaptive batch sizes for training deep neural networks. arXiv preprint arXiv:1712.02029 (2017)
8. Gridach, M.: Character-aware neural networks for Arabic named entity recognition for social media. In: Proceedings of the 6th Workshop on South and Southeast Asian Natural Language Processing (WSSANLP 2016), pp. 23–32 (2016)
9. Huang, Z., Xu, W., Yu, K.: Bidirectional LSTM-CRF models for sequence tagging. arXiv preprint arXiv:1508.01991 (2015)
10. Jain, A., Kulkarni, G., Shah, V.: Natural language processing. Int. J. Comput. Sci. Eng. **6**(1) (2018)
11. Lample, G., Ballesteros, M., Subramanian, S., Kawakami, K., Dyer, C.: Neural architectures for named entity recognition. arXiv preprint arXiv:1603.01360 (2016)
12. Li, P.-H., Dong, R.-P., Wang, Y.-S., Chou, J.-C., Ma, W.-Y.: Leveraging linguistic structures for named entity recognition with bidirectional recursive neural networks. In: Proceedings of the 2017 Conference on Empirical Methods in Natural Language Processing, pp. 2664–2669 (2017)
13. Lopez, M.M., Kalita, J.: Deep learning applied to NLP. arXiv preprint arXiv:1703.03091 (2017)
14. Ma, X., Hovy, E.: End-to-end sequence labeling via bi-directional LSTM-CNNs-CRF. arXiv preprint arXiv:1603.01354 (2016)
15. Mohit, B., Schneider, N., Bhowmick, R., Oflazer, K., Smith, N.A.: Recall-oriented learning of named entities in Arabic Wikipedia. In: Proceedings of the 13th Conference of the European Chapter of the Association for Computational Linguistics, pp. 162–173. Association for Computational Linguistics (2012)

16. Srivastava, N., Hinton, G., Krizhevsky, A., Sutskever, I., Salakhutdinov, R.: Dropout: a simple way to prevent neural networks from overfitting. J. Mach. Learn. Res. **15**(1), 1929–1958 (2014)
17. Sun, Y., Li, L., Xie, Z., Xie, Q., Li, X., Xu, G.: Co-training an improved recurrent neural network with probability statistic models for named entity recognition. In: Candan, S., Chen, L., Pedersen, T.B., Chang, L., Hua, W. (eds.) DASFAA 2017. LNCS, vol. 10178, pp. 545–555. Springer, Cham (2017). https://doi.org/10.1007/978-3-319-55699-4_33
18. Taquini, R., Finardi, K.R., Amorim, G.B.: English as a medium of instruction at Turkish state universities. Educ. Linguist. Res. **3**(2), 35 (2017)
19. Xia, L., Wang, G.A., Fan, W.: A deep learning based named entity recognition approach for adverse drug events identification and extraction in health social media. In: Chen, H., Zeng, D.D., Karahanna, E., Bardhan, I. (eds.) ICSH 2017. LNCS, vol. 10347, pp. 237–248. Springer, Cham (2017). https://doi.org/10.1007/978-3-319-67964-8_23

Movie Genre Detection Using Topological Data Analysis

Pratik Doshi[✉] and Wlodek Zadrozny

Computer Science, UNC Charlotte, Charlotte, NC 28223, USA
{pdoshi3,wzadrozn}@uncc.edu

Abstract. We show that by applying discourse features derived through topological data analysis (TDA), namely homological persistence, we can improve classification results on the task of movie genre detection, including identification of overlapping movie genres. On the IMDB dataset we improve prior art results, namely we increase the Jaccard score by 4.7% over a recent results by Hoang. We also significantly improve the F-score (by over 15%) and slightly improve the hit rate (by 0.5%, ibid.). We see our contribution as threefold: (a) for general audience of computational linguists, we want to increase their awareness about topology as a possible source of semantic features; (b) for researchers using machine learning for NLP tasks, we want to propose the use of topological features when the number of training examples is small; and (c) for those already aware of the existence of computational topology, we see this work as contributing to the discussion about the value of topology for NLP, in view of mixed results reported by others.

Keywords: Topological data analysis · Text classification · NLP

1 Introduction

In this paper we describe an experiment in using topological discourse features for text classification. We show that this new method is capable of superior performance even if trained on small data sets. The topological features are extracted using 'persistent homology' – a standard tool of Topological Data Analysis. Our task is classification of movie genres. We show that adding topological features derived from text structure improves classification accuracy, namely, we increase the Jaccard score by 4.7% compared to the recently published results by Hoang [13]. (See Sect. 4 for details).

Topological Data Analysis (TDA) is a collection of data analysis methods, derived from the mathematical field of topology, that aim at finding topological structures in data. Most frequently the term refers to *persistent homology*, which is a method for computing topological features of a space in different spatial resolutions. (we explain this in more detail in Sect. 2.2). However, its extended meaning may include clustering, manifold estimation, non-linear dimension reduction,

© Springer Nature Switzerland AG 2018
T. Dutoit et al. (Eds.): SLSP 2018, LNAI 11171, pp. 117–128, 2018.
https://doi.org/10.1007/978-3-030-00810-9_11

etc. TDA is a new and growing subfield of data analysis, with successful applications reported in neuroscience [21], bioinformatics [15], sensor networks [4,5], medical imaging [3], shape analysis [10], computer vision [9], audio processing [16] and speech [2]. More recently we see applications to the analysis of neural networks (NN), showing e.g. the architectural power of NN being closely related to the algebraic topology of decision regions [12].

Although TDA is a very active area of research, it is only very rarely applied to textual data, with only a handful of papers published so far. (We discuss them in Sect. 4).

What This Paper Is About:

We see our contribution as threefold: (a) for general audience of computational linguists, we want to increase their awareness about topology as a possible source of semantic features; (b) for researchers using machine learning for NLP tasks, we want to propose the use of topological features when the number of training examples is small; and (c) for those already aware of the existence of computational topology, we see this work as contributing to the discussion about the value of topology for NLP.

We show that when the text can be interpreted as describing a progression of events (as in movies), topological features, namely, homological persistence, when added to representation of text, can significantly improve classification accuracy. In our experiment of classification of movie genres, using IMDB data[1], we show that adding topological features derived from text structure improves classification: we significantly improve the Jaccard score by 4.7% compared to the baseline and previously published results [13]; we also slightly improve the hit rate. Our work uses the methods and tools introduced by Zhu [23].

2   Introduction to Topological Data Analysis (TDA)

Topological Data Analysis (TDA) can broadly be described as a collection of data analysis methods that find structure in data. This includes: clustering, manifold estimation, non-linear dimension reduction, mode estimation, ridge estimation and persistent homology [22]. As the name suggests, these methods make use of topological ideas. Often, the term TDA is used narrowly to describe a particular method called persistent homology (discussed in Sect. 2.2). Zhu [23] also explains that as a branch of topological data analysis, persistent homology has the advantage of capturing novel invariant structural features of documents. Intuitively, persistent homology can identify clusters (0-th order holes), holes (1st order, as in our loopy curve), voids (2nd order holes, the inside of a balloon), and so on in a point cloud.

2.1   Betti Numbers

Singh et al. [21] explains the concept of a topological invariant with an example. Consider a world where objects are made of elastic rubber. Two objects are

---

[1] ftp://ftp.fu-berlin.de/pub/misc/movies/database/.

considered equivalent if they can be deformed into each other without tearing the material. If such a transformation between X and Y exists, we say they are topologically equivalent. Thus a pyramid and a ball are equivalent. It turns out two shapes are not equivalent if they differ in the number of holes. Thus, simply counting holes can provide a signature for the object at hand. Holes can exist in different dimensions. A one-dimensional hole is exposed when a one-dimensional loop (a closed curve) on the object cannot be deformed into a single point without tearing the loop. If two such loops can be deformed into one another they define the same hole, which should be counted only once. Analogous definitions can be invoked in higher dimensions (Fig. 1).

a.   b.   c.   d.   e.

(1, 0, 0, 0, ...)   (1, 1, 0, 0, ...)   (1, 2, 1, 0, ...)   (1, 2, 1, 0, ...)   (1, 0, 1, 0, ...)

Fig. 1. Betti numbers provide a signature of the underlying topology (shape).

The notion of counting holes of different dimensions is formalized by the definition of Betti numbers. The Betti numbers of an object X can be arranged in a sequence, $b(X) = (b_0, b_1, b_2, ...)$, where b_0 represents the number of connected components, b_1 represents the number of one dimensional holes, b_2 – the number of two-dimensional holes, and so forth. An important property of Betti sequences is that if two objects are topologically equivalent (they can be deformed into each other) they share the same Betti sequence.

2.2   Persistent Homology and Barcodes

Persistent homology is a multi-scale approach to quantifying topological features in data [6–8]. That is we connect Persistent homology finds "holes" by identifying equivalent cycles [23]. The basic idea of the method is to track the different "holes" across different spatial scales of analysis. We visualize the results of the analysis by plotting "birth" and "death" intervals of individual holes of different dimensions as the spatial scale ϵ goes from zero to infinity. For each Betti number, we keep a separate graph. Connected components are drawn as horizontal lines in the b_0 graph, one-dimensional holes correspond to horizontal lines in the b_1 graph, two-dimensional holes in the b_2 graph, and so on. For each hole, the horizontal line has its endpoints at the values of ϵ at which the structure was first created and then destroyed. The set of all these lines together is called a barcode.

2.3   Topological Data Analysis for Textual Data

Zhu [23] presents one of the first applications of persistent homology for natural language processing. His "Similarity Filtration with Time Skeleton" (SIFTS) algorithm identifies holes that can be interpreted as semantic "tie-backs" in a text document, providing a new document structure representation. A brief overview of the approach is explained in [23]: imagine dividing a document into smaller units such as paragraphs. A paragraph can be represented by a point in some space, for example, as the bag-of-words vector in R^d where d is the vocabulary size. All paragraphs in the document form a point cloud in this space. Now let us "connect the dots" by linking the point for the first paragraph to the second, the second to the third, and so on. What does the curve look like? Certain structures of the curve capture information relevant to Natural Language Processing (NLP). For instance, a good essay may have a conclusion paragraph that "ties back" to the introduction paragraph. Thus the starting point and the ending point of the curve may be close in the space. If we further connect all points within some small ϵ diameter, the curve may become a loop with a hole in the middle. In contrast, an essay without any tying back may not contain holes, no matter how large ϵ is.

Although we tried to provide some intuitions about TDA, *for the purpose of this paper we can treat TDA as a black box and a provider of additional numerical features*. We do not assume any prior knowledge of topology or TDA. However, to follow the remainder of this paper the reader will benefit remembering the following three points:

– One of its key tools is *persistent homology* which tries to find geometric patterns such as clusters and holes in different dimensions and different resolutions, simultaneously.
– The result of this analysis is represented as *barcodes* or equivalently *persistence diagrams*.
– For machine learning tasks such as classification, these can be viewed as additional numerical features.

For a technical and accessible introduction to topological data analysis for text processing we refer the reader to [23]. The reader will also find there all the necessary background of the SIFTS method used in this paper.

3   Description of Experiments

In this section we explain our experiment and the data preparation process. We evaluate whether topological features are effective in text classification by predicting movie genres based on plot descriptions (as in the example below). We perform multiple preprocessing steps before generating barcodes, as explained in subsections below.

We also explain the initial experiments we performed to get a better understanding of the procedure, and this we hope might help the reader to follow up the paper.

Example	Identifying Genres of movie plots
Data Used	Movie plot summary, Movie Genre from IMDB Dataset.
Data Preparation	1. Stop words removal using NLTK 2. Removing numeric tokens using Python RegEx 3. Removing Punctuation marks 4. Using Lancaster Stemming to reduce tokens to their base form
Testing Data Conditions	1. Plot should contain >100 tokens 2. Plot should contain >3 sentences 3. Plot should belong to >1 genres

Steps	1. Perform *'Data Preparation'* for all the movie plots in dataset.
	2. Create four lists of top words, one for each genre, using TF-IDF.
	   a. Separate movies belonging to only one genre
	   b. Using TF-IDF identify top words.
	   c. Filter each list to remove common nouns like film, depicts, etc.
	3. Select the plot satisfying *'Testing Data Conditions'*.
	4. Generate Term Frequency Matrix, one for each list of top words.
	   a. Columns of the matrix represent the tokens from the list of top words
	   b. Rows represent each sentence in the plot
	   c. In a X_{MxN}^{Action} matrix, M represents number of tokens in top words list of Action genre. N represents the number of sentences in movie plot X. X_{IxJ} gives the frequency of token 'I' in sentence 'J'
	5. Using Javaplex for Matlab, generate persistent homology diagrams (barcodes) using each Term Frequency Matric as input, one at a time.
	6. Identify genres of a movie plot by comparing the number of 1-dimensional holes/loop in each barcode for the respective plot.

Results	Hit Rate: 83.3% Jaccard Index: 54.8% 1. Hit Rate: Proportion of dataset where model predicted atleast one genre correctly 2. Jaccard Index: Defined as the number of correctly predicted labels divided by the union of predicted and true labels $\frac{\|T \cap P\|}{\|T \cup P\|}$

Data Distribution	1. For Identifying Top Words for each genre:
	   Action Genre: 3286 movies Comedy Genre: 3000 movies
	   Horror Genre: 2176 movies Romance Genre: 3500 movies
	2. Testing Dataset: 250 movie plots.

Fig. 2. Outlines our entire experiment procedure. The dataset used for the experiment is the IMDB dataset. We explain Data Preparation in detail in the Sect. 3.2. The steps mentioned in the table are simplified to get a clear understanding of the experiment procedure. We perform a 4-step text preprocessing and use Lancaster Stemming to avoid writing style bias. Once we create the vector matrices, we use Javaplex with Matlab to generate the persistence diagrams i.e. barcodes (shown in the next section). Section 3.3 explains our Data Distribution and Results.

3.1 Initial Experiment

In this section we explain our initial experiment and lay the foundation for the final experiment.

The main insight of [23] experiment was that persistence diagrams can outline the strength of the main idea of a text. Following this, in an initial experiment, we compare the barcodes for two movie plots (one Action genre and one Comedy genre), from the IMDB's website, in our experiment to identify the movie plot.

We use the [1] dataset to identify the top words from the Action genre using the TF-IDF measure. Using these top words, we generate Term Frequency matrix for both the movie plots, as explained in Sect. 3.2. Understanding that an Action movie plot would have more words common with the top words list and hence the Action movie vector would present stronger looping between the sentences.

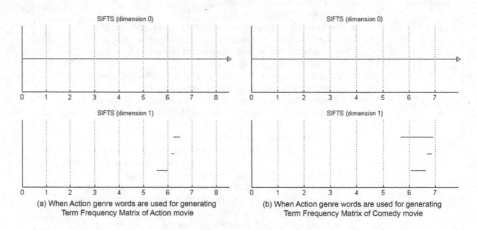

(a) When Action genre words are used for generating Term Frequency Matrix of Action movie

(b) When Action genre words are used for generating Term Frequency Matrix of Comedy movie

Fig. 3. The existence of 1-dimensional holes/loops in a document is shown by the horizontal bars in the barcodes. The count of the horizontal bar would give the number of 1-dimensional holes in the document. Length of the bar determines the persistence of holes. More the number of bars and length of the bars gives the strength of similarity between rows of the vector for a particular genre. Thus, with the presence of 1-dimensional holes/loops we say the movie belongs to the respective genre. (a) and (b) both showcase same number of 1-dimensional loops/holes. However, we can see a clear distinction in the persistence of these holes. In the (a), the holes are not as persistent as in (b), if not more. The sentences of both the movie plots were converted to vector forms using the same set of words belonging to movies exclusively from Action genre. Hence, when the Comedy movie represents stronger bond between the vectors, it indicates the ambiguity in the approach followed for generating vectors.

The barcodes in Fig. 3 indicated three major issue in our first experiments: 1. Not considering overlapping genres 2. Writing Style of the text 3. No use of semantics. Movies usually belong to more than one genres and not considering this while classifying them could result in sub-par results. We used the top words for vectors from [1] dataset while tested on an IMDB's movie plot. To account for change of writing styles and implicitly for semantics, we simply use the Lancaster stemming [14] in our final experiment (as the performance of most stemming algorithms is data specific, we observed Lancaster Stemming to be working best for our experiment and hence decided to use Lancaster Stemming over other algorithms). This is clearly a very simple solution, and others, e.g. based on word2vec-like solutions will perhaps be more appropriate for future work to produce better semantic representations.

3.2   Data Preparation and Generation of Topological Signatures

As we performed some basic preprocessing on the text and used NLTK's stop-words list for removing the stopwords. We also remove the punctuation marks and numerical characters from the sentences. Next, we separate each sentence from the text into a new line, thereby letting us handle each sentence individually. To make the experiment neutral to writing styles, we use Lancaster Stemming and reduce each token to its base form. After the data preparation, next is creating the Term Frequency Matrix for each genre in consideration per movie plot. Hence, each column in the matrix represented the top words from the respective genre and each row was the vector representation of the respective line from the text. We create this matrix for every movie plot that satisfied 'Testing Data Conditions'.

3.3   Experiment and Results

Data Selection: From the dataset we filtered out the details regarding TV episodes and short/documentary as that would not be inline with the problem statement. With the movies, we collect the plots, genres and a movie id, for uniquely identifying each movie in the database. As our major comparison is between the movies from genre Action, Romance, Comedy and Horror, we segregate the movie belonging exclusively to only these four genres i.e. no overlap. Thus we got 3286 movies belonging to only action genre, 3500 movies belonging to only comedy genre, 2176 movies belonging to only horror genre and 18000 movies belonging to comedy genre of which we randomly select 3000 movies belonging to comedy genre, to avoid the problem of over fitting.

Data Preparation: We preprocess all the movies belonging one of the four genres, individually. Thereby removing the stop words, punctuation marks, numeric tokens, stemming to reduce tokens to their same base forms. Next, we use TF-IDF to get the top 1000 words from each genre. With the four lists of 1000 top tokens of each genre, we perform subtraction of list to remove the common nouns from each list, as nouns like 'second', 'depict', etc. added noise resulting in incorrect final outputs. After manually removing the common nouns left after subtraction, we are left with top words belonging to each genres without any noise, each list is approximately 200 tokens long. We use these lists of top tokens for creating sentence vectors for the test documents.

Selection of Testing Data: While picking movies for testing, we found that one movie could have more than 1 plot summaries, provided by different authors. Hence, database had multiple entries for a movie with same name, however with a unique movie id, for each different plot summary. Hence, for each movie plot, we first assign the longest movie plot provided for each movie. For testing, we randomly pick 250 movies from the database satisfying the basic criteria, i.e. belonging to more than one genres, having more than 100 tokens in the plot and having at least 4 sentences. We found 66000 movies satisfying our above criteria and we randomly picked 250 movies, keeping no preference for genre combinations or length of the plots.

Testing: We want to find the 1-dimension holes across the sentences. Using the vectors generated with the top words from each genre as explained above, we run them through Javaplex for generating the homology complexes. We compare the four 1-dimension homology complexes generated for each movie plot to determine the genre for the respective movie. Using the barcode representation of the 1-dimension homology complexes, the program is able to correctly identify the genres of 208 movies with overlapping genres, giving a hit rate of 0.8333%. The output was considered correct if we were able to correctly predict at least one genre if a movie belonged to n genres. As hit rate is considered a weak metric, we calculate Jaccard index and F-score using the formula mention in Fig. 2. We obtained a Jaccard index of 54.8% and an F-score of 71.88%.

In Fig. 4 we present an example of the output. Here, we consider a movie plot form the IMDB dataset which is listed as Comedy and Romance genre. We, generate the Term Frequency Matrix and run TDA to generate the barcodes presented in Fig. 4. Plot of the movie tested is highlighted below.

Example Movie Plot: *Al Bennett and Alice Cook are blissfully happy and are building their house in an isolated area; using Al's savings of $7;000. Troubles begin when Al's uncle and boss; Uncle George; unaware of Al's engagement; inspects the house and announces he will live with him. Furthermore; he wants Al to marry Minnie Spring; a wonderful girl George just met; so the three of them can live happily ever after. Troubles mount when Alice's parents come to see the partially built house. They bring with them eleven other family members; some of whom expect to live with the couple when they marry. Badgered on all sides; Al finally yells "There's too many Cooks." Alice breaks their engagement; and George fires him. As if these problems weren't enough; the Carpenter's Union calls a strike; but a determined Al decides to finish the house himself. Months later; lonely and depressed; Al puts his finished house up for sale; but things are looking up for Al.*

Reproducibility: As mentioned earlier, the code and data we used for experiments is available (http://pages.cs.wisc.edu/~jerryzhu/publications.html, ftp:// ftp.fu-berlin.de/pub/misc/movies/database/). We have published the data we used, with topological features, and the classification results on data (https:// data.world/pdoshi3/movie-genre-classification-using-tda).

4   Comparison with Related Work and Discussion

TDA although a very active area of research, as mentioned above, is very rarely applied to textual data. The main reference in this space is [23], which can also serve as an excellent introduction to the field. Since the paper is accompanied by software it was relatively painless for us to run the experiments described above. The works cited here might be (as of May 2018) complete or close to

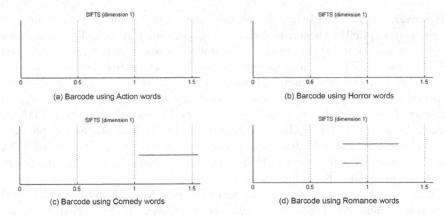

Fig. 4. Comparing the four barcodes, we can see that (c) and (d) have persistent 1-dimensional holes whereas (a) and (b) have none. For (c) and (d), top words from Comedy genre and Romance genre, respectively, were used to represent the columns for the Term Frequency Matrix. For (a) and (b), top words from Action genre and Horror genre, respectively, were used to represent the columns in the Term Frequency Matrix. This clearly shows the inclination of the movie plot in question, towards Comedy and Romance genre, which are the original genres for the movie in IMDB dataset.

complete list of papers using persistent homology for text processing (and not just mentioning it as a possibility). We briefly discuss them now.

There is substantial amount of work on classification of movie plots, as the problem appears in movie recommendations. A recent article by Hoang [13] is closest to our work, as it is focused on the same task of predicting movie genres based on plots, and contains state of the art results. The author reports results of experiments with more than 250,000 movies using neural networks for classification. The produced model achieves the Jaccard-score of 50%, the F-score of 56% and the hit rate of 80.5%. Table 1 Compares our results with Hoang's.

While our results look better, this is not exactly an apples-to-apples comparison: while Hoang performs the experiment on a very large data set, our test is limited to a sample of 250 movies. On the other hand, this limitation is also the strength of the method. Namely, we only need to train on approximately 1% of the data to obtain a very good performance.

Secondly, we perform our experiment on 4 most popular genres i.e. Action, Comedy, Horror and Romance, while Hoang [13] also considers not-so popular genres like Adventure, Sport, Mystery, Family. We believe, the F-score for TDA approach would be higher when compared to Hoang's [13] result for the same four genres, since we have better precision and recall. However we estimate the difference in the F-score of 15.88% might come down to 7% since [13] model performed better for popular genres compared to other genres. Therefore we do not want to emphasize the F-score improvements.

However, we want to bring the reader's attention to the fact that our 250 movies were explicitly chosen to belong to overlapping genres. The reason for that choice was that (a) our initial experiment on a few dozen movies showed 100% accuracy of TDA on movies with no overlapping genres; (b) we decided in late 2017 to run the experiment on overlapping categories, which arguably can be viewed as a more difficult problem. Statistically speaking 250 serves as a good sample set to compare the results. We are currently focused on testing TDA on a larger dataset that would allow us remove the limitations of this comparison. One of the issues here is that for a larger set we need to change the set of TDA tools to a more efficient program than used in the reported experiment; we are experimenting with Ripser[2] for this purpose.

There are only a few other examples of application of TDA to text. [18] perform sentiment classification on both sentence level, on the Cornell Sentence Polarity (the CSP-corpus of [19]), and on IMDB movie reviews (following Michel et al. [17]). They conclude "using persistence diagrams for text representation does not seem to positively contribute to document clustering and sentiment classification tasks". Although they leave open the possibility of topological features contributing to other NLP tasks such a parsing.

On the other hand Guan et al. [11] show that topological features can improve extraction of multiword expressions and in document summarization.

Finally, we want to mention [20] who argues for the applicability of TDA to visualization of texts; this is an important issue, but somewhat orthogonal to the tasks discussed in this paper.

Table 1. Comparison with recent prior art. See the discussion in text for the limitations of this comparison.

Methods	Jaccard	Hit rate	F-score
Hoang [13]	50%	74.2–82.9%	56%
Our results (TDA)	**54.8%**	83.3%	71.88%

5   Conclusion

In the reported experiment, we showed the ability of Topological Data Analysis (TDA) to perform text classification. TDA not only matches the performance of widely used algorithms like Multinomial Naive Bayes, Logistic Regression for binary text classification, but also can also outperform more advanced techniques like neural networks when in multi-label text classification. On the task of classification of movies according to four most common genres, we obtain Jaccard score of 54.8%, F-score of 71.88%, and hit rate of 83.3%. This is a significant improvement in 2 of the 3 measures over recently reported results of [13]: (+4.7%, +15.88%, and +0.5%)-respectively. As noted above, one limitation of our work

---

[2] https://github.com/Ripser/ripser.

is that the testing has only been performed on a (random) sample of 250 movies, moreover we limited ourselves to four categories. However, we also chose – on purpose – the data consisting of the movies which belong to multiple categories, and thus made the task harder. (And this harder task was our initial objective, as we found out about [13] after most of the experiments were done).

Clearly, the main message of this exercise is that TDA can be seriously used as a tool for discourse classification, notwithstanding mixed results of other experiments (discussed above in Sect. 4). Topology can be a source of useful features. And while this work focused on low dimensional persistence, higher dimensional topological features can be a source of additional insights by representing more complex repeating patterns.

References

1. Bamman, D., O'Connor, B., Smith, N.A.: Learning latent personas of film characters. In: Proceedings of the Annual Meeting of the Association for Computational Linguistics (ACL), p. 352 (2014)
2. Brown, K.A., Knudson, K.P.: Nonlinear statistics of human speech data. Int. J. Bifurcat. Chaos 19(07), 2307–2319 (2009)
3. Chung, M.K., Bubenik, P., Kim, P.T.: Persistence diagrams of cortical surface data. In: Prince, J.L., Pham, D.L., Myers, K.J. (eds.) IPMI 2009. LNCS, vol. 5636, pp. 386–397. Springer, Heidelberg (2009). https://doi.org/10.1007/978-3-642-02498-6_32
4. De Silva, V., Ghrist, R.: Homological sensor networks. Not. Am. Math. Soc. 54(1) (2007)
5. De Silva, V., Ghrist, R.: Coverage in sensor networks via persistent homology. Algebraic Geom. Topol. 7(1), 339–358 (2007)
6. Edelsbrunner, H., Harer, J.: Persistent homology-a survey. Contemp. Math. 453, 257–282 (2008)
7. Edelsbrunner, H., Harer, J.: Computational Topology: An Introduction. American Mathematical Society, Providence (2010)
8. Edelsbrunner, H., Letscher, D., Zomorodian, A.: Topological persistence and simplification. In: 2000 Proceedings of 41st Annual Symposium on Foundations of Computer Science, pp. 454–463. IEEE (2000)
9. Freedman, D., Chen, C.: Algebraic topology for computer vision. Comput. Vis. 239–268 (2009)
10. Gamble, J., Heo, G.: Exploring uses of persistent homology for statistical analysis of landmark-based shape data. J. Multivariate Anal. 101(9), 2184–2199 (2010)
11. Guan, H., Tang, W., Krim, H., Keiser, J., Rindos, A., Sazdanovic, R.: A topological collapse for document summarization. In: 2016 IEEE 17th International Workshop on Signal Processing Advances in Wireless Communications (SPAWC), pp. 1–5. IEEE (2016)
12. Guss, W.H., Salakhutdinov, R.: On characterizing the capacity of neural networks using algebraic topology. arXiv preprint arXiv:1802.04443 (2018)
13. Hoang, Q.: Predicting movie genres based on plot summaries. arXiv preprint arXiv:1801.04813 (2018)
14. Hull, D.A.: Stemming algorithms: a case study for detailed evaluation. J. Am. Soc. Inf. Sci. 47(1), 70–84 (1996)

15. Kasson, P.M., Zomorodian, A., Park, S., Singhal, N., Guibas, L.J., Pande, V.S.: Persistent voids: a new structural metric for membrane fusion. Bioinformatics **23**(14), 1753–1759 (2007)
16. Liu, J.Y., Jeng, S.K., Yang, Y.H.: Applying topological persistence in convolutional neural network for music audio signals. arXiv preprint arXiv:1608.07373 (2016)
17. Maas, A.L., Daly, R.E., Pham, P.T., Huang, D., Ng, A.Y., Potts, C.: Learning word vectors for sentiment analysis. In: Proceedings of the 49th Annual Meeting of the Association for Computational Linguistics: Human Language Technologies, vol. 1, pp. 142–150. Association for Computational Linguistics (2011)
18. Michel, P., Ravichander, A., Rijhwani, S.: Does the geometry of word embeddings help document classification? A case study on persistent homology based representations. arXiv preprint arXiv:1705.10900 (2017)
19. Pang, B., Lee, L.: Seeing stars: exploiting class relationships for sentiment categorization with respect to rating scales. In: Proceedings of the 43rd Annual Meeting on Association for Computational Linguistics, pp. 115–124. Association for Computational Linguistics (2005)
20. Sami, I.R., Farrahi, K.: A simplified topological representation of text for local and global context. In: Proceedings of the 2017 ACM on Multimedia Conference, pp. 1451–1456. ACM (2017)
21. Singh, G., Memoli, F., Ishkhanov, T., Sapiro, G., Carlsson, G., Ringach, D.L.: Topological analysis of population activity in visual cortex. J. Vis. **8**(8), 11–11 (2008)
22. Wasserman, L.: Topological data analysis. Ann. Rev. Stat. Appl. (2016)
23. Zhu, X.: Persistent homology: an introduction and a new text representation for natural language processing. In: IJCAI, pp. 1953–1959 (2013)

Low-Resource Text Classification Using Domain-Adversarial Learning

Daniel Grießhaber[1](✉), Ngoc Thang Vu[2](✉), and Johannes Maucher[1](✉)

[1] Stuttgart Media University, Nobelstraße 10, 70569 Stuttgart, Germany
{griesshaber,maucher}@hdm-stuttgart.de
[2] Institute for Natural Language Processing (IMS), University of Stuttgart,
Pfaffenwaldring 5B, 70569 Stuttgart, Germany
thangvu@ims.uni-stuttgart.de

Abstract. Deep learning techniques have recently shown to be successful in many natural language processing tasks forming state-of-the-art systems. They require, however, a large amount of annotated data which is often missing. This paper explores the use of domain-adversarial learning as a regularizer to avoid overfitting when training domain invariant features for deep, complex neural network in low-resource and zero-resource settings in new target domains or languages. In case of new languages, we show that monolingual word-vectors can be directly used for training without pre-alignment. Their projection into a common space can be learnt ad-hoc at training time reaching the final performance of pretrained multilingual word-vectors.

Keywords: NLP · Low-resource · Deep learning · Domain-adversarial

1 Introduction

Text classification is the generic term to describe the process of assigning a document x to a class y [1]. Depending on the nature of the class label y, text classification can be used for a variety of tasks, including sentiment analysis [24], spam filtering [34] or topic labeling [38].

Traditional approaches use sparse, symbolic representations of words and documents, such as the bag-of-words model [8]. Then, linear models or kernel methods are used for the classification [38]. This approach has obvious disadvantages. While the symbolic representation of words can not model similarities and relations between words [6], linear models often fail to understand relations in longer sentences which is particularly important for sentiment detection [29].

Current state-of-the-art natural language processing (NLP) models often use distributed representations of words [27,30] which are then feed into complex neural network models such as convolutional neural networks (CNNs) [21] or recurrent neural networks (RNNs) [36]. While these approaches proved to be successful for many NLP tasks [5,8], they often require large amounts of labeled data. However, there is often only a little training data or even no data available

© Springer Nature Switzerland AG 2018
T. Dutoit et al. (Eds.): SLSP 2018, LNAI 11171, pp. 129–139, 2018.
https://doi.org/10.1007/978-3-030-00810-9_12

when a NLP application is needed for new domains [12] or new languages [2,9, 15]. Moreover in case of adaptation to new languages, multilingual word-vectors are considered to be required. They are, however, not trivial to obtain due to the lack of parallel data [10] or multilingual dictionaries [3].

In this work we explore domain adversarial training and its interpretation as a regularizer for training of complex model architectures avoiding overfitting in low-resource and zero-resource settings. In the case of transfer learning from one to another, low-resource, language, our experimental results reveal that a projection of separate word-vectors into a common space can be automatically learnt during training, which suggests that the multilingual word-vectors are no longer needed. All code necessary to reproduce our experimental results is made available[1].

The remainder of the paper is organized as follows: In Sect. 2, we shortly summarize the most related work and emphasize the differences between our work and the previous one. Section 3 describes the model architecture and various feature extractors. In Sect. 4, we introduce the three datasets and present our experimental setups. Section 5 reports the results and our analysis on the two experiments including low-resource domain and language. The study is concluded in Sect. 6.

2   Related Work

Adversarial training [13] has recently gained considerable interest in NLP research community [7,11,14,19,23,31,33,41]. The most related works to our research are presented in [11] and [7]. [11] proposed domain-adversarial neural networks (DANN), a general approach for domain adaptive classifiers using the reversal of the gradients in an adversarial domain classifier. They showed that domain-adversarial training using gradient-reversal enables a feature-extractor to learn domain-invariant representations of an input. [7] extended it by using Wasserstein approximation over categorical cross-entropy as the loss function and used the general DANN architecture for multilingual sentiment classification by averaging multilingual word-vectors. In comparison with t*/hese works, we will explore DANN when training of more complex networks in low-resource scenarios. Furthermore, we will address the question whether multilingual word-vectors are necessary in transfer learning to low-resource languages.

3   Proposed Model

3.1   Architecture

Figure 1 shows the general network architecture. Input to the network is a document x represented by a $K \times |x|$ matrix where each row represents a K dimensional word vector and $|x|$ is the number of words in x. In the case where the

---

[1] https://gitlab.mi.hdm-stuttgart.de/griesshaber/dann-evaluation.

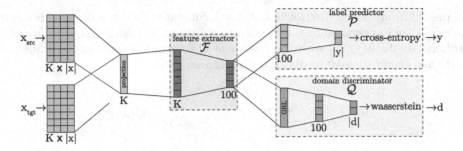

Fig. 1. The general network architecture using domain-adversarial training

documents x_{src} and x_{tgt} are from different languages, an additional layer with shape $K \times K$ for each domain is introduced to project word-vector into a common space. As this projection is learnt during training of the classifier, it optimises the alignment to the objective of the network. We argue this presents an advantage over the use of a pre-aligned embedding which may have been optimised to a different objective (i.e. using the distributional hypothesis [16] or parallel corpora).

The projected input is then fed into a feature extractor $\mathcal{F}$ (more details in Subsect. 3.2) which should learn to produce a single document vector z for any document x. The objective of $\mathcal{F}$ is to learn features that are discriminative to the class of the document but indiscriminate to the domain. To achieve this, the architecture trains 2 separate classifiers: a *label predictor* $\mathcal{P}(z) \Rightarrow y$ and a *domain discriminator* $\mathcal{Q}(z) \Rightarrow d$. Both get their input from the joint feature extractor $\mathcal{F}(x) \Rightarrow z$ and are jointly trained. While $\mathcal{P}$ is trained to minimise the loss on the label classification, the domain classifier $\mathcal{Q}$ is *adversarially* trained to minimise the loss on the domain classification. Thus, the intuition is that $\mathcal{F}$ will learn a joint feature space where elements are invariant for their domain d but distinguishable in their class label y. For the adversarial training, a gradient-reversal-layer (GRL) is used that inverts the gradients of $\mathcal{Q}$ during back-propagation. Thus, minimising the loss $L(\mathcal{Q})$ effectively trains $\mathcal{F}$ to produce features that hinder $\mathcal{Q}$ from learning a good domain discriminator. This is explained by the fact that $L(\mathcal{Q})$ approximates the divergence of the space of hyperplanes $\mathcal{H}$ of $\mathcal{F}$ that separates the training elements by their domain association. See [11] for a full mathematical elaboration. To weight the impact of the two branches, the gradients of $\mathcal{Q}$ are multiplied with the hyperparameter λ during training. Therefore a higher λ value puts more emphasis on learning $\mathcal{F}$ to produce domain-invariant features. One important property of this architecture is that it does not explicitly need labeled training samples from the target domain. Moreover, it is also possible to use any available data from the target domain for the training of $\mathcal{P}$. This makes the architecture suitable for no- and low-resource learning.

The label predictor $\mathcal{P}$ is trained to minimise the cross-entropy between the output and the document labels. As the domain discriminator effectively tries to predict from which distribution $P_\mathcal{F}$ a document vector z is drawn from, we follow [4] and approximate the Wasserstein distance by using the Kantorovich-Rubenstein duality [37] with the output of $\mathcal{Q}$ to avoid saturating the gradients and thus giving $\mathcal{F}$ good feedback during training:

$$W(P_\mathcal{F}^{src}, P_\mathcal{F}^{tgt}) \cong$$
$$\sup_{\|\mathcal{Q}\|_L \leq 1} \left(\mathop{\mathbb{E}}_{\mathcal{F}(x) \sim P_\mathcal{F}^{src}} [\mathcal{Q}(\mathcal{F}(x))] - \mathop{\mathbb{E}}_{\mathcal{F}(x\prime) \sim P_\mathcal{F}^{tgt}} [\mathcal{Q}(\mathcal{F}(x\prime))] \right)$$

where $P_\mathcal{F}^{src}$ and $P_\mathcal{F}^{tgt}$ are the distributions of the feature-representations of the elements from the source- and target-domain respectively. To meet the Lipschitz constraint $\|\mathcal{Q}\|_L \leq 1$, all weights of $\mathcal{Q}$ are clipped to the interval $[-0.01, 0.01]$.

3.2 Feature Extractors

We implement several feature extractors $\mathcal{F}$ with an increasing level of complexities in this work. The idea is to explore the effectiveness of domain adversarial learning as a regularizer when training complex networks with small amount of annotated training data or even without any training data.

Word-Vector Average. The first simple feature extractor maps a document to a single vector by averaging all embedded word-vectors in the document $w_i \in x$.

$$\mathcal{F}_{avg}(x) = \frac{1}{|x|} \sum_{w_i \in x} w_i$$

The document vector is then fed into a subsequent ReLU fully connected layer with 100 neurons [28].

tf-idf weighted Average. The second method extends $\mathcal{F}_{avg}$ by weighting all the word-vectors by its term frequency-inverse document frequency (tf-idf) [32, p. 7].

$$\mathcal{F}_{tfidf}(x) = \frac{1}{|x|} \sum_{w_i \in x} tfidf(w_i, x, X) \cdot w_i$$

Convolutional Neural Network. We also use convolutional neural networks (CNNs) following [21]. Each document x is modelled as a $N \times K$ matrix, where $N = max(|X|)$ is the maximum number of words in the set of documents X, and K is the dimensionality of the used word-embedding. Shorter documents are padded with zero vectors. This input representation is fed into a set of filters with widths $3, 4, 5$ each with 100 feature maps. The feature maps are max-over-time pooled [8] which naturally deals with the zero-padding. For regularization, dropout with a constraint on l_2-norms [18] is applied to the flattened and pooled feature maps.

Hierarchical Attention Network. The most complex feature extractor explored in this work is the Hierarchical Attention Network (HAN) presented in [40], which captures the inherent hierarchical structure of a document. Each word in a sentence is fed into a bidirectional recurrent network (RNN) consisting of 100 GRU-cells [5], the *word-encoder* with output h_{it}. Attention mechanism [5,39] is used to weight each representation. Specifically,

$$u_{it} = tanh(W_w h_{it} + b_w)$$

$$\alpha_{it} = \frac{exp(u_{it}{}^T u_w)}{\sum_t exp(u_{it}{}^T u_w)}$$

$$s_i = \sum_t \alpha_{it} h_{it}$$

where u_{it} is the hidden representation of h_{it} for the attention mechanism and α_{it} is the softmax-normalized attention for the current word as a similarity measure of the hidden representation with a word-context vector u_w that is learned during training. s_i is then the weighted sum of all word representations and used as input to the *sentence-encoder*. The *sentence-encoder* uses the sentence vectors s_i as an input and has the same general structure as the *word-encoder*.

4   Experiment Setup

4.1   Datasets

We evaluate the model across three datasets with a focus on sentiment classification:

- Amazon Reviews dataset contains 142.8M text reviews including a 5-star rating [17,26] including many different categories. We simplified the sentiment classification task to the case of binary classification. A rating of 1 or 2 indicated a negative example, while reviews with a rating of 4 or 5 got labeled positive. The categories are used as a domain-label d.
- the Arabic Social Media dataset [35] contains 1200 Arabic sentences from social media posts, annotated into 3 sentiment classes (+, 0 and -).
- the last dataset contains over 4.7M reviews from the *Yelp Open Dataset Challenge*[2] that have a 5 star rating. A subset of 600.000 reviews (120.000 entries per rating) was selected for training. To match the polarity labels of the Arabic Social Media dataset, reviews with a rating of 1 and 2 were assigned the - label, 4 and 5 rated reviews were assigned the + category and a rating of 3 was assigned the 0 label.

In order to simulate the low-resource scenario, a fixed number of 500 elements from the target category were randomly selected and used in training. In the source domain, 80% of the dataset are used for training. We conduct two different experiments:

---

[2] https://www.yelp.com/dataset.

- In the low-resource domain experiments, the five main categories `Electronics`, `Home and Kitchen`, `Beauty` and `Baby` from the Amazon Reviews corpus composed the source domain, while `Automotive` was used as low-resource target domain.
- For the low-resource language settings, Arabic was used as the low-resource target language, while the English Yelp reviews were used as the source.

4.2 Hyperparameters

We use two different word-vectors: (a) the pretrained monolingual fastText word-vectors[3] [20] and (b) the pretrained multilingual word-vectors $MUSE$[4]. Both vectors have a dimensionality of $K = 300$.

The label and domain predictors are trained using ADAM [22] with a learning-rate of $\mu_\mathcal{P} = 0.01$ resp. $\mu_\mathcal{Q} = 0.00005$. The domain discriminator $\mathcal{Q}$'s first layer is the GRL that is implemented by multiplying the gradients with -1 during back-propagation, effectively inverting them, and passing all values unaltered during the forward pass. The values are then passed to two subsequent, fully-connected layers: one hidden layer with 100 neurons and ReLU nonlinearities and the output layer with unscaled, linear outputs. Following [4, 7] we also calculate the Wasserstein loss on the output of $\mathcal{Q}$. The domain predictor is trained for $n_{critic} = 5$ iterations for each $\mathcal{P}$ step and the weights of $\mathcal{Q}$ are clipped to the interval $[-0.01, \quad 0.01]$. More details can be found in footnote 1.

5   Results and Discussion

5.1   Low-Resource Domain

Table 1 compares the accuracy of the different feature extractors on the sentiment classification tasks. The models trained only on documents of the source domain perform poorly on the target data. Moreover, the more complex $\mathcal{F}_{cnn}$ and $\mathcal{F}_{han}$ model architectures perform worse in this scenario than the simpler $\mathcal{F}_{avg}$ and $\mathcal{F}_{tfidf}$ models. This indicates, that the complex models overfit on the source domain. In comparison, the models using the adversarial training of $\mathcal{Q}$, are regularized and do not overfit on the source domain, even if no labeled target data is used.

Figure 2 compares the classification accuracy of the two extreme cases: very simple model $\mathcal{F}_{avg}$ and fairly complex model $\mathcal{F}_{han}$ varying the amount of adaptation data. Strong overfitting of the HAN architecture without adversarial training was observed when training with source and target training data. The simpler approach using word-vector averaging performs considerably better in this low-resource scenario without the domain adversarial training. All models benefit from introducing labeled training data from the target domain. With domain adversarial training, the complex $\mathcal{F}_{han}$ performs best in this experiment.

---

[3] https://github.com/facebookresearch/fastText.
[4] https://github.com/facebookresearch/MUSE.

Table 1. Classifier accuracies on the 3-class classification tasks. $DANN_n$ is the domain adversarial model trained on n labeled examples from the respective *target* domain. The *S only* column shows the accuracy of the models trained with source data without adversarial training, while for $S+T$ the model is trained on source domain data and 500 target domain data points

Features	$DANN_{500}$	$DANN_0$	S only	S+T
$\mathcal{F}_{avg}$	86.0	81.5	79.7	82.1
$\mathcal{F}_{tfidf}$	86.2	83.9	79.0	83.2
$\mathcal{F}_{cnn}$	88.8	84.7	77.2	80.6
$\mathcal{F}_{han}$	86.7	85.9	77.5	79.3

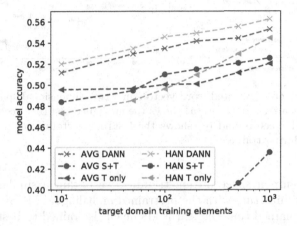

Fig. 2. Performance of the $\mathcal{F}_{avg}$ and $\mathcal{F}_{han}$ models trained on different numbers of target data

5.2   Low-Resource Language

Table 2 shows the results with different feature extractors using monolingual and multilingual word-vectors. Note that the monolingual word-vectors are trained independently and therefore are in different subspaces. The models trained only in the source domain without domain-adversarial training are not able to learn a usable classification rule for the target domain. When projecting the word-

Table 2. Model accuracies using the monolingual word-vectors ($_{ft}$) and multilingual MUSE word-vectors ($_{muse}$)

$\mathcal{F}$	$DANN_{ft-500}$	$DANN_{ft-0}$	S only$_{ft}$	$DANN_{muse-500}$	$DANN_{muse-0}$
$\mathcal{F}_{avg}$	54.6	51.2	35.3	54.4	51.1
$\mathcal{F}_{cnn}$	55.4	52.3	42.2	55.4	52.4
$\mathcal{F}_{han}$	55.3	51.8	41.5	55.7	52.0

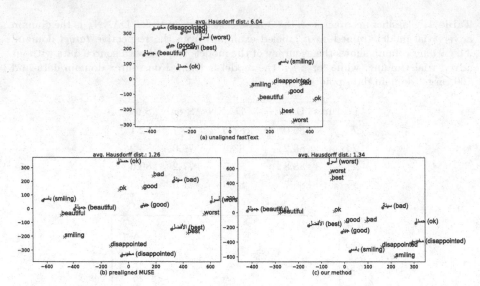

Fig. 3. Visualization of selected word-vectors in a two-dimensional space using t-SNE [25] for dimensionality reduction. (a) shows the unaligned fastText vectors, (b) are the prealigned MUSE vectors and (c) shows the fastText vectors after projection into a common space during training

vectors in a common space during training, we obtain a similar performance to the model architecture with the pretrained multilingual MUSE word-vectors. This can be explained that the learnt alignment is trained to best suit the task of the classifier, while the multilingual word-vectors may be trained towards a different objective. A visualization of our fine-tuned word-vectors in Fig. 3 supports these results. The monolingual word-vectors do not show any visible alignment between words in different languages. Using our model, they were projected into a common space during training and have overall lower average Hausdorff distance, indicating an alignment of the two embedding spaces.

6   Conclusion

We evaluated different feature extractors for the domain-adversarial training of text classifiers in low- and zero-resource scenarios. Our experimental results reveal that adversarial training of a domain discriminator works as a regularizer across different architectures ranging from simple to complex networks. All tested feature extractors were able to learn a domain-invariant document-representation. We also showed that learning a projection of word-vectors into a common space during training can improve classification performance and renders the use of pretrained multilingual word-vectors unnecessary.

Acknowledgments. This research and development project is funded within the "Future of Work" Program by the German Federal Ministry of Education and Research

(BMBF) and the European Social Fund in Germany. It is implemented by the Project Management Agency Karlsruhe (PTKA). The authors are responsible for the content of this publication.

References

1. Aggarwal, C.C., Zhai, C.: A survey of text classification algorithms. In: Aggarwal, C.C., Zhai, C. (eds.) Mining Text Data, pp. 163–222. Springer, Boston (2012). https://doi.org/10.1007/978-1-4614-3223-4_6
2. Agić, Ž., Johannsen, A., Plank, B., Martínez, H.A., Schluter, N., Søgaard, A.: Multilingual projection for parsing truly low-resource languages. Trans. Assoc. Comput. Linguist. **4**, 301 (2016)
3. Ammar, W., Mulcaire, G., Tsvetkov, Y., Lample, G., Dyer, C., Smith, N.A.: Massively multilingual word embeddings. arXiv preprint arXiv:1602.01925 (2016)
4. Arjovsky, M., Chintala, S., Bottou, L.: Wasserstein GAN. arXiv.org (2017)
5. Bahdanau, D., Cho, K., Bengio, Y.: Neural Machine Translation by Jointly Learning to Align and Translate. arXiv.org (2014)
6. Bengio, Y., Ducharme, R., Vincent, P., Janvin, C.: A neural probabilistic language model. J. Mach. Learn. Res. **3**, 1137–1155 (2003)
7. Chen, X., Athiwaratkun, B., Sun, Y., Weinberger, K.Q., Cardie, C.: Adversarial deep averaging networks for cross-lingual sentiment classification. In: NIPS cs.CL (2017)
8. Collobert, R., Weston, J., Bottou, L., Karlen, M., Kavukcuoglu, K., Kuksa, P.: Natural Language Processing (almost) from Scratch. arXiv.org (2011)
9. Fang, M., Cohn, T.: Model transfer for tagging low-resource languages using a bilingual dictionary. arXiv preprint arXiv:1705.00424 (2017)
10. Faruqui, M., Dyer, C.: Improving vector space word representations using multilingual correlation. In: Proceedings of the 14th Conference of the European Chapter of the Association for Computational Linguistics, pp. 462–471 (2014)
11. Ganin, Y., et al.: Domain-adversarial training of neural networks. J. Mach. Learn. Res. (JMLR) **17**(1), 1–35 (2016)
12. Glorot, X., Bordes, A., Bengio, Y.: Domain adaptation for large-scale sentiment classification: a deep learning approach. In: Proceedings of the 28th International Conference on Machine Learning (ICML 2011), pp. 513–520 (2011)
13. Goodfellow, I.J., et al.: Generative adversarial networks. In: Advances in Neural Information Processing Systems (NIPS) (2014)
14. Gulrajani, I., Ahmed, F., Arjovsky, M., Dumoulin, V., Courville, A.: Improved training of Wasserstein GANs. arXiv (2017)
15. Hao, S., Boyd-Graber, J.L., Paul, M.J.: Lessons from the Bible on Modern Topics - Low-Resource Multilingual Topic Model Evaluation. CoRR cs.CL (2018)
16. Harris, Z.S.: Distributional structure. In: Papers in Structural and Transformational Linguistics, pp. 775–794. Springer, Netherlands (1970). https://doi.org/10.1007/978-94-017-6059-1
17. He, R., McAuley, J.: Ups and downs - modeling the visual evolution of fashion trends with one-class collaborative filtering. In: NIPS (2016)
18. Hinton, G.E., Srivastava, N., Krizhevsky, A., Sutskever, I., Salakhutdinov, R.R.: Improving neural networks by preventing co-adaptation of feature detectors. arXiv.org (2012)
19. Hjelm, R.D., Jacob, A.P., Che, T., Cho, K., Bengio, Y.: Boundary-seeking generative adversarial networks. arXiv (2017)

20. Joulin, A., Grave, E., Bojanowski, P., Mikolov, T.: Bag of tricks for efficient text classification. arXiv preprint arXiv:1607.01759 (2016)
21. Kim, Y.: Convolutional neural networks for sentence classification. In: EMNLP 2014 (2014)
22. Kingma, D.P., Ba, J.: Adam: A Method for Stochastic Optimization. arXiv.org (2014)
23. Li, J., Monroe, W., Shi, T., Jean, S., Ritter, A., Jurafsky, D.: Adversarial learning for neural dialogue generation. In: Proceedings of the 2017 Conference on Empirical Methods in Natural Language Processing, pp. 2157–2169. Association for Computational Linguistics, Copenhagen, September 2017. https://www.aclweb.org/anthology/D17-1230
24. Liu, B., Zhang, L.: A survey of opinion mining and sentiment analysis. In: Aggarwal, C.C., Zhai, C. (eds.) Mining Text Data, pp. 415–463. Springer, Boston (2012). https://doi.org/10.1007/978-1-4614-3223-4_13
25. van der Maaten, L., Hinton, G.: Visualizing data using t-SNE. J. Mach. Learn. Res. **9**(Nov), 2579–2605 (2008)
26. McAuley, J.J., Targett, C., Shi, Q., van den Hengel, A.: Image-based recommendations on styles and substitutes. In: NIPS (2015)
27. Mikolov, T., Chen, K., Corrado, G., Dean, J.: Efficient estimation of word representations in vector space. In: NIPS (2013)
28. Nair, V., Hinton, G.E.: Rectified linear units improve restricted Boltzmann machines. In: Proceedings of the 27th International Conference on International Conference on Machine Learning, pp. 807–814 (2010)
29. Pang, B., Lee, L., Vaithyanathan, S.: Thumbs up?: sentiment classification using machine learning techniques. In: Proceedings of the ACL-02 Conference on Empirical Methods in Natural Language Processing, vol. 10, pp. 79–86 (2002)
30. Pennington, J., Socher, R., Manning, C.D.: GloVe: global vectors for word representation. In: Empirical Methods in Natural Language Processing (EMNLP), pp. 1532–1543 (2014)
31. Press, O., Bar, A., Bogin, B., Berant, J., Wolf, L.: Language generation with recurrent generative adversarial networks without pre-training. arXiv (2017)
32. Rajaraman, A., Ullman, J.D.: Mining of Massive Datasets. Cambridge University Press, Cambridge (2011)
33. Rajeswar, S., Subramanian, S., Dutil, F., Pal, C., Courville, A.: Adversarial generation of natural language. arXiv (2017)
34. Sahami, M., Dumais, S., Heckerman, D., Horvitz, E.: A Bayesian approach to filtering junk E-mail. In: Learning for Text Categorization: Papers from the 1998 Workshop. AAAI Technical Report WS-98-05, Madison, Wisconsin (1998). citeseer.ist.psu.edu/sahami98bayesian.html
35. Salameh, M., Mohammad, S., Kiritchenko, S.: Sentiment after translation: a case-study on Arabic social media posts. In: Proceedings of the 2015 Conference of the North American Chapter of the Association for Computational Linguistics: Human Language Technologies, pp. 767–777 (2015)
36. Tai, K.S., Socher, R., Manning, C.D.: Improved semantic representations from tree-structured long short-term memory networks. In: NIPS (2015)
37. Villani, C.: Optimal Transport: Old and New. Grundlehren der mathematischen Wissenschaften. Springer, Heidelberg (2008). https://doi.org/10.1007/978-3-540-71050-9
38. Wang, S., Manning, C.D.: Baselines and bigrams: Simple, good sentiment and topic classification. In: Proceedings of the 50th Annual Meeting of the Association for Computational Linguistics: Short Papers-Volume 2 (2012)

39. Xu, K., et al.: Show, Attend and Tell: Neural Image Caption Generation with Visual Attention. arXiv.org (2015)
40. Yang, Z., Yang, D., Dyer, C., He, X., Smola, A.J., Hovy, E.H.: Hierarchical attention networks for document classification. In: HLT-NAACL (2016)
41. Zhao, J.J., Kim, Y., Zhang, K., Rush, A.M., LeCun, Y.: Adversarially regularized autoencoders for generating discrete structures. arXiv (2017)

Handling Ellipsis in a Spoken Medical Phraselator

Manny Rayner[1][(✉)], Johanna Gerlach[1], Pierrette Bouillon[1], Nikos Tsourakis[1], and Hervé Spechbach[2]

[1] FTI/TIM, University of Geneva, Geneva, Switzerland
{Emmanuel.Rayner,Johanna.Gerlach,Pierrette.Bouillon,
Nikolaos.Tsourakis}@unige.ch
[2] Hôpitaux Universitaires de Genève, Geneva, Switzerland
Herve.Spechbach@hcuge.ch

Abstract. We consider methods for handling incomplete (elliptical) utterances in spoken phraselators, and describe how they have been implemented inside BabelDr, a substantial spoken medical phraselator. The challenge is to extend the phrase matching process so that it is sensitive to preceding dialogue context. We contrast two methods, one using limited-vocabulary strict grammar-based speech and language processing and one using large-vocabulary speech recognition with fuzzy grammar-based processing, and present an initial evaluation on a spoken corpus of 821 context-sentence/elliptical-phrase pairs. The large-vocabulary/fuzzy method strongly outperforms the limited-vocabulary/strict method over the whole corpus, though it is slightly inferior for the subset that is within grammar coverage. We investigate possibilities for combining the two processing paths, using several machine learning frameworks, and demonstrate that hybrid methods strongly outperform the large-vocabulary/fuzzy method.

Keywords: Phraselators · Speech understanding · Ellipsis
Medical applications · Context-dependent translation

1 Background and Motivation

In this paper, we will be examining issues that arise when building spoken medical phraselators. By this, we mean speech-enabled systems useful to medical professionals (hereafter, "doctors", though in practice they can be nurses or medical receptionists), which contain a limited repertoire of phrases, each one paired with translations in a number of target languages. The operation of the system is that the doctor speaks, and the system shows her the phrase or phrases

The work described here was funded by the Fondation privée des Hôpitaux universitaires de Genève and Unitec. We would like to thank Nuance Inc for generously making their software available to us for research purposes, and one of the anonymous referees for helpful suggestions.

© Springer Nature Switzerland AG 2018
T. Dutoit et al. (Eds.): SLSP 2018, LNAI 11171, pp. 140–152, 2018.
https://doi.org/10.1007/978-3-030-00810-9_13

which match it most closely. If the doctor selects one of the candidate phrases offered by the system, the system speaks the translation in the currently active target language. If the doctor considers that none of the phrases are a close enough match to what she said, she respeaks.

There are two points following from the above which we will mention at once. First, medical phraselators have in no way been rendered obsolete by Google Translate (GT) and similar systems. GT is known to be seriously inaccurate in medical situations; experiments carried out by ourselves and other groups suggest that it mistranslates 30–40% of all utterances [2,5]. The problem is not so much the error rate as the fact that the only feedback given to the source language user, the recognition result, is unreliable, since correctly recognised utterances can often be mistranslated. For these reasons, doctors are sceptical about systems like GT and more interested in phraselators, which are constructed to give completely reliable feedback.

Second, medical phraselators are nontrivial to build. There is a temptation to think that little more is required than to assemble a collection of useful phrases, get them translated into the target languages, and connect them to a speech recogniser, but practical experience shows this picture is deceptive. Quite apart from the fact that selection and accurate translation of the content requires substantial expertise, the fundamental challenge at the software level is the matching process. It is unreasonable to expect the doctor to remember more than a small number of fixed phrases [3], so the system must be able to support robust, accurate matching of freely expressed user input against the phrase repertoire.

The specific problem we will examine in this paper is that of incomplete (elliptical) phrases, which constitute a particularly difficult challenge for the matching process. For example, suppose that the last question was "Is the pain worse when you lean forward?". If the doctor now wants to continue by asking whether standing up also makes the pain worse, it is obviously clumsy to say "Is the pain worse when you stand up?"; a shorter and more natural phrasing is the elliptical "When you stand up?". The problem is that incomplete phrases of this kind are systematically ambiguous unless discourse context is taken into account: thus, in this particular example, "When you stand up?" could equally well mean "Is the pain better when you stand up?" or "Does it hurt when you stand up?", given suitable preceding contexts.

The paper describes approaches to the problem of translating elliptical utterances which have been implemented inside BabelDr, a medical phraselator currently being developed at the University of Geneva. Section 2 gives an overview of BabelDr, highlighting aspects of processing which are relevant here. The next three sections form the main content of the paper. Section 3 describes two solutions to the ellipsis translation problem which we have implemented, respectively using the system's "limited-vocabulary/strict grammar-based" and "large-vocabulary/fuzzy grammar-based" processing paths, Sect. 4 describes how the two solutions can be combined into a hybrid processing method, and Sect. 5 describes an initial evaluation. The final section concludes and suggests next steps.

2   The BabelDr Medical Phraselator

The BabelDr project (http://babeldr.unige.ch/) is a collaboration, initiated in mid-2015, between the Hôpitaux Universitaires de Genéve (HUG), Geneva's main hospital, and Geneva University's Faculty of Translation and Interpreting. The goal is to develop a medical phraselator usable in real medical situations, focusing initially on communication between French-speaking medical professionals and Arabic- and Tigrinya-speaking patients presenting at HUG's Accident and Emergency and Migrant Health facilities. Target languages currently being added include Spanish, Farsi, Albanian, Amharic and Swiss French Sign Language. Two evaluations with simulated patients have been carried out (the first is described in [2]). Initial clinical trials are scheduled for August 2018.

The currently popular way to create systems of the kind under consideration here is to use machine learning methods, collecting data to train a domain-specific speech recogniser, together with a classifier which maps recogniser output to the set of defined phrases. This approach is not feasible in the medical phraselator context, where no relevant data is available and data collection is difficult and expensive. Instead, it is necessary to revert to an earlier kind of architecture based on hand-coded grammars. Human intelligence makes it possible to develop usable grammars with quantities of domain data that are still insufficient for machine learning methods.

```
Utterance
Source ($avez_vous | $ça_fait | $ressentez_vous) $mal_au_ventre \
      $$depuis_durée
Source $c_est_douloureux $$depuis_durée
Source ?$votre_douleur (dure-t-elle | dure-t-il) $$depuis_durée
Source ?(est-ce (que|qu')) $votre_douleur dure $$depuis_durée
Source ?$vos_douleurs (durent-elles | durent-ils) $$depuis_durée
Source ?(est-ce (que|qu')) $vos_douleurs durent $$depuis_durée
Target/french Avez-vous mal au ventre $$depuis_durée ?
EndUtterance

TrLex $$depuis_durée source="depuis longtemps" \
      french="depuis longtemps"
TrLex $$depuis_durée source="depuis ?environ une heure" \
      french="depuis une heure"
(...)
```

Fig. 1. BabelDr rule for the question-schema *"Avez-vous mal au ventre ⟨DepuisDurée⟩"* ("Have you had abdominal pain ⟨SinceTime⟩"). We only show the source-language (French) side. Items starting with a single dollar sign ($) are simple non-terminals. $$depuis_durée is a synchronised (translated) non-terminal defined by the TrLex rules, only two of which are shown. The line starting Target/french is the canonical sentence/backtranslation. The notation is defined in the online documentation [6].

BabelDr's grammars are written in a variant of Synchronised Context Free Grammar (SCFG; [1]) which compactly associates source-language and target-language patterns. In order to allow modular development of the grammars, source- and target-language content is split into separate files, with a canonical version of the source-language used both as a pivot and as a backtranslation; thus source-language rules map source language phrases into canonical phrases/backtranslations, and target-language rules map canonical phrases into target-language phrases. Typically, on the order of tens or hundreds of thousands of possible source-language utterances will be mapped into each canonical phrase; an example of a source-language rule is shown in Fig. 1. Rules are compiled into GrXML grammars and then into grammar-based language models that can be run on a variety of recognition platforms supporting the GrXML standard. This architecture is described in detail in [7].

The key advantage of the limited-vocabulary/strict grammar-based architecture is that it is fast. Recognition, parsing and translation are all combined by compilation into a single efficient operation, yielding response latency of several times real time on the commercial Nuance 10.2 platform. The downside, as usual, is that strict grammar-based processing is fragile, with poor performance on utterances which are outside grammar coverage. For these reasons, we later added a second processing path which combines large-vocabulary recognition and robust matching of grammar rules against recogniser output.

We experimented with different methods for performing the robust matching. The conceptually simplest one is well-known (e.g. [4]): sample the grammar to create a semantically annotated corpus, and use it to train a machine learning classifier. We have found, however, that directly performing fuzzy matching of the grammar against the recogniser output is a highly competitive alternative. By weighting the words with tf-idf scores [9] and doing the match with a bottom-up dynamic programming algorithm[1], we have obtained accuracy not worse than any of the machine learning methods we have so far investigated, and much better than the strict grammar-based method [8]. The fuzzy matching process is fast enough that response times are in practice dominated by the recognition speed of the large-vocabulary recogniser.

As noted, the fuzzy matching method is much more accurate than the strict grammar-based method; the experiments in [8] show relative reductions in 1-best semantic error rate by 35% and 2-best semantic error rate by 45% on realistic unseen speech data. This is unsurprising, given that commercial large-vocabulary recognisers, with a little domain tuning, can achieve word error rates of under 15% on BabelDr data, while the grammar-based recogniser's WER is typically in the neighbourhood of 30–40%.

3   Context-Dependence and Ellipsis

We now describe how we extended the limited-vocabulary/strict grammar-based and large-vocabulary/fuzzy grammar-based processing methods sketched in the

---

[1] The matching algorithm is fully specified in [8].

previous section to make them capable of handling elliptical utterances. In the following section, we go on to consider hybrid processing.

3.1   Limited-Vocabulary/Strict Grammar-Based Method

The limited-vocabulary/strict grammar-based processing path allows an obvious approach to handling elliptical sentences. Grammar rules are extended to include plausible elliptical variants of phrases; since this makes many elliptical phrases ambiguous, a method is added to prefer readings coherent with the preceding dialogue context to ones which are not. We examine the details.

The first question is how to extend the grammar. The example rule in Fig. 1 immediately suggests one plausible strategy: look for rules which are parametrized by synchronised/translation variables, then include the variable as an elliptical alternative. So in the example, which gives different French expressions meaning "Have you had abdominal pain ⟨SinceTime⟩?", we add "⟨SinceTime⟩" as an elliptical variant. This means that e.g. the French version of "for a long time" (*depuis longtemps*) will be included as an elliptical form of "Have you had abdominal pain for a long time?", the French version of "for a few hours" (*depuis plusieurs heures*) will be included as an elliptical form of "Have you had abdominal pain for a few hours?", and so on. So far, all the elliptical rules added to the grammar have basically used this approach. In a few cases, the parametrization of the rule is not explicit, and the grammar contains several related rules. Here, the elliptical variant is in effect the element which would been the translation variable if the rules had been parametrized.

In the initial version, we have also used a minimal approach to defining the preference method which chooses between ambiguous readings of an elliptical utterance: we compare the canonical sentences/backtranslations for the different readings of the current utterance against the canonical sentence/backtranslation for the preceding accepted utterance, and pick the one which has the smallest edit distance. Thus, adapting the French examples to English for convenience, suppose the preceding sentence was "Initially, was the pain most intense in the upper part of the abdomen?", with canonical form "When the pain first appeared, was it strongest in the upper part of the abdomen?". If the following utterance is "Around the navel?", there are two possible interpretations, with canonical forms "Is the pain strongest around the navel?" and "When the pain first appeared, was it strongest around the navel?". The edit distance is smaller for the second alternative, so this one is preferred.

3.2   Large-Vocabulary/Fuzzy Grammar-Based Method

The strict grammar-based solution is conceptually straightforward, but it is not obvious how to add enough rules to give good coverage of plausible elliptical sentences. The strategy of adding rules for the parameters/translation variables is too simplistic. A straightforward example of a type of ellipsis not conforming to this pattern is provided by the words for "left" and "right". The doctor will often ask a question which refers to a side of the body, e.g. "Did the pain start in the left side?" Here, the parametrized element is "in the left side". The doctor can continue "In the right side?", which fits the pattern; but they can equally well shorten the question to the single word "Right?", which does not fit.

The fuzzy grammar-based processing route offers a more principled way to address the problem. Rather than add any special rules, we simply say that fuzzy matching of rules can take input both from the current input string and from the discourse context. In the initial implementation, we define the discourse context to be the matched string from the most recent accepted sentence. Thus in the example above, we assume that the system has just successfully recognised "Did the pain start in the left side?", making this sentence the context. It can then correctly interpret "Right?" as "Did the pain start in the right side?" by matching the word "right" against the current input, and the remaining words against the context.

This simple idea appears to work remarkably well, with just two minor enhancements. First, we need to enforce the constraint that words in the current input are preferred to words in the context. We do this by multiplying the tf-idf scores for words taken from the context by a discounting factor $k_{context}$; the value of $k_{context}$ is unimportant, as long as it is small enough that context words always have lower scores than non-context words. Second, we prefer matches which are similar to the context by adding a component to the global score for the match, consisting of the word edit distance between the candidate match and the context multiplied by another constant $k_{parallel}$. Again, performance does not appear to be sensitive to the value of the parameter, as long as it produces parallelism scores small compared to the normal tf-idf scores. In Sect. 5, we describe an initial evaluation.

4   Hybrid Processing and Machine Learning

It is possible to improve on the performance of the "fuzzy" method by exploiting the fact that grammar-based recognition platforms like Nuance 10.2 deliver fairly reliable confidence scores. This lets us create a hybrid system which uses the pure grammar-based result when the confidence score is over a threshold, otherwise defaulting to the "fuzzy" result. The point is that the grammar-based recogniser's WER is much lower on the high-confidence portion of the data, and with a suitable threshold can be reduced to a point substantially under that of the large-vocabulary recogniser. The experiments in [8] show the hybrid method achieving a relative reduction in 1-best semantic error rate by 8% and 2-best semantic error rate by 20%, compared to the plain fuzzy matching method.

The reason why this simple method worked well in [8] is the fact that text processing on plain utterances is normally trivial. If a plain utterance is correctly recognised, we can be almost sure that it will also produce a correct interpretation. Utterances where the grammar-based recogniser gives a high confidence score have a high probability of being correctly recognised, hence are also likely to give correct interpretations. The argument is however not valid for elliptical utterances, where text processing poses more challenging problems, and a correctly recognised utterance can easily be misinterpreted. It seemed reasonable to hope that a better procedure for deciding between the strict and fuzzy processing paths could be crafted by including a larger number of features and training a classifier. In our initial experiments, we have used the following set:

1. Grammar-based recogniser confidence score. A low score suggests strict grammar-based processing is wrong.
2. Edit distance between the current strict grammar-based canonical sentence and the previous strict grammar-based canonical sentence. A low score suggests that strict grammar-based processing is right.
3. Fuzzy match score. A high score suggests that fuzzy processing is right.
4. Number of words in current large-vocabulary recogniser input that are not in the fuzzy match string. A high score suggests fuzzy matching is wrong.
5. Number of words in the fuzzy match string that are neither in the current recogniser input nor in the previous match. A high score suggests fuzzy matching is wrong.
6. Edit distance between the current fuzzy match string and the previous fuzzy match string. A low score suggests fuzzy processing is right.
7. Length in words of the large-vocabulary recognition result. Short results tend to be elliptical.

We used these features, together with the SVM, NaiveBayes, J48, Random-Forest, DecisionTable and KStar methods from the Weka toolkit, to train several classifiers on the task of predicting which of the two kinds of processing was more likely to yield a correct result: in other words, the hybrid output for each example is the result of the classifier choosing between the "strict" and "fuzzy" outputs, and the machine learning problem is to make this choice as accurate as possible. Experiments and results are described in the next section.

5   Experiments

This section describes preliminary experiments to investigate the performance of the ellipsis processing mechanisms just described. We describe the data, experiments on each individual ellipsis processing method, and experiments on hybrid processing.

5.1   Data

Collecting spontaneous data in the medical interpretation domain is costly and time-consuming. For example, the experiments described in [2], which produced less than a thousand utterances of high-quality annotated data, required over three person-months of work. Support for ellipsis processing was only introduced recently; previous data collection exercises threw up few examples of ellipsis, in part because subjects were explicitly advised in the pre-experiment instructions not to use incomplete phrases.

We have consequently begun by using an artificial corpus, which was produced as follows. The project member responsible for grammar development first

selected 191 sentences currently inside grammar coverage where an elliptical continuation was intuitively plausible, writing down an example of a continuation
in each case. The intention was that the sentences and fragments would provide
as broad a range of examples as possible. Five native francophone subjects, all
students at Geneva University, were then asked to read the pairs in a natural
voice, freely varying the wording if possible under the constraint that the frag-
ment would still be a plausible follow-on to the sentence. Data was collected
using a web tool which prompted the students and recorded their responses.
This produced a total of 955 recorded spoken sentence/fragment pairs.

Each utterance was then transcribed and semantically annotated, using a
web tool, by a project member familiar with the grammar. Semantic annotation consisted of labelling each utterance with the canonical sentence that the
annotator considered closest in meaning to the utterance, or with a null token
if there was no sufficiently close canonical sentence. Sentences were divided into
pairs consisting of a plain utterance and a follow-on elliptical utterance; pairs
were removed in cases where this was not possible, most frequently because the
subject had failed to follow the instructions and had not produced an elliptical
follow-on utterance. Semantic annotation assumed a null context in the case of
the plain utterance, and a context consisting of the associated plain utterance
in the case of the elliptical sentence. This process finally produced 821 recorded,
transcribed and annotated utterance pairs. The average utterance length for
the plain utterances was 8.96 words, and 73.0% were inside grammar coverage;
for the elliptical utterances, the average length was 3.14 words and 51.6% were
inside grammar coverage.

5.2   Different Types of Ellipsis Processing

We first processed the corpus just described, in both spoken and text form,
through three different offline versions of the system:

Strict Grammar-based speech and text processing using the commercial Nuance
10.2 recogniser, strict grammar-based ellipsis processing.

Fuzzy/NTE Large-vocabulary recognition using the commercial Nuance Transcription engine, fuzzy grammar-based text processing. The version of NTE
used a language model created as an interpolation between a domain-specific
model trained on data sampled from the grammar, and a general model.

Fuzzy/Google Large-vocabulary recognition using Google Speech API, fuzzy
grammar-based text processing. Google Speech API offers considerably more
restricted possibilities for domain tuning than NTE, and we decided it was
most interesting to maximise the contrast by using an untuned recogniser.

Since the focus of the experiment is processing of elliptical utterances and the
data is any case artificial, we used an idealised "best-case" approach to define
the context. Consistent with the annotation scheme, utterances were processed
in pairs, where the first sentence in each pair was a plain utterance and the second was a follow-on elliptical utterance. The plain utterance was processed with

a null context. The elliptical utterance was processed with a context where the canonical sentence used by grammar-based processing was the correct canonical sentence for the preceding plain utterance, and the context string used by fuzzy processing was the match string resulting from fuzzy processing of the transcription from the preceding plain utterance.

The above definition is more natural than it may first seem. During normal operation of the phraselator, the doctor will abort processing on all sentences which have been misunderstood, so it is reasonable to assume that processing of the "plain" sentence in the pair will be correct. Another possible methodological objection is that the processing methodology ignores a problem which can arise in the general setting, where fuzzy processing of a plain utterance yields an incorrect result due to words being inappropriately taken from the preceding context. This occurs, but it is rare on the data we have so far examined. As a check, we processed the (non-artificial) corpus from [8] in a mode where each sentence provided the context for the following one. The results were almost unchanged, with a marginal difference in semantic error rate of less than 1% absolute.

Finally, we used the different machine learning methods described in Sect. 4 to create a number of hybrid systems that combined two different processing paths. Experiments were carried out using the combinations **Strict + Fuzzy/NTE** and **Strict + Fuzzy/Google**.

5.3   Results

We now present the results of the experiments just described. Table 1 shows raw recognition performance in terms of Word Error Rate (WER) and Sentence Error Rate (SER), contrasting one limited-vocabulary grammar-based recogniser, Nuance Recognizer 10.2, against two large-vocabulary recognisers, Nuance Transcription Engine and Google Speech API. Several points stand out. First, WER is much higher for the grammar-based recogniser than for the large-vocabulary recognisers (34.8% versus 6.4% and 9.9% for plain utterances, 42.1% versus 23.3% and 14.2% for elliptical utterances). Second, the difference between WER on in-coverage and out-of-coverage utterances is very large for the grammar-based recogniser (26.8% versus 53.4% for plain, 15.4% versus 67.9% for elliptical), but quite small for the large-vocabulary recognisers (5.3% and 9.0% versus 9.1% and 8.6% for plain; 21.4% and 14.4% versus 25.2% and 14.6% for elliptical). Third, WER is much higher on elliptical utterances than on non-elliptical for the Nuance Transcription Engine (23.3% versus 6.4%), but only moderately higher for the other two recognisers (42.1% versus 34.8% for Nuance Recogniser; 14.2% versus 9.9% for Google Speech API). The unexpected result here is the WER for the Nuance Transcription Engine, which is dramatically worse on elliptical utterances compared to plain utterances, the difference corresponding to a factor of 3.6.

Table 2 presents figures for semantic error rate, which, as previously, we define as the proportion of utterances producing an incorrect canonical sentence. For the whole set of plain utterances, the semantic error rate for the tuned NTE

Table 1. Recogniser performance for plain and elliptical utterances on in-coverage, out-of-coverage and all data, using three recognizers: grammar-based/Nuance Recognizer 10.2, large-vocabulary/Nuance Transcription Engine and large-vocabulary/Google Speech API.

Recogniser	IC		OOC		All	
	WER	SER	WER	SER	WER	SER
Plain utterances						
Nuance Recognizer	26.8	63.1	53.4	100.0	34.8	73.1
Nuance Transcription Engine	5.3	20.9	9.1	52.7	6.4	29.5
Google Speech API	9.0	44.6	8.6	44.1	9.9	45.9
Elliptical utterances						
Nuance Recognizer	15.4	23.6	67.9	100.0	42.1	60.5
Nuance Transcription Engine	21.1	35.6	25.2	56.7	23.3	45.8
Google Speech API	14.4	33.6	14.6	31.8	14.2	35.5

recogniser on speech input is about half that for the grammar-based recogniser (18.9% versus 35.2%). The difference for elliptical utterances is slightly smaller (30.5% versus 53.1%), but still represents a reduction in error rate by 43%. This is consistent with the results presented in our paper from last year [8].

The semantic error rates are roughly in line with the WER figures from Table 1. Looking first at the in-coverage part of the data, we find that the semantic error rate on plain utterances is much lower for the NTE large-vocabulary recogniser than for the grammar-based one (10.7% versus 23.7%, 56% relative reduction); but for elliptical utterances, the grammar-based recogniser narrowly outperforms NTE (27.8% versus 29.7%). When we compare the untuned Google Speech API recogniser to the tuned NTE recogniser, we see a similar pattern. For plain utterances, it performed much worse than NTE (26.2% versus 18.9%), but for elliptical utterances the two large-vocabulary recognisers delivered almost the same performance (30.5% versus 30.3%).

Over the 1642 utterances in the corpus, the balance between the two processing methods is as follows when the NTE recogniser is used to provide input for fuzzy processing. For 790 utterances, both methods give a correct result, and for 282 they both give an incorrect result. Out of the 570 remaining utterances, there are 443 (78%) where fuzzy processing is correct and strict grammar-based is incorrect, and 127 (22%) where strict grammar-based processing is correct and fuzzy processing is incorrect. With Google Speech API, the breakdown is 727 both correct, 279 neither correct, 446 (62%) fuzzy correct/strict incorrect, and 279 (38%) strict correct/fuzzy incorrect.

The results for hybrid methods are shown in Table 3. Unexpectedly, since we had thought the problem of deciding between strict and fuzzy processing was challenging and there was little data, machine learning delivered very substantial gains. Several different methods were able to reduce the semantic error rate on

Table 2. 1-best semantic classification error for three different recognisers, distinguishing plain and elliptical utterances. "Speech" = spoken input processed by recogniser; "Text" = simulated perfect recognition.

Version	IC		OOC		All data	
	Speech	Text	Speech	Text	Speech	Text
Plain utterances						
Nuance Recognizer 10.2	23.7	(0)	66.2	(100)	35.2	27.0
Nuance Transcription Engine	10.7	1.7	41.0	32.9	18.9	10.1
Google Speech API	21.5	1.7	38.7	32.9	26.2	10.1
Elliptical utterances						
Nuance Recognizer 10.2	27.8	(0)	80.1	(100)	53.1	48.4
Nuance Transcription Engine	29.7	14.6	31.2	17.1	30.5	15.8
Google Speech API	28.8	14.6	32.0	17.1	30.3	15.8

elliptical utterances from about 30% to 22–23%, a relative reduction of around 25%. With the Google recogniser, there was also a large improvement in semantic error rate on plain utterances, from 26% to 17–19%. The surprising consequence is that the hybrid system with the untuned Google recogniser is approximately equivalent to the hybrid system with the tuned NTE recogniser; it is slightly less accurate on 'plain' and slightly more accurate on 'ellipsis'.

Table 3. 1-best semantic classification error on speech data for hybrid strategies using different ML methods to combine strict and fuzzy grammar-based processing.

| | Nuance Trans. Engine | | | | | | Google Speech API | | | | | |
| | Plain | | | Elliptical | | | Plain | | | Elliptical | | |
Version	IC	OOC	All	IC	OOC	All	IC	OOC	All	IC	OOC	All
Baseline	10.7	41.0	18.9	29.7	31.2	30.5	21.5	38.7	26.2	28.8	32.0	30.3
NaiveBayes	9.1	37.8	16.6	26.9	32.0	29.5	10.5	36.0	17.6	27.8	32.7	30.3
KStar	10.0	37.8	17.5	17.9	31.5	25.2	9.3	35.5	17.9	16.0	31.2	23.1
SVM	9.5	38.7	16.7	17.2	32.0	24.2	10.0	38.3	17.7	15.3	32.7	23.1
J48	7.7	39.6	16.8	17.0	30.2	24.7	11.5	37.8	19.4	15.3	31.0	23.3
DecisionTable	9.2	39.6	16.8	16.5	31.0	24.1	12.2	38.3	19.4	14.9	31.7	22.8
RandomForest	8.0	37.4	15.6	16.5	30.5	23.9	9.0	34.6	17.2	14.8	30.7	22.5

6   Conclusions and Further Directions

We have presented two general methods that can be used to extend the functionality of a grammar-based spoken phraselator so that it includes support for elliptical utterances, and evaluated them inside the BabelDr prototype. The first method is uses only strict grammar-based methods for both recognition and language processing, and the second combines large-vocabulary recognition with fuzzy grammar-based matching. On our initial artificial corpus, the fuzzy method strongly outperforms the strict grammar-based method, reducing the semantic error rate on elliptical utterances from 53% to 30%. Despite this, we were surprised to find that a hybrid system combining the two methods strongly outperforms plain fuzzy processing, further reducing the error rate to 22.5%.

To progress beyond this point, one plausible idea is to address the speech recognition component. On plain utterances, Nuance Transcription Engine, whose language model had been tuned to the domain, achieved by far the best performance. It however did no better than the untuned Google Speech API on elliptical utterances, and its WER on elliptical data was over three and a half times higher than on the plain data. It may well be significant that the data used to train the Nuance Transcription Engine domain language model so far only contains plain utterances sampled from the grammar. The next step will consequently be to investigate strategies for adding elliptical utterances to the language model training corpus.

As noted, the experiments described here tell us nothing about the impact the methods would have in real situations. In the next BabelDr system evaluation, scheduled for August 2018 and involving real patients, we will use a version of the system which includes support for ellipsis processing. This will let us make an initial evaluation of its relevance at the level of system usability.

References

1. Aho, A.V., Ullman, J.D.: Properties of syntax directed translations. J. Comput. Syst. Sci. **3**(3), 319–334 (1969)
2. Bouillon, P., Gerlach, J., Spechbach, H., Tsourakis, N., Halimi, S.: BabelDr vs Google Translate: a user study at Geneva University Hospitals (HUG). In: Proceedings of the 20th Conference of the European Association for Machine Translation (EAMT), Prague, Czech Republic (2017)
3. Day, K.J., Song, N.: Attitudes and concerns of doctors and nurses about using a translation application for in-hospital brief interactions with Korean patients. J. Innov. health Inf. **24**(3), 262–267 (2017)
4. Jurafsky, A., et al.: Using a stochastic context-free grammar as a language model for speech recognition. In: Proceedings of the IEEE International Conference on Acoustics, Speech and Signal Processing, pp. 189–192 (1995)
5. Patil, S., Davies, P.: Use of Google Translate in medical communication: evaluation of accuracy. BMJ **349**, g7392 (2014)
6. Rayner, M.: Using the Regulus Lite Speech2Speech Platform (2016). Online documentation. http://www.issco.unige.ch/en/research/projects/Speech2SpeechDoc/build/html/index.html
7. Rayner, M., Bouillon, P., Ebling, S., Strasly, I., Tsourakis, N.: A framework for rapid development of limited-domain speech-to-sign phrasal translators. In: Proceedings of the workshop on Future and Emerging Trends in Language Technology, Sevilla, Spain (2015)

8. Rayner, M., Tsourakis, N., Gerlach, J.: Lightweight spoken utterance classification with CFG, tf-idf and dynamic programming. In: Camelin, N., Estève, Y., Martín-Vide, C. (eds.) SLSP 2017. LNCS (LNAI), vol. 10583, pp. 143–154. Springer, Cham (2017). https://doi.org/10.1007/978-3-319-68456-7_12
9. Sparck Jones, K.: A statistical interpretation of term specificity and its application in retrieval. J. Document. **28**(1), 11–21 (1972)

Text Processing and Analysis

Knowledge Transfer for Active Learning in Textual Anonymisation

Laura García-Sardiña[✉], Manex Serras, and Arantza del Pozo

Speech and Natural Language Technologies, Vicomtech,
Mikeletegi Pasealekua 57, 20009 Donostia-San Sebastán, Spain
{lgarcias,mserras,adelpozo}@vicomtech.org

Abstract. Data privacy compliance has gained a lot of attention over
the last years. The automation of the de-identification process is a challenging task that often requires annotating in-domain data from scratch,
as there is usually a lack of annotated resources for such scenarios. In this
work, knowledge from a classifier learnt from a source annotated dataset
is transferred to speed up the process of training a binary personal data
identification classifier in a pool-based Active Learning context, for a
new initially unlabelled target dataset which differs in language and
domain. To this end, knowledge from the source classifier is used for seed
selection and uncertainty based query selection strategies. Through the
experimentation phase, multiple entropy-based criteria and input diversity measures are combined. Results show a significant improvement of
the anonymisation label from the first batch, speeding up the classifier's
learning curve in the target domain and reaching top performance with
less than 10% of the total training data, thus demonstrating the usefulness of the proposed approach even when the anonymisation domains
diverge significantly.

Keywords: Knowledge Transfer · Active Learning · Seed selection
Query selection strategy · Textual anonymisation

1 Introduction

Due to the growing amount of data (and especially textual data) created every
day through social network posts, official documents, etc. that contain personal
information, data privacy has gained a lot of attention over the last few years.
Furthermore, valuable data which could be beneficial for research or trans-
parency purposes may be kept unshared if it contains personal information
because of the prohibitively high costs of its manual anonymisation and the
legal repercussions of not doing it correctly. Even if datasets are not too large,
manual anonymisation is a tedious and time-consuming task: Dorr et al. [6]
assessed that manually de-identifying medical notes containing an average of 7.9
Personal Health Information items took around 87.3 s per note to complete. In
this scenario, the automation of data sanitisation while preserving its usefulness
has been widely researched [4, 8, 12, 28].

© Springer Nature Switzerland AG 2018
T. Dutoit et al. (Eds.): SLSP 2018, LNAI 11171, pp. 155–166, 2018.
https://doi.org/10.1007/978-3-030-00810-9_14

Different approaches oriented to the anonymisation of unstructured textual data have been proposed in [4,16], where techniques of suppression, tagging/categorisation, and substitution are described. In this paper, the step previous to applying these techniques, i.e. personal data identification, is tackled. This step can be seen as a binary classification task, where the positive label corresponds to the words in an utterance that refer to sensible data such as personal names, organisations, passwords, and so on that need to be anonymised.

Lack of annotated data is a common issue when automating de-identification in supervised machine learning (ML) settings. In this context, the use of Active Learning (AL) [3] can optimise the data annotation phase, resulting in better ML models with fewer data. In a typical pool-based AL scenario the input is a small set of labelled instances (*seed*) and a large set of unannotated ones (*pool*). A classifier (*base learner*) is trained on the labelled instances and then asks an *oracle* to label the instance (in *serial* AL) or set of instances (in *batch mode* AL) which the classifier considers more informative according to some criterion (*query selection strategy*). The newly labelled data are moved from the pool to the labelled set and the classifier is retrained following this process iteratively until some *stopping criterion* is satisfied or the pool is empty. Two of the main questions that need to be answered in every AL framework are: (1) how to select the seed, and (2) which AL query selection strategy will be best to speed up the classifier's learning curve.

Very little attention has been paid to the seed selection aspect in the literature. Olsson [17] compared using a random seed against using cluster-centroid based sampling with little to no improvement for a NERC annotation task. Tomanek et al. [29,30] compare multiple kinds of seeds checking instances against manually created entity gazetteers, reporting significant improvements over the random selection. Other automatic approach presented by Dligach and Palmer [5] uses unsupervised language model (LM) sampling to select a seed containing the examples with lowest LM probability in a word sense disambiguation task, obtaining significantly better results than using a random seed.

As surveyed by Settles [21,22], there are multiple approaches for serial query selection in AL. In Uncertainty Sampling [10] scenarios, the learner uses an uncertainty measure (e.g. entropy) to query the most uncertain instances. Query-by-Committee [24] strategies use a committee of classifiers that present different hypotheses and query the instances with most disagreement. Expected classifier change methods query those instances which may cause the greatest change in the classifier. In Expected error reduction methods the classifier estimates the expected future error of the instances in the unlabelled pool and queries those with the minimal expected risk. In variance reduction strategies the learner queries those instances which minimise the output variance and thus the classifier's generalisation error. Finally, Density-weighted methods [2,20,23] query those instances which are both uncertain to the classifier and representative of the data's underlying distribution. Batch mode query strategies also attempt at selecting the best batch taking into account notions like information overlap in the set. Not much attention has been paid to this type of strategies in the literature even if batch mode AL is a more realistic practice scenario, as the overhead of re-training the ML model for each annotated instance often renders serial query selection unusable.

The Knowledge Transfer (KT) or Transfer Learning paradigm encompasses the idea of re-using existing annotated resources to improve learning in new domains or tasks [18]. As the anonymisation task may re-use information extracted from different corpora that may vary in domain and language, it is sensible to consider combining KT with AL. There have been some previous works in the Natural Language Processing (NLP) field that combine KT with AL. Rai et al. [19] propose hyperplane-based distances to choose the most divergent samples from the source and target domains as seed in a sentiment analysis task. However the existence of this hyperplane narrows down the possibilities of classification algorithms and may not be suitable for sequential data [1]. Shi et al. [27] use a set of labelled instances in the target domain to train a text classifier with data from both domains, the oracle is only asked to label when the classifier's confidence is too low. In a sentiment classification task, Li et al. [11] train one classifier on the source data and another one on the target data and then both are used to select the most informative samples using a Query-By-Committee strategy.

The motivation of this paper is to speed up the process of training a robust classifier for textual data anonymisation using KT from available corpora within the Active Learning framework. Our main contribution is a previously unexplored method for transferring the knowledge from a classifier trained on a source corpus, differing from the target corpus both in language and domain, to improve the AL process both at seed selection and query selection strategies, and accelerating the learning curve in the target domain from the very first labelled batch. The source classifier's uncertainty is combined using different scoring methodologies to select the best possible seed and query selection criteria. Also, to the extent of our knowledge, the Active Learning paradigm is tested for the first time in an anonymisation task. Finally, a strong baseline for the anonymisation task using the publicly available ES-Port corpus [7] is set.

The paper is structured as follows: in Sect. 2 the proposed methods to exploit Knowledge Transfer for Active Learning from a theoretical point of view are described; then the feature sets and corpora used for the selected anonymisation task are introduced in Sect. 3; in Sect. 4 the methods are tested and their results are presented focusing on the two topics of interest of the paper: seed and query selection strategy in the AL setting; final remarks and conclusions are given in Sect. 5, as well as some ideas on future work directions.

2 Knowledge Transfer for Seed and Query Selection Strategy

In this section, the different query strategies used in this work and how the knowledge from the source domain is used to improve the Active Learning process are explained in detail.

2.1 Active Learning

The traditional pool-based Active Learning process as described in Sect. 1 is shown in Algorithm 1.

Algorithm 1. Pool Active Learning typical setting

---
input : set of labelled instances L, pool of unlabelled instances U, query
        strategy ϕ, batch size B, stopping criterion S
repeat
    // Train model M on L
    Q = best set in U of size=B according to ϕ
    // Ask Oracle to label Q
    $L = L + Q$
    $U = U - Q$
until S or size(U)=0
return M, L

The anonymisation task is approached as a binary classification problem, where the positive label corresponds to the words to anonymise. Due to the sequential nature of the task, a discriminative model based on Conditional Random Fields [9] is used. These models have been intensively used for sequence labelling and segmentation [1,15,25].

2.2 Entropy Score Query Strategies

Being $I = (w_1, w_2, ...w_{|I|})$ an instance (i.e., a sentence or utterance) composed of words of a corpus and given the stochastic nature of the CRF classifiers, the uncertainty over the binary decision for each word $w_i \in I$ can be measured using the Shannon entropy [26]:

$$H(w_i) = -P(\hat{y}_i = A|\ I)log_2(P(\hat{y}_i = A|\ I))$$

$$-(1 - P(\hat{y}_i = A|\ I))log_2(1 - P(\hat{y}_i = A|\ I))$$

where $P(\hat{y}_i = A\ |\ I)$ is the probability of the classifier assigning the *anon* label A to the word w_i. As each instance is a sequence of words, the entropy score of the whole instance can be defined in multiple ways:

1. **H Sum:** Sum of all its word entropies: $H(I) = \sum_{w \in I} H(w)$
2. **H Mean:** Mean of its word entropies: $H(I) = \frac{1}{|I|} \sum_{w \in I} H(w)$
3. **H K-Max:** Mean of its K-Max word entropies: $H(I) = \frac{1}{K} \sum_{i=0}^{K} H(w)$, where the K words with highest entropy of the instance I are chosen.
4. **H Max:** Maximum entropy: $H(I) = max_{w \in I} H(w)$

The entropy scorers can be used to measure how certain the classifier is about a taken decision, yielding a robust query strategy to select the instances with high information content in the AL process.

2.3   K-Means-Centroids Query Strategy

The K-Means clustering algorithm [13] can be used to split the sample set into K clusters or groups. Then, the closest candidate to each cluster's centroid is selected. Being B the batch size of the instances to select from the pool, let $K = B$ in the clustering algorithm, splitting the pool in B clusters. Then, being $c_1, c_2, \cdots, c_B$ the centroids of each cluster and I_{c_k} the instances that encompass the cluster of centroid c_k, the closest instance I_k to the cluster centroid according to the Euclidean distance is chosen for each cluster:

$$I_k = argmin_{I \in I_{c_k}} ||c_k - I|| \ \forall \ k = 1, \cdots, B$$

2.4   K-Means-Centroids-Entropy Query Strategies

As the K-Means algorithm measures the input diversity and the $H(I)$ entropy scorers measure the base learner's uncertainty, both measures can be combined to select the instance I_k for each cluster centroid:

$$I_k = argmin_{I \in I_{c_k}} ||c_k - I|| \cdot (1 - rescale(H(I))) \tag{1}$$

where the $H(I)$ results are rescaled so they are within the range $[0, 1]$.

2.5   Entropy-Based Knowledge Transfer

In this section the proposed Knowledge Transfer methodology is explained. As depicted in Fig. 1, the entropy measures from the source classifier (S-H Sum/Mean/K-Max/Max) are used for both seed selection and query strategy in the target domain.

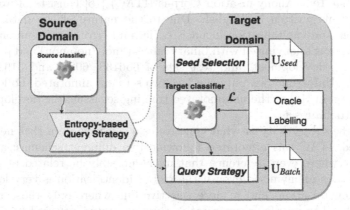

Fig. 1. KT schema, where entropy-based query strategies from the source classifier are used first for seed selection and then for query selection in the target domain

For seed selection, one cannot rely on knowledge from the target classifier or base learner since there is no labelled data in the target domain on which to train it. To overcome this limitation, the source domain classifier's entropy score S-H can be used to sample the most uncertain instances ($\mathcal{U}_{seed}$) of the target domain as seed. After annotation, these labelled instances $\mathcal{L}(\mathcal{U}_{seed})$ can be used to start training the target base learner. In addition, S-H can be combined with the target domain classifiers' entropy scorers (T-H) for query selection, in order to select the next batch $\mathcal{U}_{batch}$ of instances for the oracle to label.

3 Corpora

Two publicly available anonymised corpora differing in language, style, and domain have been used: ITAC and ES-Port. Both resources are briefly described below and their main characteristics are summarised in Table 1.

Table 1. ITAC and ES-Port corpora comparison

Characteristics	ITAC	ES-Port
Main language	English	Spanish
Language switching	No	Yes
Language form	Written, planned (emails)	Spoken, spontaneous (phone calls)
Domain	various (personal, corporate)	IT, telecommunications
Training utterances	473	47073

3.1 ITAC

The Informal Text Anonymisation Corpus (ITAC) [16] consists of about 2500 personal emails written in English. Due to the nature of the data, spelling, punctuation, and capitalisation inconsistencies and errors are common.

The corpus is anonymised with binary labels (anon/no-anon) and partitioned into training, development, and test sets of 666138, 6026, and 31926 tokens respectively. Unfortunately, only the last two sets are annotated. Following the solution given in [16] to the unannotated training set issue, the development set is used as training set.

Given the subjectivity of what constitutes a sensitive item that needs to be anonymised, ITAC was annotated following two different schemes: a comprehensive one where every reference that might possibly be related to people or organisations is anonymised even if the risk of identification is very low, called *blanket* anonymisation, and a more selective one where only those references directly related to people or organisations are annotated, referred to as *selective* anonymisation. In this work the blanket version is used as source corpus.

3.2   ES-Port

The Spanish Technical Support (ES-Port) corpus [7] consists of transcriptions of 1170 dialogues from calls to the technical support service of a telecommunications provider. Due to its nature, the corpus includes numerous turn overlaps, unfinished sentences and words, mispronunciations, filler words, grammatical errors, and other phenomena alike typical of spontaneous spoken language. Although Spanish is the main language of the corpus, various code switching events take place adding up to six other languages, of which English is the most common one.

The corpus is fully anonymised by token substitution. The types of items which are anonymised include basic personal information, contact information and digital trace items. Despite the anonymised items are annotated with their specific anonymisation categories, for the experiments reported in this paper the categorised labels have been converted to a simple 'anon' label to accommodate to our binary identification task.

As opposed to ITAC, ES-Port is not pre-partitioned, so for our tests we chose to divide the corpus by taking the first 900 dialogues (47073 utterances after the removal of turns not containing any text, e.g. silences, unintelligible speech) as training set and the rest (around 23% of the data) as test set.

3.3   Feature Selection

As the proposed methodology is used on cross-lingual data, two source classifiers were trained over the ITAC corpus, one with language independent features and another one with language dependent features. Beginning/End of Sentence (BOS/EOS), punctuation, case, NERC and Part of Speech (PoS) tags[1] were used as language independent features. For the language dependent case, features also included lower cased word forms and prefixes and suffixes (two and three first and last characters in the word). The selected features in a $[-2, +2]$ word context window were also included. The features used for each instance (i.e., sentence or utterance) are the concatenation of the word-level features for each token in the sequence. The target classifier was trained over the ES-Port corpus with language dependent features only.

4   Experiments

In this section, the experiments carried out and their results are presented. Since the ITAC annotated training set is too short (473 utterances), we have tested the KT for AL setting using ES-Port as target, but not in the opposite direction. That being so, we will be referring to ITAC as *Source* and to ES-Port as *Target*. All results are reported on the ES-Port test set, taking into account the positive ('anon') label only.

---

[1] NERC and PoS tags were automatically extracted using the Stanford CoreNLP tool [14] for both languages and normalised to share the same values, e.g. both Spanish tag 'LUG' and English tag 'LOCATION' refer to place entities.

CRF classifiers were trained passively on the whole ES-Port training data to test their top performance, achieving 0.935 of F1 score on the 'anon' label. Source CRF models were trained using the blanket data, achieving 0.803 of F1 score with language dependent features and 0.785 without on ITAC's test set.

4.1 Seed Selection Evaluation

For seed selection, various methods have been implemented:

- **Random:** the seed is selected at random. This is used as a weak baseline.
- **Maximum Utterance Length:** the samples with largest number of words are chosen as seed.
- **K-Means-Centroids (K-MC):** the K-Means algorithm is used to split the corpus and choose a representative sample in each cluster to build the seed.
- **Source entropy (S-H):** a source classifier is used to calculate the target instances' entropy score and select the ones with highest uncertainty as seed. Both language dependent (S_D) and independent (S_I) models are tested.
- **S-H and K-MC Combination:** the top ranked instances are selected as seed according to their entropy and K-MC combination score following Eq. 1.
- **S-H and Length Combination:** the instances are ranked according to their entropy and length combination score and the top ones are chosen as seed. The combination score of an instance is the product multiplication of its rescaled (range 0–1) length with its entropy score.

Table 2. F1 and standard error results for different seed selection methods and sizes

Method	B = 100	B = 250	B = 500	B = 1000
Random	$0.598 \pm .024$	$0.735 \pm .013$	$0.793 \pm .004$	$0.829 \pm .004$
Length	0.749	0.811	0.834	0.851
K-MC	$0.655 \pm .016$	$0.8 \pm .004$	0.832 ± 002	0.864 ± 001
K-MC & Length	$0.665 \pm .021$	$0.794 \pm .003$	$0.831 \pm .004$	$0.864 \pm .001$
S_D-H Sum	0.746	0.809	0.838	0.845
S_D-H Mean	0.108	0.456	0.627	0.66
S_D-H K-Max	0.717	0.762	0.828	0.854
S_D-H Max	0.69	0.737	0.783	0.849
S_I-H Sum	0.777	0.806	0.831	0.862
S_I-H Mean	0.08	0.289	0.432	0.609
S_I-H K-Max	0.769	0.797	0.821	0.863
S_I-H Max	0.67	0.762	0.807	0.862
S_I-H Sum & K-MC	$\mathbf{0.79} \pm .005$	$\mathbf{0.839} \pm .003$	$\mathbf{0.858} \pm .002$	$\mathbf{0.876} \pm .001$
S_I-H K-Max & K-MC	$0.756 \pm .007$	$0.805 \pm .005$	$0.845 \pm .002$	$\mathbf{0.879} \pm .002$
S_I-H Sum & Length	0.77	0.786	0.842	$\mathbf{0.878}$
S_I-H K-Max & Length	0.766	0.786	0.842	0.873

Table 2 shows the results obtained for each explored configuration using practical seed sizes for a real environment. For the K-Means and Random selectors, their mean and standard error over 5 iterations are shown. As expected, the random baseline performs the worst. Selecting instances according to their length gives good results, although performance decreases as the number of selected instances increases. The K-MC sampling method yields better results as the batch size increases, demonstrating that input diversity plays an important role for instance sampling. Nevertheless, results for smaller seeds are lower than using other methods because information content is not taken into account. When transferring knowledge from the source classifier using the entropy scorers Sum and K-Max[2], S_I models perform slightly better than S_D models in smaller seeds, although such difference gets narrower in bigger seeds. While both S-H K-Max and S-H Sum demonstrate to be useful, the latter has direct relation with instance length, as the longer it is the more likely it is to have a higher entropy sum. It also shows similar patterns to the utterance length method, no longer being among the top methods in the largest seed size tested. The reason for this could be that it takes into account all the words of the instance, thus being sensitive to noise. On the other hand, the S-H K-Max scorer takes into account only the K words with highest entropy of the instance so it is more agnostic to length and low-entropy words in the utterance, making it more robust to noisy instances. As S_I models yield better results in general, only this method was combined with length and KMC.

The best results for seed selection are rendered by combining the K-MC method with the S_I-H Sum scorer, as this method takes into account the divergence between the input data, the length of the input samples, and their uncertainty. Likewise, the combination of K-MC with the S_I-H K-Max model yields better results as the seed size increases. It is interesting to note that when K-MC is combined with S-H the standard error intervals are reduced, improving the robustness of the method.

4.2   Query Selection Strategy Evaluation

In this section, the AL process is evaluated using different query strategies. To visualise the impact on learning speed, the learning curves for the base learners trained on the first 10.000 selected samples of the target corpus are plotted in Fig. 2. The classifiers were asked to stop learning when they reached top performance[3]. The best configuration of Sect. 4.1 is used as seed. The query strategies evaluated are: Random baseline (R), Target domain T-H Sum/K-Max, the product multiplication of T-H Sum/K-Max with S_I-H Sum/K-Max, and the K-MC combination with T-H Sum/K-Max following Eq. 1. The selected size for both seed and query batches was 250 instances.

The reported learning curves show that all the proposed query selection methods perform significantly better than passive random selection, showing a much

---

[2] K = 3 is used throughout the experiments.

[3] Instead of using the hard 0.935 top performance score, a minimally softened breakpoint of 0.9345 was set.

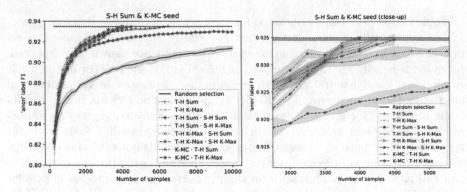

Fig. 2. F1 results of using the different query strategies for AL (left), and close up look of the top performance reaching iterations of the best methods (right). The standard deviation over 5 iterations appears shadowed

steeper curve and reaching top performance in fewer iterations. The two methods which consider target domain information only (T-H Sum and T-H K-Max) perform equally well, reaching top performance trained on 4250 instances only. Methods which combine target and source model information are in the top positions of best possible query strategies. Although the former has a slightly less steep curve in the first iterations, both the **T-H K-Max · S-H Sum** and the **T-H Sum · S-H Sum** combinations reach the top score with just 4000 training instances (less than 10% of the target training corpus), outperforming methods which do not use source model information. On the other hand, the combination of target and source H K-Max scores performs moderately worse than the mentioned methods, even the ones which do not consider S-H. Considering that H K-Max is agnostic to instance length we may conclude that this aspect may actually play a somewhat important role in best query selection. This hypothesis is supported by the fact that K-MC combination with T-H Sum has better results than its combination with T-H K-Max as the number of instances in the training set gets larger, although the two combinations perform the worst among the AL strategies tested.

5 Conclusions and Future Work

In this paper, new methods combining Knowledge Transfer and Active Learning to approach the lack of available annotated data for textual anonymisation have been proposed and compared. This has been done taking advantage of existing resources from a different language and domain. Exploiting classifiers trained on the source data, we demonstrate that the learning process on the target data for the anonymisation task at hand can be notably speeded up from the very first batch, or seed, given to the target classifier.

Different scoring methods considering input divergence, length, uncertainty, and their combinations have been tested for seed selection and as AL query strategy criteria. Best seeds were achieved using scorers that considered all three aspects. For query strategy, methods that combined information from the source and the target models were the ones which performed better. With such query strategy methods and best seed selection, top classifier performance was reached using less than 10% of the full training data.

As future work, we plan to test this methodology for non-binary classification tasks, and to explore new ways to exploit information from multiple source model classifiers from different domains for textual anonymisation and other tasks.

References

1. Álvarez, A., Martínez-Hinarejos, C.D., Arzelus, H., Balenciaga, M., del Pozo, A.: Improving the automatic segmentation of subtitles through conditional random field. Speech Commun. **88**, 83–95 (2017)
2. Baker, L.D., McCallum, A.K.: Distributional clustering of words for text classification. In: Proceedings of the 21st Annual International ACM SIGIR Conference on Research and Development in Information Retrieval, pp. 96–103. ACM (1998)
3. Cohn, D., Atlas, L., Ladner, R.: Improving generalization with active learning. Mach. Learn. **15**(2), 201–221 (1994)
4. Dias, F.M.C.: Multilingual automated text anonymization. Master's thesis, Instituto Superior Técnico de Lisboa (2016)
5. Dligach, D., Palmer, M.: Good seed makes a good crop: accelerating active learning using language modeling. In: Proceedings of the 49th Annual Meeting of the Association for Computational Linguistics: Human Language Technologies: Short Papers, vol. 2, pp. 6–10. Association for Computational Linguistics (2011)
6. Dorr, D.A., Phillips, W., Phansalkar, S., Sims, S.A., Hurdle, J.F.: Assessing the difficulty and time cost of de-identification in clinical narratives. Methods Inf. Med. **45**(03), 246–252 (2006)
7. García-Sardiña, L., Serras, M., del Pozo, A.: ES-Port: a spontaneous spoken human-human technical support corpus for dialogue research in Spanish. In: Proceedings of the Eleventh International Conference on Language Resources and Evaluation (LREC 2018), Miyazaki, Japan, 7–12 May 2018 (2018)
8. Kleinberg, B., Mozes, M., van der Toolen, Y., et al.: NETANOS-named entity-based text anonymization for open science (2017). Preprint on Open Science Framework
9. Lafferty, J., McCallum, A., Pereira, F.C.: Conditional random fields: probabilistic models for segmenting and labeling sequence data (2001)
10. Lewis, D., Gale, W.: A sequential algorithm for training text classifiers. In: Proceedings of the 17th Annual International ACM SIGIR Conference on Research and Development in Information Retrieval. Springer, New York (1994)
11. Li, S., Xue, Y., Wang, Z., Zhou, G.: Active learning for cross-domain sentiment classification. In: IJCAI, pp. 2127–2133 (2013)
12. Li, X.B., Qin, J.: Anonymizing and sharing medical text records. Inf. Syst. Res. **28**(2), 332–352 (2017)
13. MacQueen, J., et al.: Some methods for classification and analysis of multivariate observations. In: Proceedings of the Fifth Berkeley Symposium on Mathematical Statistics and Probability, Oakland, CA, USA , vol. 1, no.14, pp. 281–297 (1967)

14. Manning, C.D., Surdeanu, M., Bauer, J., Finkel, J., Bethard, S.J., McClosky, D.: The Stanford CoreNLP natural language processing toolkit. In: Association for Computational Linguistics (ACL) System Demonstrations, pp. 55–60 (2014)
15. McCallum, A., Li, W.: Early results for named entity recognition with conditional random fields, feature induction and web-enhanced lexicons. In: Proceedings of the Seventh Conference on Natural Language Learning at HLT-NAACL 2003, vol. 4, pp. 188–191. Association for Computational Linguistics (2003)
16. Medlock, B.: An introduction to NLP-based textual anonymisation. In: Proceedings of 5th International Conference on Language Resources and Evaluation (LREC), Genes, Italy (2006)
17. Olsson, F.: Bootstrapping named entity annotation by means of active machine learning: a method for creating corpora. Ph.D. thesis, University of Gothenburg (2008)
18. Pan, S.J., Yang, Q.: A survey on transfer learning. IEEE Trans. Knowl. Data Eng. **22**(10), 1345–1359 (2010)
19. Rai, P., Saha, A., Daumé III, H., Venkatasubramanian, S.: Domain adaptation meets active learning. In: Proceedings of the NAACL HLT 2010 Workshop on Active Learning for Natural Language Processing, pp. 27–32. Association for Computational Linguistics (2010)
20. Settles, B.: Curious machines: active learning with structured instances. Ph.D. thesis, University of Wisconsin-Madison (2008)
21. Settles, B.: Active learning literature survey. Computer Sciences Technical Report 1648 (2010)
22. Settles, B.: Active learning. Synth. Lect. Artif. Intell. Mach. Learn. **6**(1), 1–114 (2012)
23. Settles, B., Craven, M.: An analysis of active learning strategies for sequence labeling tasks. In: Proceedings of the Conference on Empirical Methods in Natural Language Processing. Association for Computational Linguistics (2008)
24. Seung, H.S., Opper, M., Sompolinsky, H.: Query by committee. In: Proceedings of the Fifth Annual Workshop on Computational Learning Theory. ACM (1992)
25. Sha, F., Pereira, F.: Shallow parsing with conditional random fields. In: Proceedings of the 2003 Conference of the North American Chapter of the Association for Computational Linguistics on Human Language Technology, vol. 1, pp. 134–141. Association for Computational Linguistics (2003)
26. Shannon, C.E.: A note on the concept of entropy. Bell. Syst. Tech. J. **27**(3), 379–423 (1948)
27. Shi, X., Fan, W., Ren, J.: Actively transfer domain knowledge. In: Daelemans, W., Goethals, B., Morik, K. (eds.) ECML PKDD 2008 Part II. LNCS (LNAI), vol. 5212, pp. 342–357. Springer, Heidelberg (2008). https://doi.org/10.1007/978-3-540-87481-2_23
28. Szarvas, G., Farkas, R., Busa-Fekete, R.: State-of-the-art anonymization of medical records using an iterative machine learning framework. J. Am. Med. Inf. Assoc. **14**(5), 574–580 (2007)
29. Tomanek, K., Laws, F., Hahn, U., Schütze, H.: On proper unit selection in active learning: co-selection effects for named entity recognition. In: Proceedings of the NAACL HLT 2009 Workshop on Active Learning for Natural Language Processing, pp. 9–17. Association for Computational Linguistics (2009)
30. Tomanek, K., Wermter, J., Hahn, U.: Efficient annotation with the Jena annotation environment (JANE). In: Proceedings of the Linguistic Annotation Workshop, pp. 9–16. Association for Computational Linguistics (2007)

Studying the Effects of Text Preprocessing and Ensemble Methods on Sentiment Analysis of Brazilian Portuguese Tweets

Fernando Barbosa Gomes[✉], Juan Manuel Adán-Coello,
and Fernando Ernesto Kintschner

Pontifícia Universidade Católica de Campinas, Campinas, Brazil
fernando60794@hotmail.com,
{juan, fek}@puc-campinas.edu.br

Abstract. The analysis of social media posts can provide useful feedback regarding user experience for people and organizations. This task requires the use of computational tools due to the massive amount of content and the speed at which it is generated. In this article we study the effects of text preprocessing heuristics and ensembles of machine learning algorithms on the accuracy and polarity bias of classifiers when performing sentiment analysis on short text messages. The results of an experimental evaluation performed on a Brazilian Portuguese tweets dataset have shown that these strategies have significant impact on increasing classification accuracy, particularly when the ensembles include a deep neural net, but not always on reducing polarity bias.

1 Introduction

People, from different places, genders and ages, use social media to express their opinions regarding all kinds of subjects such as events, services and products. These opinions could be a source of very useful feedback for people and organizations; this feedback allows them to come up with new and better products and services. The analysis of these opinions could partially replace traditional opinion polls, which are usually slow and expensive.

However, social media content is huge and grows at a tremendous rate which makes it unfeasible to analyze it manually, requiring the use of computational tools to automate the task. An undertaking that is also difficult since social media users frequently use slang, comparative text, metaphors, sarcasm and many other language elements that make automatic text analysis a non-trivial challenge. When the analysis task is concerned with identifying the polarity (positive and negative) of the text it is usually referred to as sentiment analysis.

In sentiment analysis, two main approaches are widely used and studied: lexicon-based methods and statistical/machine learning based methods [1]. Lexicon-based method aim to identify the opinion lexicons which help in analyzing the data; one of the major drawback of these methods is that they depend heavily on the language they are designed to work with. On the other hand, machine learning algorithms can learn

© Springer Nature Switzerland AG 2018
T. Dutoit et al. (Eds.): SLSP 2018, LNAI 11171, pp. 167–177, 2018.
https://doi.org/10.1007/978-3-030-00810-9_15

how to provide sentiment analysis for any language after being exposed to a large collection of text documents of that language [2].

There are many machine learning algorithms that can be applied to sentiment analysis, each processes the data in a different way and therefore can produce different results for the same document, and some algorithms work better on a set of domains and not very well on others [3]. Several studies show that this limitations can be partially overcome using ensemble methods [4] and text preprocessing heuristics. However, these approaches are usually not used in combination. On the other hand, there is a shortage of papers that analyze the impact of each preprocessing heuristic, as well as their combined effect.

2   Machine Learning Algorithms

All algorithms used in this research belong are supervised machine learning algorithms. They classify input data into pre-determined classes, to do that they must pass through a process called training, in which they are provided with a series of pre-classified example data that allow them to develop a model on how to classify the next data they are inputted with.

Although there are some algorithms that use the same data representation for inputs and produce models with similar structures, this elements are usually algorithm specific.

In the experimental study discussed in this paper three popular algorithms were chosen: Naïve Bayes (NB), Logistic Regression (LR) and Support Vector Machine (SVM) [5], and a deep learning algorithm, the Recursive Neural Tensor Network (RNTN) [6].

Naïve Bayes is a probabilistic machine learning algorithms. It applies the Bayes theorem with the assumption that terms are independent (that is why it is called naïve).

Logistic Regression, also a probabilistic machine learning algorithms, produce classifiers based on regression. Its output has the form of a percentage that represents the cumulative logistic distribution, which is then transformed into a categorical binary value (belong or not belong to a class). LR considers that input terms are dependent.

Support Vector Machine is a linear non-probabilistic classification algorithm, it represents data inputs as points in a space and its output is generated based on the position of the data in a hyperplane defined by support vectors.

Naïve Bayes, Logistic Regression and Support Vector Machines input format is a vector of features. The meaning of each feature depends on the type of data that will be classified. The Recursive Neural Tensor Network is a classifier organized as a neural network. The neural networks layering approach produces models more complex than those seem in the other three algorithms. With enough data, neural network algorithms often perform better than most other classifier algorithms. However, in environments that are not data rich they can produce complex bad models, and the added complexity makes them more computationally expensive.

The literature shows that ensemble methods can be used to combine multiple models (classifiers) to produce improved results. Ensemble methods usually produce more accurate solutions than a single model would. This can be confirmed by several machine learning contests where the winning solutions used ensemble methods, as for example the Netflix prize[1] and many Kaggle competitions[2].

We used Logistic Regression and Support Vector Machine implementations available in LIBLINEAR [7], with regularization L2 and minimum frequency feature selection of two (selects terms that appears at least twice); Naïve Bayes was implemented with chi-square feature selection; the Recursive Neural Tensor Network used was Stanford's implementation [8] and in the construction of ensembles we adopted the majority voting method [9].

3 Data Representation

Machine learning algorithms are usually generic and can be used in a plentitude of domains. Each algorithm does have a format to which input data must fit. Naïve Bayes, Logistic Regression and Support Vector Machines receive as input feature vectors. In sentiment analysis, the input data is composed of text documents that must be transformed into feature vectors to be processed by the algorithms. In this study, this was done using the bag-of-words representation that does not retain word positions in text documents.

The bag-of-words representation firstly requires the construction of a conversion table between words and vector positions. This table includes all the words in the vocabulary used for training; the table maps each word to a position into a feature vector, so text documents can be transformed into a vector of word occurrences. Upon analyzing new documents, words that are not present in the conversion table are discarded.

The Recursive Neural Tensor Network does not use the bag-of-words representation, instead, it uses word vectors and a parse tree to compute vectors for higher nodes in the tree using a tensor-based composition function. This data representation allows the RNTN to capture the compositionality of phrases, allowing it to detect negation and other language phenomena.

4 Text Preprocessing

Noise is a relevant issue when trying to perform sentiment analysis in tweets, it appears in diverse forms, including terms that are not relevant to express sentiments, terms with wrong spelling and shortened terms. For example, algorithms are incapable of knowing that "mate" and "m8" should have the same meaning. Without text preprocessing, they are treated as different terms. There are many ways to reduce noise on text data; in this work, the following heuristics are used:

A. Bigrams.
B. All characters are converted to lower case.
C. Accentuation removal.

---

[1] http://blog.echen.me/2011/10/24/winning-the-netflix-prize-a-summary/.

[2] https://www.kaggle.com/.

D. Special character treatment.
E. Stop-words removal.
F. Twitter user names removal.
G. Twitter topics removal.
H. Reduction of laugh expressions to a common token.

An important issue to address in sentiment analysis is the way data is represented. In a bag-of-words, the position of words in sentences is lost. In this scenario, the order in which words appear becomes irrelevant for sentiment classification. To try to cope with this problem we can associate words before mapping them into the bag-of-words representation. For example, words can be represented in the frequency vector as individual terms (unigrams) and pairs of terms (bigrams), this way "not like" turns into "not", "like" and "not_like". In the data representation used by RNTN, the parse tree, the position and association of words is not lost, which means there is no need for bigrams with this representation.

Lower-casing characters makes sure that common writing variation of words, such as "good", "Good" and "gOOd" are treated as the same word. Often a difference in the letter case might be related to an intensity variation on the text meaning, for example: "I HATE THIS" and "I hate this" have different intensities. Usually though, the polarity of the sentence stays the same. In addition, to counter balance the loss of intensity, higher-case typed words could be duplicated during this process, increasing their frequency in the text.

While accentuation is not a problem in the English language, in Romance languages, such as Portuguese, there is heavy use of accentuation. Nevertheless, it is often ignored in social media writing. For example, words such as "não" ("no" in Portuguese) can easily be seen written as "nao". Without accentuation removal, algorithms would treat these words as different terms. In most cases, this heuristic is helpful. Nonetheless, there are exceptions. Some words with different meanings are written the same except for the accentuation. Nevertheless, as will be seen in the experimental evaluation section, the benefits of this heuristic outweigh its problems.

Special character treatment, in this work, consists of removing characters that represent emoticons (character sequences which show faces with expressions, such as ":)"). This was done because some research, as [10], have found that emoticons are able to reverse the polarity of the true sentiment values of sentences. That means that while very important to sentiment analysis they need a special treatment that is out of the scope of this work.

Stop-word removal is a strategy to remove very common words which tend to be of little value in associating sentiment to texts.

Removal of Twitter user names and topics is used to reduce data sparsity and noise.

Reduction of laugh expressions to a common token helps to diminish data noise generated by the many forms of expressing laughs in social media, in Portuguese it is common to represent laugh with the following patterns: "kkkkkkkk", "kkkk", "hahahaha", "hehehehe", "rsrsrsrs", "lol", and others. With laugh reduction, most laugh patterns are transformed into the same token "_laugh_", holding the meaning of a laugh while removing the data noise it would cause.

After text preprocessing, documents pass through different steps to be prepared as inputs for the machine learning algorithms. For Naïve Bayes, Support Vector Machines and Logistic Regression the documents go through the bag-of-words conversion table, in a process called tokenization. After tokenization, words are represented as positions in a vector where their magnitude is given by their frequency of occurrence in the document they came from. For the RNTN, the document goes through the Stanford NLP Pipeline that parses, tokenizes and transform the text into a tree.

5 Dataset

For the task of evaluating the algorithms performances, we created a dataset collecting tweets written in Brazilian Portuguese over a six months period. The dataset is generic and comprises tweets from a range of different subjects, specifically: brands, social networks, telecommunication companies, companies with active marketing campaigns, sports, regions, videogames, movies, books, food, government and events.

A total of 12076 tweets were manually classified in the classes positive, negative, ambiguous and non-opinionated. Tweets are considered ambiguous when they have more than one kind of expressed opinion, such as "I love tulips but I hate roses" and are considered non-opinionated when they have no opinion expressed, such as in "The president arrives today".

Out of the 12076 tweets, 5034 were classified as non-opinionated, 582 as ambiguous, 3280 as negatives and 3180 as positives.

To use the dataset with the RNTN it was necessary to parse it using the Stanford Parser [6], generating a treebank dataset in the Portuguese language.

6 Experimental Evaluation

The performance of the algorithms was measured using the metrics accuracy, overall polarity, r, and polarity bias, b [11, 12]. The accuracy of a model is the fraction of its classifications that are correct. Overall polarity, r, is the ratio of positive tweets to the number of positive plus negative tweets. Polarity bias, b, is the absolute difference between the predicted r' and the real r. The best b value is zero, denoting that the algorithm is unbiased.

To evaluate each algorithm and the effects of text preprocessing on sentiment analysis several experiments were performed, using fivefold cross validation[3].

Initially, Naïve Bayes (NB), Logistic Regression (LR), and Support Vector Machine (SVM) were run with all combinations of text preprocessing heuristics. As it is impractical to present here the results of all 785 executions performed, Tables 1 and

---

[3] Fivefold cross validation is a method in which 80% of the dataset is used to train the algorithm, while the rest 20% are used to test its accuracy. The 80–20% chunks of data are swapped five times until all data have been used for both testing and training.

2 present only the lower (Min) and higher (Max) values for accuracy and polarity bias according to the number of heuristics used. Each cell shows the heuristics used and the corresponding accuracy or polarity bias values.

Table 1. Accuracy (in %) with text preprocessing heuristics (higher is better). A. Bigrams; B. Lower case; C. Accentuation removal; D. Special character treatment; E. Stop-words removal; F. User names removal; G. Topics removal; H. Reduction of laugh expressions.

	LR		NB		SVM	
	Min	Max	Min	Max	Min	Max
0		59.68		68.53		56.93
1	B 60.79	D 67.33	B 71.43	G 72.67	C 54.18	D 62.08
2	BF 60.79	DE 68.88	BE 70.38	FG 72.67	BH 54.25	DE 64.78
3	BFG 60.79	CDE 71.31	ABE 70.08	BDF 73.03	ABG 53.51	DEG 65.47
4	CDE 71.31	BCDE 72.77	ABEF 70.08	BCDG 73.51	ACFH 53.52	CDEG 67.63
5	ABFGH 60.96	ABCDE 73.00	BCDEF 69.54	BCDGH 73.54	ABFGH 55.05	BCDEF 67.74
6	ABEFGH 60.97	ABCDEG 72.96	BCDEFH 69.53	BCDFGH 73.00	ABCFGH 54.86	ABCDEG 67.58
7	ABCEFGH 61.93	ABCDEGH 72.74	BCDEFGH 70.20	ABCDFGH 72.45	ABCEFGH 57.91	BCDEFGH 68.44
8		ABCDEFGH 72.58		ABCDEFGH 71.26		ABCDEFGH 65.88

Table 2. Polarity bias with text preprocessing heuristics (lower is better). A. Bigrams; B. Lower case; C. Accentuation removal; D. Special character treatment; E. Stop-words removal; F. User names removal; G. Topics removal; H. Reduction of laugh expressions.

# of heuristics	LR		NB		SVM	
	Min	Max	Min	Max	Min	Max
1	D 0,001	E 0.204	D 0.001	E 0.040	F. 0.024	C 0.186
2	DH 0.002	BE 0.209	BD 0.002	EH 0.041	DH 0.005	FG 0.223
3	DGH 0.003	BCE 0.212	BDF 0.004	ACE 0.045	CGH 0.001	AEF 0.294
4	ACDF 0.001	BCEG 0.212	BDFH 0.004	ABCE 0.047	DEGH 0.000	ABCG 0.234
5	ACDFH 0.000	BCEFG 0.212	BCDGH 0.001	ABCEG 0.047	ACDEF 0.003	ABCEG 0.270
6	ACDFGH 0.000	BCEFGH 0.211	ABCDFH 0.003	ABCEFG 0.047	ABDFGH 0.001	ABCEGH 0.280
7	ABCDFGH 0.000	ABCEFGH 0.210	ABCDFGH 0.008	ABCEFGH 0.047	ABCDEFG 0.001	ABCEFGH 0.053
8	ABCDEFGH 0.025		ABCDEFGH 0.030		ABCEFGH 0.053	

As can be seem in Tables 1 and 2, different combinations of the same number of heuristics can produce substantially diverse results, and each algorithm has a different best heuristics combination. It is also easy to see that the heuristics combinations that increase accuracy are usually not the same that decrease polarity bias. That means that depending on the application objectives a different set of heuristics should be use. But, for all the algorithms a good set of heuristics can provide noticeable increases on accuracy.

Naïve Bayes presented its higher accuracy of 73.54% when using the heuristics B, C, D, G and H; the same heuristics that account for its the lower polarity bias of 0.001 (see Table 2). The higher Logistic Regression accuracy of 73.00% is due to using also five heuristics, in this case A, B, C, D and E, that is associated with polarity bias of 0.025 (not shown on Table 2). Finally, the highest accuracy of Support Vector Machine, 68.44%, when using B, C, D, E, F, G and H, having an associated bias of 0.010, is the lowest of the three algorithms.

Text preprocessing impacted most Logistic Regression, its accuracy rose 22.3%, from 59.68 to 73.00%. Support Vector Machine was the second most impacted algorithm by text preprocessing with an increase of 20.21% on accuracy. Naïve Bayes was the least affected, it received a small boost in accuracy of 7.31%.

For the sake of evaluating different ensembles we also used Recursive Neural Tensor Network (RNTN). When executed alone it took a good advantage from text preprocessing, it was unable to surpass LR, NV and SVM in accuracy but was the only algorithm that got better in both accuracy and bias, its accuracy rose from 65.32 to 69.38% and its bias got a bit closer to zero, from 0.0097 to 0.009.

Table 3 presents the results for the ensembles combining NB, LR, SVM and RNTN, with all the algorithms using text preprocessing. All ensembles used the majority voting method for computing their final predictions.

Table 3. Ensembles accuracy (in %) and polarity bias with text preprocessing

	Accuracy	Polarity bias
NB+LR+SVM	73.53	0.0376
NB+SVM+RNTN	75.06	0.0173
SVM+LR+RNTN	73.09	0.0328
NB+LR+RNTN	76.14	0.0217

As shown in Table 3, all ensembles yielded better results than each individual algorithm. Naïve Bayes, Logistic Regression and Recursive Neural Tensor Network (NB+LR+RNTN) formed the best ensemble in accuracy, reaching 76.14%; and had the second lowest bias 0.0217 within the ensembles.

Naïve Bayes, Support Vector Machines and Recursive Neural Tensor Network (NB +SVM+RNTN) formed the second best ensemble with 75.06% accuracy and the lowest bias 0.0173 among the ensembles.

The top two performing ensembles both had Recursive Neural Tensor Network as a member, what suggest that it is an important factor in raising ensemble accuracy. RNTN produce more complex models than the other algorithms, and can better detect some linguistic facts that simpler models cannot, such as the effects of nearby terms and negations. Alone, RNTN did not show good results, yet, in an ensemble it seems to complement the simpler algorithms, this might be what makes these ensembles present better performance.

The ensemble with Naïve Bayes, Support Vector Machines and Logistic Regression (NB+LR+SVM) reached 73.53% accuracy and 0.0373 bias.

Logistic Regression, Support Vector Machines and Recursive Neural Tensor Network (SVM+LR+RNTN) was the less performing ensemble with three algorithms, with 73.09% accuracy, yet it was still better than the individual algorithms.

One commonality the two less performant ensembles share is that both include Logistic Regression and Support Vector Machines, which use the same feature selection method (minimum frequency). These two algorithms also have in common that both form a decision boundary, which linearly separates the feature vector hyperplane. This kind of similarity usually is not good for ensembles, as they benefit from algorithms that produce complementary models.

7 Discussion

Our experiments show that each machine learning algorithm alone could barely reach 70% accuracy when performing sentiment analysis on our Brazilian Portuguese Tweets dataset. The experiments also showed that text preprocessing has a very positive impact in accuracy for all algorithms and a varied impact in polarity bias.

Each algorithm had its accuracy boosted differently by text preprocessing. With the highest boost being of 22.3% and the smallest 7.31%.

For Naïve Bayes, the least affected, the small boost was probably due to the fact that text preprocessing reduced the effectiveness of its chi-square feature selection.

For the algorithms that used minimum frequency feature selection, Support Vector Machine and Logistic Regression, text preprocessing had a very positive outcome, since it removed high frequency non-relevant terms and merged misspelled words, raising their frequency.

Overall, text preprocessing showed itself to be a good way to raise algorithms accuracy, regardless of the machine learning algorithm used. It is interesting to note that in [10] it has been found that emoticons are able to reverse the polarity of the true sentiment values of sentences. Our experiments seems to confirm this observation, as the highest accuracies were obtained when the removal of emoticons was one of the heuristics used. In the case of using a single heuristic, two of the three algorithms, LR and SVM, reached their higher accuracy when using this heuristic, and two others, NB and SVM, presented their lower polarity bias.

Ensembles also proved effective on raising the accuracy on sentiment analysis. However in their construction it is important to consider that their outcomes are highly affected by the characteristics of the combined individual algorithms.

The experimental evaluation confirms what is known form the literature that there are two conditions to create effective ensembles: (1) the algorithms should have similar performances so each could have a positive effect on the ensemble; (2) the algorithms should produce different and complementary models. The showed that similar algorithms usually do not produce good ensembles, as it was the case with Logistic Regression and Support Vector Machines. When algorithms are too similar they do not add value to the ensemble decision boundary, instead they reinforce their own outputs, diminishing the added effectiveness of other less similar algorithms.

Finally, the literature points out that neural networks usually yield good results with abundant datasets, but, as shown here, they can also contribute to produce good results with smaller datasets when used in ensembles.

8   Related Work

There is a number of works that describe the construction of corpora of Brazilian Portuguese texts for sentiment analysis. Some well-kwon examples are TweetSentBR [13] and ReLi [14]. TweetSentBR has 15,000 manually annotated tweets on the domain of TV shows, and ReLi 12,000 manually annotated book reviews, at the phrase and syntag levels. These and other data sets differ from ours by not collecting Twitter texts or by focusing on a specific topic. Our corpus consists of tweets of more than ten different topics.

In [15] it is described an opinion mining application over a dataset of app reviews written in Brazilian Portuguese extracted from the Google Play. The authors apply several text preprocessing heuristic and concluded that they have an insignificant role in the opinion mining task for the considered domain. Our corpus consists of tweets related to more than 10 different subjects, and the use of text preprocessing proved to be very relevant to increase the accuracy of the evaluated classifiers. Several other papers deal with sentiment analysis text in Brazilian Portuguese, as, for example, [16–19], but, they differ from ours by not focusing on Twitter, or by dealing with a single topic, and, mainly, for not doing a detailed analysis of different combinations of text preprocessing heuristics.

9   Conclusion

The focus of this paper was to present a study on the effects of text preprocessing and ensembles of machine learning algorithms on accuracy and polarity bias when performing sentiment analysis.

An experimental evaluation showed that both approaches contribute to expressive increases in classification accuracy, although not always on reducing the classification polarity bias.

It also was found that classification algorithms such as Naïve Bayes, Logistic Regression and Support Vector Machine combined with neural networks, such as the RNTN, can form very effective ensembles, raising the classification accuracy even for small datasets.

In future work we intend to expand our study including other deep learning models, in particular Convolutional and Recurrent Neural Networks.

References

1. Astya, P.: Sentiment analysis: approaches and open issues. In: 2017 International Conference on Computing, Communication and Automation (ICCCA), pp. 154–158. IEEE (2017)
2. Liu, B., Zhang, L.: A survey of opinion mining and sentiment analysis. In: Aggarwal, C., Zhai, C. (eds.) Mining Text Data, pp. 415–463. Springer, Boston (2012). https://doi.org/10.1007/978-1-4614-3223-4_13
3. Ng, A., Jordan, M.: On discriminative vs generative classifiers: a comparison of logistic regression and Naive Bayes. In: Advances in Neural Information Processing Systems, vol. 14 (2002)
4. Xia, R., Zong, C., Li, S.: Ensemble of feature sets and classification algorithms for sentiment classification. Inf. Sci. **181**(6), 1138–1152 (2011)
5. Nasrabadi, N.M.: Pattern recognition and machine learning. J. Electron. Imaging **16**, 049901 (2007)
6. Socher, R., et al.: Recursive deep models for semantic compositionality over a sentiment treebank. In: Conference on Empirical Methods in Natural Language Processing (2013)
7. Fan, R., Chang, K., Hsieh, C., Wang, X., Lin, C.: LIBLINEAR: a library for large linear classification. J. Mach. Learn. Res. **9**, 1871–1874 (2008)
8. Stanford CoreNLP – Natural language software. https://stanfordnlp.github.io/CoreNLP/
9. Zhou, Z.-H.: Ensemble Methods: Foundations and Algorithms. Chapman and Hall, Boca Raton (2012)
10. Teh, P.L., Rayson, P., Pak, I., Piao, S., Yeng, S.M.: Reversing the polarity with emoticons. In: Métais, E., Meziane, F., Saraee, M., Sugumaran, V., Vadera, S. (eds.) NLDB 2016. LNCS, vol. 9612, pp. 453–458. Springer, Cham (2016). https://doi.org/10.1007/978-3-319-41754-7_48
11. Powers, D.: Evaluation: from precision, recall and F-measure to ROC, informedness, markedness & correlation. J. Mach. Learn. Technol. (2011)
12. Rosenthal, S., et al.: SemEval-2015 task 10: sentiment analysis in Twitter. In: Proceedings of the 9th International Workshop on Semantic Evaluation, SemEval 2015, Denver, Colorado (2015)
13. Brum, H.B., das Nunes, M.G.V.: Building a sentiment corpus of Tweets in Brazilian Portuguese. In: Proceedings of the Eleventh International Conference on Language Resources and Evaluation (LREC 2018), Miyazaki, Japan (2018)
14. Freitas, C., Motta, E., Milidiú, R., César, J.: Vampiro que brilha... rá! Desafios na anotação de opinião em um corpus de resenhas de livros. Encontro de Linguística de Corpus **11**, 22 (2012)
15. dos Santos, F.L., Ladeira, M.: The role of text pre-processing in opinion mining on a social media language dataset. In: 2014 Brazilian Conference on Intelligent Systems (BRACIS), pp. 50–54. IEEE (2014)
16. Antonio, J.D., Santin, A.C.L.: "Haters gonna hate": challenges for sentiment analysis of Facebook comments in Brazilian Portuguese. In: Proceedings of the 6th Workshop on Recent Advances in RST and Related Formalisms, pp. 64–72 (2017)

17. Balage Filho, P.P., Pardo, T.A.S., Aluísio, S.M.: An evaluation of the Brazilian Portuguese LIWC dictionary for sentiment analysis. In: Proceedings of the 9th Brazilian Symposium in Information and Human Language Technology (2013)
18. Cirqueira, D., Jacob, A., Lobato, F., de Santana, A.L., Pinheiro, M.: Performance evaluation of sentiment analysis methods for Brazilian Portuguese. In: Abramowicz, W., Alt, R., Franczyk, B. (eds.) BIS 2016. LNBIP, vol. 263, pp. 245–251. Springer, Cham (2017). https://doi.org/10.1007/978-3-319-52464-1_22
19. de Araujo, G.D., Teixeira, F.O., Mancini, F., de Paiva Guimarães, M., Pisa, I.T.: Sentiment analysis of Twitter's health messages in Brazilian Portuguese. J. Health Inform. **10** (2018)

Text Documents Encoding Through Images for Authorship Attribution

Daniel Lichtblau[1] and Catalin Stoean[2]([⊠])

[1] Wolfram Research, 100 Trade Center Dr, Champaign, IL 61820, USA
danl@wolfram.com
[2] Faculty of Sciences, University of Craiova, A.I.Cuza, 13, Craiova, Romania
catalin.stoean@inf.ucv.ro

Abstract. In order to use a machine learning methodology for classifying text documents, relevant features have to be first extracted from them. The current approach uses the chaos game representation to produce an image out of a text document, flattens the images into vectors, while further reduces the dimension via singular value decomposition. Finally, a neural network learns the features relevant for each author and the built model is used to classify new samples. The results obtained on some well known benchmark data sets approach or exceed those in prior literature, and encourage further research within this unexplored area.

Keywords: Author attribution · Chaos game representation
Machine learning

1 Introduction

Authorship attribution (AA) represents the task of determining the author of a text out of several candidates based on text samples written by all these authors [17, 22]. In order to achieve AA automatically, the process involves the use of a machine learning (ML) technique that learns characteristics from a training set of documents written by the authors. The found characteristics specific to each author are then used to discover the best matches for new texts.

Jeffrey [6] introduced the Chaos Game Representation (CGR) as a means to visualize the structure of a DNA sequence. Such a sequence contains a long string built on an alphabet of only 4 letters, usually G, C, A and T. The CGR produces a grayscale image for a given DNA sequence that can be interpreted as a symbol (akin to a fingerprint) of that long sequence of characters. The current approach proposes the use of CGR for texts written in the Latin alphabet to generate symbolic images that can be further used for AA.

The application to authorship attribution proceeds as follows. Using some adjustments, CGR is applied to Latin alphabet texts that are written by various authors, and images, each associated to its corresponding author, are produced. The images can be intuitively regarded as signatures or fingerprints of the authors. When new texts are considered, the same CGR procedure is applied

© Springer Nature Switzerland AG 2018
T. Dutoit et al. (Eds.): SLSP 2018, LNAI 11171, pp. 178–189, 2018.
https://doi.org/10.1007/978-3-030-00810-9_16

for producing new fingerprint images that can be compared to the previous ones. In order to automate such comparison, a Neural Network (NN) learns characteristics from a training set comprised of the symbolic representations for each author. The built model recognizes images that correspond to new manuscripts written by authors that had assigned texts in the training set. In order to simplify the NN task, the images are transformed into numerical vectors in the current study, first by flattening them and then by an extra reduction in dimension via Singular Value Decomposition (SVD).

2 Related Work

The AA task assumes that there is a data set of text samples that is split into training items for which the authors are known and a test corpus of distinct text documents with unknown authorship, but for which the authors should be identified from a set of known candidates. The ML methods need to extract relevant features from both the training and the test text samples. These can refer to lexical characteristics, like word frequencies or richness of the vocabulary, character attributes (n-grams are the most extensively used ones), syntactic observations, e.g. structure of the sentence, or even semantic ones [17,22]. As the extracted characteristics can be very numerous, usually feature selection is used as a subsequent step to keep only the most relevant attributes and to allow the successful application of a ML approach.

Some of the most successful methods that are applied for the considered data sets in English are next briefly presented. A support vector machines (SVM) with bag of local histograms is used in [2]. In [5] and a SVM is applied to a set of values obtained from 3-, 4- and 5-grams, after applying feature selection. Test are made for each n-gram size separately and in combinations, while varying the size of features selected from 2000 to 10000. Other methods consider different types of n-grams and apply SVM [13], or utilize continuous n-grams representation with a NN [15], use tensors for representation and apply SVM [11], distort text for eliminating terms that do not possess information [18] or use orthogonal similarity relations [14].

As concern the applications to the Portuguese data set considered in the experiments, Varela et al. [19] selects syntactic attributes, use a SVM as a wrapper and also employ a multi-objective genetic algorithm for AA, while Oliveira et al. [10] uses compression models and again SVM for the same purpose.

. As opposed to the standard AA methods, that usually establish a numerical data set from texts, the currently proposed work uses a completely different perspective. The text samples are transformed into images through CGR and these are next transformed into numerical data to be used by a ML technique. Although the CGR holds information related to n-grams, the representation is completely different from the usual ones that use character attributes.

We previously proposed the use of CGR for AA and text categorization [9] with very competitive results. The current work drives forward the general methodology by further improving results with the following alterations:

- Characters have a different grouping, one that is better balanced (as measured on the CCAT-50 data set).
- After the CGR representations are flattened, further dimensionality reduction is achieved via SVD.
- After SVD, a NN classifier is used to handle the obtained samples.

Advantages over [9] can be enumerated as follows.

- NN does not face the *curse of dimensionality* due to significant reduction in the number of dimensions achieved through SVD and hence scales well.
- The overall methodology becomes computationally faster.
- The quality of results is considerably higher. It now exceeds the best prior literature on all benchmarks considered. Prior to this, no method has given best results on multiple benchmarks, let alone in more than one language.
- There are fewer parameters to tune and the method is essentially automated.

3   Chaos Game Representation

CGR is used to produce graphical representations of DNA sequences which are represented using a 4 letters alphabet, A, C, G and T. The representation starts from a blank square having the corners labeled each with one of the 4 letters and the starting (and current) point is the middle of the square. Then, each nucleotide of the sequence is taken in turn and plotted as the middle point between the corner labeled by that letter and the current point. This new point becomes the current one and is used to represent the next nucleotide and the process continues until the letter sequence is finished.

The graphical representation will be in the form of a grayscale square. Given its size of $2^k \times 2^k$ pixels, every pixel represents a distinct k-mer [6]. The number of times a k-mer occurs in the DNA sequence determines the gray level of the corresponding pixel, relative to the total number of k-mers. Subsequence repetitions (like words occurrences in an alphabet) lead to similar patterns represented in the image. It is interesting to see that the CGR representations of various species have distinct patterns [7]. The existence of such specific prototypes associated to diverse species led us to the hypothesis that some patterns might be formed from Latin text that would tend to correlate with their author.

Deschavanne [1] proposed a modified CGR procedure known as Frequency CGR (FCGR), equivalent to the former once the pixelation level is fixed, but easier to implement [20]. FCGR is adopted in the current work.

4   Proposed Methodology

The FCGR procedure is applied on sequences of text that use a 4 letters alphabet so, for its application for a text written with a Latin alphabet, several alterations are required. It is necessary that the text is transformed into an alphabet of only 4 characters to be able to apply FCGR directly, and a base 4 representation is adopted. Similarly to [9], 16 symbols are considered for transforming the initial text in the current study, with each element now regarded as a base 4 pair. Thus, like DNA sequences, the obtained alphabet contains 4 distinct characters, denoted by 0, 1, 2 and 3. Subsequently, the application of the FCGR procedure is straightforward [1,7]. Algorithm 1 briefly illustrates the work flow of the proposed FCGR-SVD-NN methodology for AA. There are no other preprocessing procedures applied to the texts.

Algorithm 1. Overview of the proposed FCGR-SVD-NN methodology

---

Data: Input text documents with their known authors split into training and test

Result: Assignation of test samples to candidate authors, depending on the problem

1 Reduce the alphabet of the input document samples to 16 characters;
2 Transform the obtained documents into base 4 representation, i.e. 2 digits per input character;
3 Produce FCGR images for each distinct sample;
4 Flatten FCGR representations to numerical vectors;
5 Use SVD to further reduce dimensionality of the vectors;
6 Apply NN to learn corresponding numerical features from the training cases and use the model to classify test samples;

4.1 From Latin Alphabet to Base Four

No distinction is made between upper and lowercases and all non-Latin characters are omitted. In order to keep the size of the transformed text low, it is decided to represent each character from the initial material with 2 digits of base 4. This leads to a number of 16 distinct symbols that can be represented each as a pair from the set $\{00, 01, \dots, 33\}$. To reduce to a character set of size 16 without discarding from the texts, sets of characters are merged so that we only use 16 distinct "character groups" (where some groups are in fact singletons). The process to test various combinations in groups and permutations of the ordering of character sets was carried out on the CCAT-50 benchmark. The character grouping was done with the goal to have a crude balance in counts for each group of characters. The sets are shown in Fig. 1. As the plot illustrates, an acceptable balance is obtained with this separation: on the maximal side there is the character *space*, with characters m and u at the low end. It should be noted that this character grouping and ordering is dissimilar to the one from [9]. The latter was done by a modest amount of trial and error tests, and while it led to reasonable results, it did not perform so well as the one proposed herein.

4.2 Classification

A pixelation level of 7 is considered, as suggested to be the most suitable in [9], where tests were made on the Federalist Papers using different levels. After

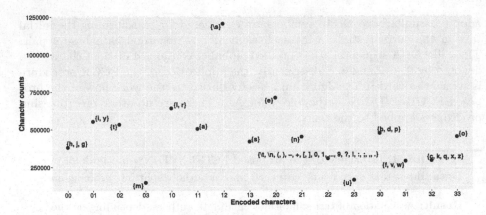

Fig. 1. Chosen sets of characters and their corresponding base 4 representation are represented on the horizontal axis. The number of counts for the sets of characters, as found in the CCAT-50, are shown on the vertical axis.

transformation into a base 4 representation, all texts are fed into the FCGR procedure, which produces images of 128×128 pixels, that is $2^7 \times 2^7$. Subsequent processing takes place at the pixel level. Each matrix of values behind an image is flattened to a vector of 16384 numerical values between 0 and 256. All the vectors that derive from the training set are gathered as separate rows of a large matrix that will be subsequently used by the SVD. Naturally, the labels (authors) are retained for each row in turn. Similarly, the images from the test set are each flattened to long vectors.

Singular Value Decomposition. The SVD on the training matrix is then computed. Recall that the full SVD of a matrix M returns a triple of matrices U, W, V such that U and V are orthogonal matrices, W is a diagonal matrix of nonnegative values, and $MV = UW$ due to orthogonality of V (that is, $VV^* = I$) [3]. In the current study, only the k largest singular values are retained, along with the corresponding singular vectors from U and V. UW is thus the best rank k approximation to MV in Euclidean norm. The left singular vector matrix U has rows that correspond to each particular author, one row per initial document. UV is then fed to the NN classifier.

The right singular vectors V from the largest singular values are needed for the test phase. The test samples to be classified are multiplied with the transpose of the V matrix and then fed to the NN model in order to determine their classes.

During pre-experimental testing, it was observed that normalizing the values of the involved matrices led to better results, so that was consequently applied.

Neural Network. NN [4] simulates the biological neural connections from the animal brain. The structure is comprised of a network of units (or neurons) that transfer information from the training data and adjusts the synaptic weights with the aim of reducing the loss between the true label and the predicted one. The NN architecture can have a certain number of units, layers, various functions and learning schemes. Once the training phase is accomplished, the model receives new samples and decides their labels.

Each neuron is associated with a set of synaptic weights $\mathbf{w}$, which are used in order to compute a function of its inputs. The expression of a neuron u is represented in (1), where $\mathbf{in}$ is its input received from a predecessor neuron, $\mathbf{w}$ is the vector of synaptic weights and b is the bias.

$$u = \mathbf{w} \cdot \mathbf{in} + b \tag{1}$$

Its output is given by (2), where φ is the activation function.

$$out = \varphi(u) \tag{2}$$

The architecture that led to the most accurate results during pre-experimentation, when tests were made on the CCAT-50 data set (which is presented in the following section), is next described. A fully connected layer receives the initial sample vectors, then a ramp function is applied to the inputs followed by a hyperbolic tangent activation function. The output results from another hyperbolic tangent function and a subsequent softmax layer. The cross-entropy loss is computed by comparing input class probability vectors with indices representing the target class. The Adam optimizer method is used for minimizing the model outputs and the actual ones. For every training sample $\mathbf{x}_i$ in turn, the information is forwardly propagated from the input layer to the output through hidden units. All computations, including the NN, were done in version 11.3 of Mathematica [21].

5   Experimental Results

Two corpora are considered for testing the proposed methodology and the results are compared to the most successful ones found in the literature.

5.1   Benchmark Data Sets

One corpus contains texts written in English, while the other one is in Portuguese. CCAT is in English and represents a subset of the Reuters Corpus Volume 1 [8] and it was used before for AA in [13,16]. There are two subsets used, CCAT-10 and CCAT-50. The numbers in the names indicate that they have 10 and 50 authors, respectively. Each author has 100 articles, and in both sets 50 articles per author are used for training and 50 for testing. The topic of the documents is corporate/industrial news.

The other corpus is represented by articles published in newspapers from Brazil, written by 100 distinct authors, and is firstly presented in [19]. In the initial data set, each author has 30 articles, but some duplicates are found and removed within the experiments, so a few authors remain with only 28 or 29 articles. Specifically, 2 texts are removed from author 26 and one from authors: 3, 17, 49, 59, 60, 88, 90 and 92. The total number of remaining articles is 2990. The data set consists of 10 separate genres and there are 10 authors that contributed for each one of them. The information about the publication and author name is removed from each article. In order to keep the methodology unchanged, all diacritical marks from the Portuguese language are erased.

5.2   Experimental Setup

The CCAT subsets have pre-defined settings as concerns the splitting into training-test sets, and this simplifies the comparison to other techniques. Each author has 100 articles and they are split into a set of 50 for training and 50 for testing.

Varela et al. [19] does not provide a similar direct separation, but they use 60% of the articles for training and the rest for testing. Next is described how the training and test sets were extracted from the data set in the present work, so that further replication of the experiments can be done. From each block of 5 articles from the same author, the second and fourth are withheld for testing, except for the sixth block where instead the second and third are kept out. Consequently, there are 1200 articles used for testing and the remaining 1790 are kept for training, so the separation is similar as concerns percentages to the one in [19]. The chosen separation could be useful to make the experiments repeatable.

A pixelation level of 7 is used for all situation and an FCGR representation is obtained for each distinct document, that is each text is transformed into an image of $2^7 \times 2^7$ pixels.

The NN uses 300 units for CCAT-10 and 500 for the other two data sets. The number of training rounds is set to 300 for CCAT-10, and 100 for both the CCAT-50 and Brazilian data sets; in all cases the number was set based on where the incremental improvement in the training phase was observed to tail off. As mentioned in Subsect. 4.2, the optimizer is Adam and the β_1 parameter is set to 0.9. The values for these parameters are chosen based on fine tuning performed on CCAT-50.

The number of singular values to keep is chosen as 500 for CCAT-10 and 1000 for the other two data sets. A larger value was considered for CCAT-50 and Brazilian data sets because they are more complex both as regards the number of classes and documents, and therefore we considered a larger number of features to represent the samples. For CCAT-10 the value is taken as the maximal one, since 500 is the number of samples in the test set. For the other two data sets greater values than 1000 were tried during pre-experimentation, but no significant improvements were reached. For smaller sizes however, losses in classification accuracy were observed. With these settings, the reduction in size for each training and test sample exceeds a factor of 16.

Due to the stochastic nature of the classifier, in order to reach objective results, all classification settings presume the execution of 10 runs for the same configuration. The usual average over the 10 runs is reported in the results. Also an aggregate output over all repeated runs is computed as follows. In each run, for one test sample, probabilities of assigning it to each class are computed. Subsequently, the 10 probabilities for each class are summed and the maximal value decides the class of the sample. Experimentally it was observed that this aggregation has two advantages over individual runs: it reduces variance and, for the two larger corpora, sometimes outperforms all individual runs. Both results will be presented in next subsection, the former under the name *average* and the latter as *aggregated*. For all data sets the 10 runs were repeated five times, and one with the median aggregated score is reported.

5.3   Results and Discussion

Figure 2 illustrates the FCGR representation of 4 distinct documents: the first 2 belong to the same author, while the others correspond to documents written by a different person. At a glance, it is difficult for the human eye to observe similarities or differences between these images. Nevertheless, these representations are very useful for comparing texts (as they were previously for DNA sequences) by means of computing machines, as they discern between FCGR representations remarkably well.

Fig. 2. From left to right, the FCGR representations of the first and last documents for the first author and the same first and last texts for the second author in CCAT-10.

Table 1 shows a comparison over the results obtained by several recent techniques for the CCAT tasks. Besides the proposed method, a similarly good result for CCAT-10 is reported in [2]. Nevertheless, there are several works like [15] and [12] which demonstrate that the result in [2] is difficult to replicate, perhaps due to sensitive parameters that require specific values. While their implementations of the technique in [2] performed reasonably well, i.e. 77% and 75.4% respectively, they are significantly far from the 86.4% reported in the original publication. Our previous attempt [9] applies linear regression to the FCGR images directly (without any dimension reduction) and the results are presented under the name FCGR+LR. Although FCGR+LR accuracy is very competitive for both data sets, the ones we put forward herein (denoted by FCGR-SVD-NN) are better by more than 3%. Alternatively, an application of the NN directly on the FCGR representation (without the SVD reduction) is achieved on the

CCAT-10 data set and the classification accuracy results reached only 78%. This variant is therefore not considered for the rest of the comparison.

The second best result for CCAT-50 is reported in [5]. The result presented in Table 1 is obtained for 4-grams and for 10000 features.

Table 1. Classification accuracy results compared to other methods on CCAT-10 and CCAT-50 data sets. The best results are written in bold.

Method	CCAT-10(%)	CCAT-50(%)
FCGR-SVD-NN average	**86.5**	**74.3**
FCGR-SVD-NN aggregated	85.9	73.7
FCGR+LR [9]	82.2	70
SVM [5]	–	74
SVM [2]	86.4	–
SVM [13]	78.8	69.3
n-gram char $(1, 2)$ [15]	77.8	70.2
n-gram char $(2, 3, 4)$ [15]	74.8	72.6
SVM [11]	80.8	–
Character n-grams [18]	80.6	–
MSMF+FLF [14]	78.8	69.5

It is also important to mention that for the aggregated score for CCAT-10, beside 84.5% text documents with correctly identified authors, there are another 13% (63 samples) that have the correct author as second choice. For CCAT-50 11.6% of documents have the correct author as second choice.

Figure 3 illustrates a confusion matrix for CCAT-10 and also how many times the texts are assigned to each author, both correctly and incorrectly. As it can be noticed from both plots, the author that is hardest to recognize is the fourth. 22 of the texts written by A4 are labeled as belonging to A10. This is also the reason why author 10 has so many samples assigned in the second plot. On the other hand, there is also A5 that is very clearly distinct from the rest: texts of A5 are both precisely identified and moreover none of the other documents are misattributed to A5 (but neither to A7).

For CCAT-50 the confusion matrix is too large to be included in the manuscript. Four authors are accurately identified for all 50 of their documents in the test set (authors 11, 16, 21, and 29), while at the low end A44 is correctly attributed in only 13 cases, and A7 in only 14.

Table 2 presents a comparison to the best performing methods as presented in [9,10,19]. The result of the proposed technique clearly outperforms those of the other methods applied for the same data set, with the next best result more than 5% lower. Also the second choice guess for the proposed method remains relatively high, at 5.75%. It should be noted that no change was required, other

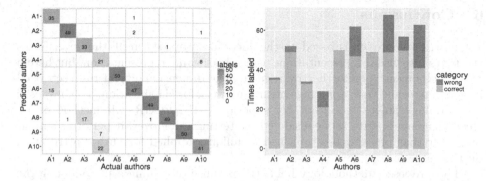

Fig. 3. Confusion matrix for CCAT-10 on the left plot and the number of documents correctly and wrongly attributed to each author in turn for the same data set.

than preprocessing to remove diacritical marks, in applying this method to the Portuguese data set.

The FCGR+LR in [9] is also applied for genre classification and the accuracy obtained for this task is identical to the aggregated one of the proposed approach for AA. As a side experiment, the current method is also applied for genre recognition, but the classification accuracy is similar to the one for the AA task. Having no significant increase in result quality for the text categorization task, we decided to keep the focus of the study only on AA.

Table 2. Comparison of classification accuracy results in percentages for AA for the Brazilian newspaper data set. The last column shows the percent of samples attributed to the correct author as second choice.

Classifier	Correct author	Correct second author
FCGR-SVD-NN average	**89.2**	4.4
FCGR-SVD-NN aggregated	87.8	–
FCGR+LR [9]	82	6.9
SVM [19]	72	–
SVM [10]	77	–

The results of the proposed approach are seen to be generally better than other successful techniques applied to these benchmark data sets. Moreover these results are achieved despite a rough truncation of the initial alphabet and no other modifications to the text. For instance, text distortion similar to [18] might be very useful as a preprocessing step, as the FCGR images would perhaps be more informative for the classifier. Such a preprocessing step will be tried in future research.

6 Conclusions

The current approach is based on the encoding proposed in [9] that transforms the texts into visual representations using chaos game representation, but herein the development goes further by reducing the dimensionality of the vectorized image matrix and then applying a neural network for classification. The proposed methodology proves to be notably superior to the FCGR+LR method on all three benchmark data sets considered for testing. Moreover, it performs similar or better than other well established techniques applied for author attribution on the same corpora.

The proposed methodology holds the promise of gaining a place among the state-of-the-art techniques for author attribution, since it already proves successful when applied to several benchmark problems, without a thorough investigation of all the possible settings for the process. For instance, tasks of future research analysis might involve other transformations of the initial text into the base 4 representation, as there might still exist important information loss at this point. A change of the classifier or even other means of reducing dimensionality could also prove favorable for boosting the classification accuracy.

Acknowledgments. We thank the anonymous reviewers for their careful reading of our manuscript and their many insightful comments and suggestions.

References

1. Deschavanne, P.J., Giron, A., Vilain, J., Fagot, G., Fertil, B.: Genomic signature: characterization and classification of species assessed by chaos game representation of sequences. Mol. Biol. Evol. **16**(10), 1391–1399 (1999)
2. Escalante, H.J., Solorio, T., Montes-y Gómez, M.: Local histograms of character n-grams for authorship attribution. In: Proceedings of the 49th Annual Meeting of the Association for Computational Linguistics: Human Language Technologies, HLT 2011, vol. 1, pp. 288–298. Association for Computational Linguistics, Stroudsburg (2011)
3. Golub, G.H., Reinsch, C.: Singular value decomposition and least squares solutions. Numerische mathematik **14**(5), 403–420 (1970)
4. Haykin, S.: Neural Networks: A Comprehensive Foundation, 2nd edn. Prentice Hall PTR, Upper Saddle River (1998)
5. Houvardas, J., Stamatatos, E.: N-gram feature selection for authorship identification. In: Euzenat, J., Domingue, J. (eds.) AIMSA 2006. LNCS (LNAI), vol. 4183, pp. 77–86. Springer, Heidelberg (2006). https://doi.org/10.1007/11861461_10
6. Jeffrey, H.J.: Chaos game representation of gene structure. Nucleic Acids Res. **18**(8), 2163–2170 (1990)
7. Karamichalis, R., Kari, L., Konstantinidis, S., Kopecki, S., Solis-Reyes, S.: Additive methods for genomic signatures. BMC Bioinform. **17**(1), 313 (2016)
8. Lewis, D.D., Yang, Y., Rose, T.G., Li, F.: Rcv1: a new benchmark collection for text categorization research. J. Mach. Learn. Res. **5**, 361–397 (2004)
9. Lichtblau, D., Stoean, C.: Authorship attribution using the chaos game representation. CoRR abs/1802.06007v1 (2018)

10. Oliveira, W., Justino, E., Oliveira, L.S.: Comparing compression models for authorship attribution. Forensic Sci. Int. **228**(1), 100–104 (2013)
11. Plakias, S., Stamatatos, E.: Tensor space models for authorship identification. In: Darzentas, J., Vouros, G.A., Vosinakis, S., Arnellos, A. (eds.) SETN 2008. LNCS (LNAI), vol. 5138, pp. 239–249. Springer, Heidelberg (2008). https://doi.org/10. 1007/978-3-540-87881-0_22
12. Potthast, M., et al.: Who wrote the web? Revisiting influential author identification research applicable to information retrieval. In: Ferro, N., et al. (eds.) ECIR 2016. LNCS, vol. 9626, pp. 393–407. Springer, Cham (2016). https://doi.org/10.1007/ 978-3-319-30671-1_29
13. Sapkota, U., Bethard, S., Montes-y-Gómez, M., Solorio, T.: Not all character n-grams are created equal: a study in authorship attribution. In: Human Language Technologies: The 2015 Annual Conference of the North American Chapter of the ACL, pp. 93–102 (2015)
14. Sapkota, U., Solorio, T., Montes-y-Gómez, M., Rosso, P.: The use of orthogonal similarity relations in the prediction of authorship. In: Gelbukh, A. (ed.) CICLing 2013. LNCS, vol. 7817, pp. 463–475. Springer, Heidelberg (2013). https://doi.org/ 10.1007/978-3-642-37256-8_38
15. Sari, Y., Vlachos, A., Stevenson, R.: Continuous n-gram representations for authorship attribution. In: Lapata, M., Blunsom, P., Koller, A. (eds.) European Chapter of the Association for Computational Linguistics (EACL 2017), vol. 2. ACL, April 2017
16. Stamatatos, E.: Author identification: using text sampling to handle the class imbalance problem. Inf. Process. Manag. **44**(2), 790–799 (2008). Evaluating Exploratory Search Systems Digital Libraries in the Context of Users Broader Activities
17. Stamatatos, E.: A survey of modern authorship attribution methods. J. Am. Soc. Inf. Sci. Technol. **60**(3), 538–556 (2009)
18. Stamatatos, E.: Authorship attribution using text distortion. In: Proceedings of the 15th Conference of the European Chapter of the Association for Computational Linguistics: Volume 1, Long Papers, pp. 1138–1149. Association for Computational Linguistics, Valencia, April 2017
19. Varela, P., Justino, E., Oliveira, L.S.: Selecting syntactic attributes for authorship attribution. In: The 2011 International Joint Conference on Neural Networks, pp. 167–172, July 2011
20. Wang, Y., Hill, K., Singh, S., Kari, L.: The spectrum of genomic signatures: from dinucleotides to chaos game representation. Gene **346**, 173–185 (2005)
21. Wolfram Research Inc.: Mathematica 11, Champaign, USA (2018). http://www. wolfram.com
22. Zhang, C., Wu, X., Niu, Z., Ding, W.: Authorship identification from unstructured texts. Knowl.-Based Syst. **66**, 99–111 (2014)

Author Index

Printed in the United States
By Bookmasters